ALBERT SHAW LECTURES ON DIPLOMATIC HISTORY

1899. JOHN H. LATANÉ. The Diplomatic Relations of the United States and Spanish America. (Out of print.)

1900. JAMES MORTON CALLAHAN. The Diplomatic History of the Southern Confederacy. 1901. (Out of print.)

1906. JESSE SIDDALL REEVES. American Diplomacy under Tyler and Polk. 1907. $1.75.

1907. ELBERT JAY BENTON. International Law and Diplomacy of the Spanish-American War. 1908. $1.75.

1909. EPHRAIM DOUGLAS ADAMS. British Interests and Activities in Texas, 1838-1846. 1910. $1.75.

1911. CHARLES OSCAR PAULLIN. Diplomatic Negotiations of American Naval Officers, 1778-1883. 1912. $2.25.

1912. ISAAC J. COX. The West Florida Controversy, 1798-1813. 1918. $3.00.

1913. WILLIAM R. MANNING. Early Diplomatic Relations between the United States and Mexico. 1916. $2.50.

1914. FRANK A. UPDYKE. The Diplomacy of the War of 1812. 1915. $2.75.

1916. PAYSON JACKSON TREAT. The Early Diplomatic Relations between the United States and Japan, 1853-1865. 1917. $2.75.

1921. PERCY ALVIN MARTIN. Latin America and the War. 1925. $3.50.

1926. SAMUEL FLAGG BEMIS. Pinckney's Treaty. A Study of America's Advantage from Europe's Distress, 1780-1800. 1926. $3.00.

1927. BRUCE WILLIAMS. State Security and the League of Nations. 1927. $2.75.

1928. J. FRED RIPPY. Rivalry of the United States and Great Britain Over Latin America (1808-1830). 1928. $2.75.

Rivalry of the
United States and Great Britain
Over Latin America
(1808-1830)

THE ALBERT SHAW LECTURES ON DIPLOMATIC HISTORY

By the liberality of Albert Shaw, Ph.D., of New York City, the Johns Hopkins University has been enabled to provide an annual course of lectures on Diplomatic History. The lectures are included in the regular work of the Department of History and are published under the direction of Professor John H. Latané.

**THE ALBERT SHAW LECTURES ON
DIPLOMATIC HISTORY, 1928**

Rivalry of the United States and Great Britain Over Latin America
(1808-1830)

BY

J. FRED RIPPY

PROFESSOR OF HISTORY IN DUKE UNIVERSITY

BALTIMORE
THE JOHNS HOPKINS PRESS
1929

Copyright 1929
By THE JOHNS HOPKINS PRESS

The Industrial Printing Company
BALTIMORE, MD.

To
MY FRIENDS IN LONDON

TABLE OF CONTENTS

CHAPTER		PAGE
I.	Political and Economic Issues (1808-1823)	1
II.	The Destiny of the Spanish Borderlands	22
III.	Texas and Cuba	71
IV.	The Antagonism of Canning and Adams; Rivalry in Southern South America	107
V.	Rivalry in Northern South America	150
VI.	Friction in Central America; The Panama Congress	217
VII.	Spirited Contests in Mexico	247
VIII.	Conclusion—A Century of Subsequent Contests	303

PREFACE

"At last the Briton is beginning to be conscious of the development of a real challenge to his naval supremacy. For three hundred years his instinct has been to meet that challenge by fighting. Spain, France, and Germany have in turn gone down to defeat because each has ventured to challenge British mastery on the high seas.

". . . American economic invasion . . . has been a circumstance which has more and more attracted attention. While British industry has been passing through crisis after crisis, American prosperity and expansion have been constant. . . .

"Rich, prosperous, progressive, we continue to advance into the areas of British supremacy; and now at last, visibly, unmistakably, we are giving evidence of the purpose to invade the last field. . . .

"To-day the appalling fact for the [British] Admiralty in the American naval program is not that we are likely to have a large superiority over the British in 10,000-ton cruisers. No one calculates that these boats will fight each other. The disaster from the British naval standpoint is that we shall have . . . the type of boat which is best calculated to challenge the British blockade all over the world. . . ."[1]

[1] Frank Simonds, in *The American Review of Reviews*, Feb., 1928.

These excerpts taken from a very recent article written by a famous American journalist suggest that the work now submitted is not concerned merely with dead issues. For the contest which it describes is one that related largely to questions of commerce and maritime supremacy. It began more than a century ago and is keen at the present time when, despite the settlement of several old disputes, the merchants and capitalists of the two nations are engaged in rivalry all over the world and disarmament conferences are made futile because neither is willing to trust the other in the matter of sea power. In addition to contests regarding trade and maritime predominance, only two other important issues arose—territorial expansion and political forms and affiliations—and one of these was connected with the control of the high seas.

In the contest described in the present volume England often appeared as the villain and the United States the hero. Or, to put it in other words, Britain usually faced the past and the United States faced the future. Yankee diplomacy championed the cause of democracy, freedom of trade, and the rights of those who considered peace the normal state of man. In doing so it not only attacked the navigation laws and maritime rules of England, but encouraged the suppressed and latent forces of British democracy and even threatened British naval supremacy itself. English statesmen, on the contrary, clung to the old forms, systems, and privileges with all the tenacity of the race. Few and unimportant, indeed, were the concessions wrung from them prior to 1830. But the "spirit of the age" was against them. The process of undermining was begun and during the course of the next few decades many of the ancient structures gave way. The old navigation system began to be abandoned in 1849; the contentions of the United States with regard to neutral rights and the power of blockade were accepted in 1856; and soon afterwards the common people were granted a larger participation in the government of England and of several of her colonies.

Yet, through it all, the supremacy of British industries, capital, and sea power was maintained; and the World War revealed that international law and diplomatic agreements had not yet erected a bulwark adequate to safeguard neutrals from English encroachments in times of crisis, just as prior and subsequent events have shown that the economic and maritime rivalry of the two nations has not ceased. Professor E. D. Adams has attributed the growing harmony which developed between them subsequent to 1868 to the fact that they had become sister democracies. To this should probably be added the further circumstances of the temporary decline of our merchant marine and the danger of a European combination against England.

It has not been my purpose, however, in preparing these lectures to furnish explosives for those who would like to destroy the foundation of Anglo-Saxon harmony. Whoever reads the concluding chapter of this volume will find reason to appreciate the accommodating spirit which England has revealed in dealing with some of the more recent difficulties of the two Powers in the Western Hemisphere.

Nor do I wish to be understood as asserting that the United States has always played the rôle of the high-minded hero. On the contrary, it must be admitted that its policy has sometimes been inconsistent and characterized by selfishness of a somewhat sordid kind. The champion of the inviolability of private property upon the high seas refused to sign the Declaration of Paris (1856) because it provided for the abolition of privateering.[2] The apostle of the rights of neutrals expanded belligerent operations during the Civil War and the World War until it can never again defend the old cause with perfect grace. The former advocate of freedom of trade has erected high tariff walls, refused to admit foreign vessels on equal terms with national ships to its coasting trade, and has even been accused of a disposition to transform the Monroe Doctrine into a weapon of economic exclusiveness. Louisiana was acquired in a manner which suggests the analogy of purchasing property known to have been stolen, and Florida and the great Southwest by methods not entirely above reproach. Descendants of men who are said to have placed human freedom above material gain have been charged with supporting military

[2] It is only fair, however, to note that the refusal was due to the failure to include in the Declaration a statement exempting the private property of belligerents, other than contraband of war, from capture.

despots in the interest of dollars. Statesmen whose ancestors strictly opposed all intervention in the domestic affairs of other nations and had firm faith in the capacity and natural right of peoples for self-government are said to believe that half of the Latin-American nations cannot get along without a Yankee protectorate. Without accepting everything which the hostile critics have written, we may at least venture to remove the halo while we reiterate the statement that for the period and events treated by the volume here presented the record of the United States has in it something of the heroic.

It ought to be noted at the outset that the encounters of the rivals over Hispanic America were in some respects futile and in others unnecessary and premature. So far as rivalry for trade and investment opportunities was concerned, there was no need for bitterness at all for the simple reason that the Yankees could not raise capital for investment abroad nor, with the exception of salt fish and household furniture, offer for sale large quantities of commodities which competed with anything that the British had to sell. Nor was the suspicion which each held of the grasping commercial tendencies of the other justified. Except in Brazil, where the English were loath to give up advantages obtained during the colonial period, neither ever officially sought special trade concessions. Both greatly magnified the economic and political importance of Spanish America and conceived that new states which could neither avoid wars among themselves, nor maintain stability, nor even pay the expenses of their governments, might affect the balance of the entire world not only in matters of economics but also in those of politics and maritime regulations. In a century they were to achieve some significance in all of these lines, but it may be doubted whether at the present time they have the importance which was attributed to them more than a hundred years ago. With reference to their influence upon the status of democracy, it must probably be admitted that their history has been a reflection upon rather than a credit to this form.

Yet, these facts were of little weight in determining the conduct of the rivals prior to 1830. In international affairs, as elsewhere, erroneous opinions are often more influential than the truth. The plunging of the contestants at spectres, their charging at the shadows of their own embittered imaginations, furnish amusement at the expense of both; and the historian of the struggle finds himself somewhat in the position of the cynical gods who view from their lofty station the illusions and vain strivings of men. I must confess that I have been much interested in this phase of the contest, and for this reason, among others, I have quoted freely from the letters of the diplomats and consuls, in order that their mental operations might be placed more vividly before the reader.

In the preparation of this study I have been greatly assisted by the works of Temperley, Webster, Manning, Lockey, Perkins, and W. S. Robertson, which I

Preface

have frequently cited, but it is also based upon the manuscript sources of the Public Record Office and the State Department, whose keepers have aided me with all the generosity that I could ask. The time at my disposal has not permitted the examination of the contemporary newspapers and periodicals or the archives of the Latin-American nations, but the wide variety of opinions expressed by the official agents whose correspondence I have read appears to justify the hope that this omission has not materially detracted from the reliableness of the facts stated and the conclusions reached. It ought also to be noted that I have not attempted to present an exhaustive account of the rivalry of Great Britain and the United States in Latin America during the period treated. I have merely tried to set forth its important aspects.

I am indebted to the Guggenheim Foundation for a subsidy which enabled me to pursue my investigations in England, to Professor Louis Martin Sears for a careful reading of the manuscript, and to Professor John H. Latané for many helpful suggestions while the work was going through the press. I must also record here my deep appreciation of the generous sacrifices which my wife has made in connection with this little volume.

J. Fred Rippy.

Baltimore, February 21, 1928.

CHAPTER I

POLITICAL AND ECONOMIC ISSUES (1808-1823)

The relations of the United States and England with respect to Hispanic America during the first three decades of the nineteenth century were affected not only by old animosities, which require no discussion in this introductory chapter, but also by fundamental antagonisms of policy and interests. They were likewise influenced by the relations of both countries with the European Powers.

1. CLASHING POLICIES

Almost from the beginning of its history the foreign policy of the United States was directed toward four main objectives: the extension of its boundaries, particularly to the south and west; the enlargement of the rights of neutrals; the achievement of greater commercial freedom through the removal of the restrictions of the old commercial system; and the reduction of the points of contact between Europe and America. Moreover, from the very manner of their own nation's origin, most North Americans looked with favor upon all struggles for liberty, although a certain political caution and moderation set a limit to the support which they were willing to extend to such struggles.

The pursuit of the objectives of this policy necessarily involved the future of Hispanic America. The territory especially desired by the United States was Spanish-American and its acquisition would be facilitated by a revolution in the adjacent provinces. The independence of the whole of Hispanic America and the adoption by the new states of liberal commercial and maritime policies would constitute important steps in the shattering of the old commercial and maritime systems. Furthermore, the independence of these peoples would diminish European influence in the New World and at the same time satisfy that political idealism which caused many Americans to sympathize with movements for liberation wherever they occurred. This would be particularly true if Spanish-American independence resulted in the establishment of democratic republics.

Neither could these objectives be attained without encountering British opposition and rivalry upon almost every hand. After the formation of the Anglo-Spanish alliance in 1808 the British government felt itself under obligation to defend Spanish territorial interests in America against all attacks; the maritime rules of England were those of a great belligerent sea power contemptuous of the rights of neutrals and jealous of competitors in the shipping trade; and, so far as its own colonies were concerned, Britain still clung to the old colonial system with most of its ancient restrictions. Moreover, conservative English statesmen, who were uneasy with reference to the

POLITICAL AND ECONOMIC ISSUES

fate of their own colonial empire, somewhat fettered by their connections with reactionary Europe, and constitutionally opposed to democracy and popular uprisings, could not view with unalloyed pleasure the revolt of the Spanish colonies and the establishment of republics in the New World. Nor could they look with favor upon a policy which, like that of the United States, demanded a gradual separation of America and Europe. In their opinion the future of the British Isles was bound up with all parts of the world, America included. In fact, the commercial and political fate of Spanish America was supposed by many British statesmen to have a most intimate relation to English and European politics. George Canning was not alone in looking upon the New World as a possible means of redressing the balance of the Old.

Yet there were certain factors which tended to put a check upon British opposition to the policy of the United States and sometimes even to suggest a community of interests. Those very commercial and industrial groups who often dictated British policy were opposed to the severe restrictions of the Spanish colonial system. They forced the English government to press upon Spain the advisability of a more liberal course and the opening of the Spanish colonies to English trade, preserving only a fair preference—whatever that term meant—for the mother country. Moreover, statesmen who knew that their own government was founded in revolt and were aware of the violent strength of outraged peoples, statesmen who, after all, were more liberal than their contemporaries in Europe, could not follow the European reactionaries in all of their repressive movements. They were also suspicious and jealous of France and Russia, whose intrigues compelled them to adopt the policy of nonintervention and even to suggest a *rapprochement* with the United States. Thus potentialities of harmony were not absent, but they were usually smothered by mutual rivalries and suspicions, which will become evident as the story unfolds.[1]

II. DISAGREEMENTS WITH REFERENCE TO THE SPANISH-AMERICAN INSURGENTS

After 1808, British statesmen frowned upon insurgent movements in Spanish America. They were engaged in a terrific struggle against Napoleon and looked with disfavor upon disturbances which tended to weaken their Spanish ally. They sent naval officers and other agents to Spanish America in order to counteract French designs and recommend loyalty to the mother country; and insurgent agents who came to London were told that they could serve the great com-

[1] The authorities upon which this section is based are too numerous to cite in detail. See the standard editions of the works of Jefferson, Madison, Monroe, Clay, and J. Q. Adams; F. L. Paxson, *The Independence of the South-American Republics* (Philadelphia, 1916); and Dexter Perkins, *The Monroe Doctrine* (Cambridge, 1927). See also, on the British side, the published correspondence of Viscount Castlereagh, the Duke of Wellington, and George Canning; C. K. Webster, *The Foreign Policy of Castlereagh* (London, 1925); and Harold Temperley, *The Foreign Policy of Canning* (London, 1925).

mon cause best by helping to preserve the integrity of the Spanish empire.

Yet, there was one respect in which British policy indirectly promoted the interests of the insurgents. The Spanish government was strongly urged not to divert its energies from the Napoleonic struggle in Europe by dispatching armies to America, and to settle the colonial issue by certain political concessions to the colonists. It was also informed that access of British merchants to the Spanish-American markets was absolutely essential to effective British coöperation in the important task of driving the French out of the Spanish peninsula. Unless the colonial ports were thrown open to English commerce, British statesmen argued, the means of accomplishing this common objective would be lacking. Such a policy may have weakened Spanish opposition to the incipient American revolutions, and it certainly furnished the insurgents with finances, in the form of customs duties, which were very necessary to the organization of their resistance to Spanish rule.

American statesmen, on the contrary, looked with favor upon the Spanish-American revolution from the very outset. Such democratic idealists as Jefferson, Madison, Monroe, and young Henry Clay—men who had learned to hate the "tyranny" of England and who felt that it made little difference whether Spain was dominated by a "conqueror roaming over the earth with havoc and destruction" or by a "pirate spreading misery and ruin over the face of the ocean" [2]—found cause only for jubilation in this new struggle for liberty and self-government. It not only weakened an old enemy (Spain), but it also furnished an opportunity to enlarge the area of freedom, increase American trade, and extend the boundaries of the United States to the Gulf. It was a part of a "momentous epoch," said American statesmen, and in 1810 and 1811, when a settlement of their difficulties with Napoleon appeared not impossible, they apparently thought seriously of granting more than sympathy to their "Southern Brethren." Russia and France, possible coadjutors in the struggle against British maritime pretensions, were sounded and plans for recognition and more effective support seem to have been considered.[3] But the eventual revelation of the deception of Napoleon and the outbreak of the war with England (1812) soon put a stop to these larger contemplations and confined the efforts of American statesmen to the pursuit of the Floridas.

The overthrow of Napoleon and the termination of the war with the United States brought no important changes in British policy either toward the United States or Spanish America. Although English states-

[2] Jefferson, *Writings* (P. L. Ford ed.), IX, 274.

[3] W. R. Manning, *Diplomatic Correspondence of the United States concerning the Independence of the Latin-American Nations* (N. Y., 1925), I, 6-14; Madison, *Writings* (Gaillard Hunt, ed.), VIII, 116; Foster to Wellesley, No. 33, Dec. 20, 1811, F. O. (5), 77.

men revealed an inclination toward more cordial relations with their American kinsman, they were not willing to purchase them at the price of a modification in their maritime and commercial system; and in regard to Spanish America and Spain they adopted a policy of neutrality while insisting upon the continuation of their Spanish-American trade and pressing mediation on the old basis of larger autonomy for the colonists and free access to their markets.

In these latter respects British policy seemed to accord with that of the United States; for the Yankees, now hoping to acquire Spanish territory by negotiation with Spain, likewise adopted a policy of strict neutrality and insisted upon an open door in matters of trade. Indeed, between 1816 and 1823 the two nations seemed more nearly in harmony with reference to their Hispanic-American policy than ever before.

But the accord was more apparent than real. So far as Spanish America was concerned their commercial policies were the same, but their merchants were potential competitors in the insurgent markets. Their political policies were in some respects similar; for both proclaimed neutrality and both desired to ward off European assistance to Spain in her attempt at a colonial reconquest which involved a threat to their trade as well as the possibility of an increase of French influence in Spanish America. But their maritime antagonism, in no way relieved by the Peace of Ghent, persisted. Each was jealous of the political influence and territorial designs of the other, and the United

States favored republics in the New World while England preferred monarchies. In the face of a menace from Russia, France, or the Neo-Holy Alliance, as in 1817-1818 and in 1823, they talked of coöperation, but coöperation was in fact only a very remote possibility so long as their views so widely diverged on maritime rules and political principles.

Such overtures as the Powers made to each other represented an eagerness to checkmate a rival or counteract the schemes of the diplomats of the Continent rather than a disposition for a frank and cordial pooling of interests. In order to promote the setting up of monarchies in Spanish America, England stood for delay in extending recognition to the new states. In order to encourage those republican institutions which represented the first political impulses of the insurgents, the United States felt that an early acknowledgment was important.

The results of these negotiations, of this fencing for advantages, were meager enough. Each Power received a clearer insight into the motives of the other; the recognition of the United States was possibly delayed while that of England was hastened; but the rivalry and antagonism of the two nations continued as before.[4]

[4] On this section, see (in addition to the references given in notes 2 and 3) C. D. Yonge, *The Life and Administration of Robert Banks, Second Earl of Liverpool* (London, 1868), II, 300-303; C. W. Vane, *Correspondence, Despatches, and other Papers of Viscount Castlereagh* (London, 1851 ff.), VII, *passim*; Adams, *Memoirs* (Philadelphia, 1874), III, *passim*. See also

III. EARLY ENCOUNTERS IN HISPANIC AMERICA

While foreign ministers and secretaries of state were sparring with each other, the agents and nationals of England and the United States carried on a spirited contest for trade and political influence and said what they thought of their rivals. The official representatives of the United States were consuls, commercial agents, naval commanders, and commissioners, whereas England depended mainly upon naval officials. Only a few illustrations can be given, for a complete story of their early encounters and mutual jealousies would expand these introductory remarks beyond their proper limits.

Lively contests took place in Buenos Aires and Chile, with Consul-General Joel R. Poinsett as the storm center. He arrived at the mouth of the Plate early in 1811, disguised as an Englishman and on board a British merchant vessel. He began at once to encourage a movement for independence from Spain and soon afterwards negotiated a commercial agreement "in the face of violent British opposition." He then set out for Chile, arriving in Santiago on February 14, 1812. Captain Peter Heywood of the British Navy paid his respects to him and other Americans in the following language: "Some citizens of the United

---

Castlereagh to Sir James Cockburn, Oct. 8, 1808, Liverpool to Layard, two instructions dated June 29, 1810, Colonial Office (66), 3; Lord Wellesley to Sir Arthur Wellesley, No. 18, May 4, 1811, F. O. (72), 108.

States ... have been very busy in the politics of these people, endeavouring to persuade them that the government of the United States has taken the most lively interest in their concerns, and to make them believe that they may expect the most active assistance from it. Many of these gentlemen, and particularly a Mr. Poinsett, who is styled the Consul-General of the United States, and who went over to Chile from hence when I was here last year, are particularly diligent and active in propagating doctrines and opinions prejudicial to the British government and subjects."[5]

When Poinsett reached Chile he quickly became a partisan of the insurgent leader José Miguel Carrera, assisting his provisional government to draft a constitution and assuming command of a division of his army. He also promised military supplies from the United States. The Chileans responded with enthusiasm and the house of Poinsett became a social center. The people were in fact so thoroughly sympathetic with the United States that when Captain Porter arrived in the American warship *Essex*, with British prizes which he had captured, he was allowed to sell the cargoes and fit out the newly acquired vessels for further attacks on English commerce.

Captain Heywood and his successor at the Rio de la Plata station, William Bowles, both wrote in high irritation concerning Poinsett's activities in Chile. Heywood said that the American agent was "circulating

[5] Edward Tagart, *A Memoir of Peter Heywood* (London, 1832), 247-248.

POLITICAL AND ECONOMIC ISSUES

poison" and "contaminating the whole population on that side of the continent," by which he meant that he was encouraging revolution and denouncing the British. Bowles remarked that the Carrera brothers were "entirely guided by . . . Poinsett," and that Poinsett was serving the interests of France as well as of the United States.[6]

Early in 1814 Poinsett's position became critical. Heywood had advised that an English war vessel be stationed at Valparaiso in order to encourage British commerce and "counteract" the propaganda of "Mr. Poinsett, the American agent or consul, or whatever else he is." The Admiralty followed his advice, sending out Captain Hillyar, whose influence was felt at once. When Captain Porter returned to Valparaiso his ship *Essex* was trapped in the harbor, "not a cable length from shore," and captured in spite of all Poinsett could do. Shortly afterwards British pressure forced the Chilean government to urge Poinsett's departure. He returned to Buenos Aires and soon made his way back to the United States.[7] The British had gotten rid of one trouble-maker.

For the next few years Captain Bowles watched

[6] *Ibid.*, 256-257; Bowles to the Lords of the Admiralty, Nov. 9, 1813, Admiralty (1), 1556.

[7] For Poinsett's activities and the correspondence relative to his mission, see Manning, *Dip. Cor.*, *index* under "Poinsett"; Henry Clay Evans, *Chile and Its Relations with the United States* (Durham, 1927), 14 ff.; "Correspondence and Miscellaneous Manuscripts of Joel Roberts Poinsett," I (Penn. Historical Society).

the agents and citizens of the United States in southern South America with a critical eye. Early in 1814 he reported that there were two parties in Buenos Aires: those who favored mediation under British auspices, and those who aspired to absolute independence. To the latter party belonged "all the North Americans" and the greater part of the "anti-English faction." In the former were found, among others, San Martín and his followers and associates. Bowles said that this leader appeared to be friendly to the British, but hostile to France and the United States. For this attitude perhaps the English were responsible, for Bowles admitted that he himself was trying to keep San Martín and other leaders "clear of French and American influence," and he also stated with "much pleasure" that the "American influence" was on the decline.

San Martín, after his descent upon Chile early in 1817, requested Bowles to come to Santiago for an interview. The following October found the Captain (now promoted to the rank of Commodore) in that port. San Martín soon confided to him his desire to establish monarchies under British protection in South America and the information was sent at once to the Foreign Office. During the interview Bowles also learned that certain Americans were in San Martín's army, whereupon he warned him against them and soon concluded that they had no influence.

Bowles was still at Valparaiso when United States agent John B. Prevost arrived on board the U. S. S.

Ontario early in 1818. He thought that Prevost was "charged with some political mission," perhaps with a negotiation for the acquisition of the Island of Chiloe. He did not feel, however, that there should be "any fear of the Americans becoming too popular."

But Prevost received an entirely different impression. On April 9, 1818, he wrote: "I am really gratified in being enabled to say, after a residence of nearly three months, that the impression first produced by the arrival of the *Ontario* has been daily augmenting and that this measure . . . has been the most happy in its result. It has not merely defeated the influence which Great Britain has been struggling to acquire but has confirmed a sentiment in favor of the U States which will not easily be eradicated."[8] Nor was his optimism damped by further observation. In June he said there was "little room to fear that Chile will [would] give special advantages to England." He remarked further, that the Chileans seemed to "understand her crooked policy . . . and to regard her with contempt." Moreover, in 1821 he was still doubtful of the great influence which the British were alleged to have on the Pacific Coast.[9]

From Valparaiso Bowles sailed for Rio de Janeiro, where he arrived a few weeks after the American Commissioners Rodney, Graham, and Bland had passed through on their way to Buenos Aires. The

[8] Manning, *Dip. Cor.*, II, 921.

[9] Evans, *Chile*, 38.

attitude of the minister at Rio aroused Bowles's suspicion, for he thought that the United States was determined to "interpose in some way or other" in the projected mediation of the European Powers. With reference to the reception and activities of the commissioners at Buenos Aires, Bowles wrote: "The Director [Juan Martín de Pueyrredón] did not receive them until four days after their arrival, and no great cordiality appeared to prevail between them." Bowles did not think that they harbored any secret commercial intentions or had "produced much impression." They had told the political leaders that Russia, France, and Spain were planning to reduce Spanish America to its former state of dependence, but that England and the United States would oppose this. Moreover, in arranging for an interpreter for their secret interviews with Pueyrredón they had stipulated that he "should neither be English nor in any way connected with an English house or family." [10] But Bowles felt that there was no need for alarm.

The commissioners themselves were thoroughly conscious, and thoroughly envious, of British commerce and influence. When Bland conferred with the Chilean chief executive, Bernardo O'Higgins, in 1818, he tried to arouse his hostility against the British; and in his final report to Adams he spoke of English procedure at Buenos Aires in an unfriendly manner. He said: "The British Government and its authorities, with a con-

[10] The Bowles Correspondence is found in Admiralty (1), 23, 1556.

tinually wakeful regard to their commercial interests, have endeavored to pursue the incongruous and difficult policy of thwarting and confounding the republican principles of the people; and, at the same time, of discountenancing the inveterate hostility of the chiefs of the provinces, so wasteful of the productions of the country. The English admiral, Bowles, concluded a treaty . . . with General Artigas, regulating the British commerce with the people whom he controls; and an English consul, resident in Buenos Ayres, with a ship of war always near, without promoting the establishment of free institutions anywhere, insures an unrestrained trade with all the warring provinces." [11] The other commissioners also revealed jealously of England only slightly less pronounced.

Moreover, Poinsett, who had been asked for information in connection with their report, responded with a letter filled with envy and apprehension. "Great Britain," he said, "will probably encourage the intervention of the [Continental] Allies, to effect a pacification. She will insist upon the removal of . . . restrictions on their [*i. e.*, British] industry and their trade." In this manner England would attempt to gain the commerce of all Spanish America, where her influence was already powerful. As for the successive governments of the state of Buenos Aires, whose recognition President Monroe was now contemplating, they had "invariably acted towards this country as towards a

[11] Manning, *Dip. Cor.*, I, 435-436. Bland probably referred to Robert Staples, but Staples was not actually a consul.

Secondary power" and "the fear of exciting the jealousy of Great Britain . . . would prevent their making a treaty with us upon the footing of the most favored nation. . . . This disposition . . . was especially manifested during the late war between this Country [the United States] and Great Britain. They avoided as much as possible all public communication with our citizens: They suffered the British officers to examine all foreign letters, so as to enable them to intercept our correspondence; and they permitted the British Cruisers to capture our Ships in the Outer roads, within sight of Buenos Ayres, without remonstrance or complaint. . . . And they will never willingly adopt any measures, which might give umbrage to Great Britain."

For these and other reasons, Poinsett reluctantly advised that the government of the United Provinces of Rio de la Plata not be recognized. The democratic crusader then closed his letter with a retrospective view in which he sounded a note of melancholy disillusionment. "It is scarcely necessary," he said, "for one, who has made so many sacrifices to promote the independence of So. America, and whose enthusiasm in the cause of freedom carried him to the utmost limits of his duties as a Citizen of the United States, to disclaim all hostility to the Emancipation of these Colonies. The interest I take in their success yields only to my regard for the welfare of my own Country."[12] But his efforts in behalf of liberty were as

[12] Manning, *op. cit.*, I, 440-441.

POLITICAL AND ECONOMIC ISSUES

yet far from complete. The future was to call for more service and more disillusionment.

In other parts of Latin America contests similar to those in Argentina and Chile occurred. Space will only permit, however, a brief account of those in Great Colombia, which embraced most of the northern portion of the Southern Continent.

There is ample evidence of friction between the Yankees and the English in this region. As early as July, 1810, the commercial agent of the United States at La Guayra (Venezuela) reported from Baltimore that a British agent from the island of Curaçao was negotiating at Caracas for special commercial concessions. He urged that a government vessel be sent to cruise along the Spanish Main in order to "place us on a footing with our competitors," meaning the British, of course. In 1813 another agent, who had been sent with American relief to earthquake victims, wrote that he and another American representative had been ordered out of the country. The Spanish party, "under the influence of British counsels," he said, had been responsible for this hostile measure.[13]

The irritations of this earlier period continued. In 1819 President Monroe sent Captain Oliver H. Perry on a mission to the government of Simón Bolívar. He was authorized to explain the delay of the United States in granting recognition to the new governments of Spanish America and to negotiate, in an informal manner, concerning claims, piracy, and other matters.

[13] *Ibid.*, II, 1167.

Owing to Perry's death, the duty of reporting the results of his service devolved upon Purser Charles O. Handy, and Handy did not fail to note the activities of the British in this part of the country.

"The people of Venezuela," said Handy, "generally think that the U. S. regard with an eye of indifference their struggle for independence, and that they have never really enlisted our sympathies. . . . These sentiments are encouraged and actively propagated by the English in Venezuela, who are the avowed favorites of the Government. . . . The arrival of a vessel with about a hundred English soldiers during the stay of the Commodore [*sic*], excited a very strong sensation in Angostura in favor of England and against the United States." Handy then added somewhat hopefully: "The enlightened part of the population (and this comprehends but a small portion,) look with distrust at the apparent interest of Great Britain in their welfare. They know of the attempt heretofore made by that power [namely, in the La Plata region, 1806-1807] to establish a footing on their continent, and seriously apprehend that in the event of any open and active efforts in their favor from Great Britain, they would proceed from motives of national aggrandizement, terminating in the acquisition of additional territory." [14] What Perry did to strengthen this impression Handy does not say, but one may be sure that he did nothing to weaken it.

From the many instances of subsequent jealousies,

[14] *Ibid.*, II, 1181.

only one can now be selected. Early in 1823 Confidential Agent Charles S. Todd wrote in alarm from Bogotá of rumors to the effect that England was planning to take possession of "the Musquito Shore, Maracaibo, and the South bank of the Orinoco," thus placing Colombia absolutely under British control. He also mentioned reports of special commercial concessions which the English were pursuing elsewhere.[15]

These jealousies and alarms could doubtless be matched in the reports of British naval and colonial officials, but such reports must give place to two other documents, both of which were probably—one certainly—written by agents with experience in Hispanic America. The first of these is an unsigned memorandum prepared for the Foreign Office and bearing the date May 12, 1811.[16] The second is an address to the South Americans and Mexicans, published by James Henderson in 1822 and circulated in these countries with the view of counteracting alleged designs of the United States.[17]

The memorandum of 1811 notes that, "The United States have not swerved from the policy of fomenting the spirit of Revolt [in Spanish America], and even of absolute separation from Spain." "It is not un-

[15] Manning, *op. cit.*, II, 1247-1248.

[16] F. O. (72), 108.

[17] *Representación á los Americanos del Sud y Mexicanos; para disuadirles de que concedan ventajas comerciales á otros naciones, en perjuicio de Inglaterra, por causa de su retardo en reconocer su independencia.*

known," the writer added, "that they have offered every aid to the French agents [of 1808-1809 and 1810-1811] who have been engaged in the same designs. . . ." He went on to note, however, that the insurgents looked to England above every other nation in the world and would prefer her mediation or alliance to that of any other Power.

In a memorandum of his services, which Henderson transmitted to the Foreign Office years later, he explained his early connection with Spanish-American affairs and the motives which led to the preparation of his address in 1822.[18] He had sailed to South America in 1818 with the expectation of employment in the consular service, but had been disappointed. He later became engaged in furnishing information on the revolting provinces to the Board of Trade and the Foreign Office. "The great importance of our opening commerce with the new states of South America was daily becoming more manifest," said Henderson, "and our supposed rival, the United States, had already preceded us in the recognition of their independence, when the suggestion of Mr. Henderson, that an address to the South Americans dissuading them from giving a commercial preference . . . to any other nation, in consequence of the delay by Great Britain of their acknowledgment, was not only approved, but regarded by *several members of His Majesty's Government, as likely to be very beneficial.*"

[18] The memorandum bears the date of April 9, 1831, and was found in F. O. (18), 85.

Political and Economic Issues 21

Henderson then went on to tell how the document had been prepared, broadcasted and received in Hispanic Amercia. "Mr. Henderson immediately set about the preparation of such a document and had it translated into the Spanish language, and circulated throughout the new Republics of America. Extracts from it were introduced into the local Gazettes of those countries," and it apparently had "much influence" on their policy. The address could not have been responsible, however, for the failure of the United States to obtain special commercial concessions, for Monroe and Adams would not have accepted them if they had been offered. Yet it may have succeeded in shaking the confidence of some of the Spanish-American leaders in their Republican brothers of the North.

Such were the early rivalries and animosities of the United States and England with reference to Hispanic America as a whole. Attention must now be directed to the antagonisms which arose in connection with certain specific areas.

CHAPTER II

THE DESTINY OF THE SPANISH BORDERLANDS

With reference to the territorial phases of this rivalry over Hispanic America, Great Britain did not pursue in all respects a consistent policy. There was no departure from the conclusion formed by British statesmen in 1808 that it was undesirable for England to acquire any of the American possessions of Spain or Portugal. There was a steady conviction dating from a much earlier period that France should not be permitted to secure any portion of Spain's American empire, and there was a fairly persistent spirit of opposition to the southward expansion of the United States, but British opposition to Napoleon's acquisition of France was not actively manifested in 1801-1803, and the intensity of resentment at the expansion of the United States varied with the changing aspect of affairs in the Old World and in the New.

The political leaders of the United States revealed more consistency and aggressiveness. Long before 1808 they reached the conviction that none of the larger Powers of Europe should be permitted permanently to secure any portion of Spanish dominions which lay adjacent to the United States. Many of them also, long before this time, formed the resolution to acquire some of these dominions from the feeble hands of Spain, but this resolution was perhaps arrived at less from a desire for the territory *per se* than from the fear that France or England would acquire it.

I. THE FRENCH MENACE

During a conference with Rufus King which occurred near the last of May, 1801, Lord Hawkesbury, British secretary for foreign affairs, alluded to reports that Spain had ceded Louisiana and possibly the Floridas to Napoleon. Hawkesbury "very unreservedly expressed the reluctance with which" Englishmen would "be led to acquiesce in a measure that might be followed by the most important consequences; the acquisition might enable France to extend her influence up the Mississippi and thro' the lakes even to Canada; this would be realising the plan, to prevent the accomplishment of which the seven years' war took place, besides the vicinity of the Floridas to the West Indies and the facility with which the trade of the latter might be interrupted and the Islands even invaded, should the transfer be made, were strong reasons why England must be unwilling that this territory should pass under the dominion of France."[1]

This was a frank and significant statement. Louisiana and the Floridas must not be permitted to fall into the hands of a nation with power to menace Canada and the British West Indies. It was a true representa-

[1] *The Life and Correspondence of Rufus King* (Charles R. King, ed., New York, 1896), III, 414, 469.

tion of English official attitude in 1801, and it would doubtless have applied with equal force to the period between 1783 and 1801 if not indeed to that subsequent to 1801. France was thought to be such a nation, and the United States was probably feared for a similar reason, although not to the same extent.

To this attitude toward France must be referred, for the most part, the English government's refusal to give up the military posts in the Northwest until 1796, as well as its anxiety to keep on friendly terms with the Indians and the Western settlers. If Frenchmen, still regretting their loss of an empire in North America, persistently dreamed of the recovery of Louisiana and Canada, Britain must hold itself in readiness to defeat these dreams.[2]

To this attitude must likewise be attributed the eagerness with which Robert Liston, British minister to the United States, gave ear to the schemes of the American conspirators Chisholm and Blount. Liston believed that they were planning to take Louisiana and the Floridas from Spain in order to prevent them from coming into the possession of France. "I had convincing proofs," said Liston in this connection, "of the existence of a plan formed by the French to extend their arms and their influence over the whole of this

[2] F. J. Turner, "The Diplomatic Contest for the Mississippi Valley," in *The Atlantic Monthly*, XCIII (1904), 678 ff.; *Canadian Archives Report* (1891), pp. xxxvi-xlii, 88, 98, 108; Liston to the Foreign Office, Nov. 18, 1796; July 19, 1797; Apr. 2 and Aug. 12, 1898; F. O. (5), 14, 18, 22.

Northern Continent of America.... Means were suggested of preventing its execution; and I could not resist the temptation of making His Majesty's Ministers judges of the propriety of adopting or rejecting those means." [3]

It was for this reason, then, that Liston was interested in the project. It was likewise for this reason, apparently, that the British officials paid Chisholm's passage to London and took care of some of his bills while he was there. They decided not to support the plan when they began to doubt the ability of its promoters and when they ascertained that it would not only encounter the opposition of the Washington government but would involve an alliance with the Indians of the American Southwest and a violation of the neutrality of the United States; but the affair was none the less a significant comment on the motives of British policy.[4] The French menace was the important consideration.

British statesmen probably did not covet territory in the region. In 1783 Lord Lansdowne, British foreign secretary, had indeed desired to give up Gibraltar and demand Louisiana along with the Floridas, but "a cry arose agt. the cession of Gibraltar, the King refused his sanction to it," and the plan was abandoned. Louisiana and the Floridas accordingly had gone to

[3] Liston to Grenville, No. 3, Feb. 6, 1798, F. O. (5), 22.

[4] F. O. to Liston, April, 1797; Liston to Grenville, January 25, February 13, March 16, May 10, 1797, and *passim*, all in F. O. (5), 18.

Spain, and British statesmen were probably content that they should remain in Spanish hands. In order to prevent their acquisition by France they might under desperate circumstances have occupied them, but the acquisition would probably not have been permanent. At any rate, this is what the prime minister told Rufus King in April, 1802. "Mr. Addington desired me to be assured," [5] reported King, "that England would not accept the Country, were all agreed to give it up to her. . . ." [6] The prime minister was referring particularly to Louisiana, which was then supposed to have been ceded to France, but there is no reason to believe that the same assertion might not have been made in regard to Florida.

The United States was not actuated by a similar restraint, and its avowals were equally frank. In the important interview of May, 1801, King had remarked to Lord Hawkesbury that he thanked God for the Turks and the Spaniards. "The purport of what I said," wrote King to the secretary of state, "was that we are content that the Floridas remain in the hands of Spain, but should be unwilling to see them transferred except to ourselves." [7] During the conversation with Addington in April, 1803, King had been more explicit. He had told the prime minister that the seizure of Louisiana either by England or France could not be viewed "with indifference." "We had no objec-

[5] *The Life and Correspondence of Rufus King*, IV, 93.
[6] *Ibid.*, IV, 241.
[7] *Ibid.*, III, 469.

Destiny of Spanish Borderlands

tion to Spain continuing to possess it; they were quiet neighbors, and we looked forward without impatience to events which ... must, at no distant day, annex this Country to the United States."

In thus expressing himself to Addington, King did not proceed in opposition to the views of his chief at Washington—not if the report of British Minister Edward Thornton can be accepted as true. During the course of an interview with President Jefferson near the end of May, 1803, the conversation turned to the likelihood of a renewal of the war between Great Britain and France and the possible procedure of England in that event. Thornton asked Jefferson "half laughingly" whether the United States would "object to the invasion of the Floridas and the capture of New Orleans—adding after a pause, for the purpose of offering them on certain conditions to the Americans." Jefferson "answered in the same tone, that perhaps this step might endanger their neutrality; but that some day these possessions would become of indispensable necessity to the United States." Thornton then wrote home the following summary of the position of the United States as it appeared at that time: "They would prefer (I mean the present American Government) the continuance of the Spaniards in the possession of these countries and their own enjoyment of their present or greater privileges in the navigation and outlet of the Mississippi until acquiring greater strength and involved from whatever cause in a war with Spain they could dispossess the latter entirely of the Eastern Bank." [8]

Such, therefore, was the dilemma which Britain faced with reference to Louisiana and the Floridas at the opening of the nineteenth century. Both France and the United States were coveting these possessions. Their acquisition by either would constitute a possible threat to Canada and the English West Indies. Rufus King was urging Lord Hawkesbury to prevent France from obtaining Louisiana and to assist the United States to acquire it. For several years British ministers at Washington had been trying to frighten the United States into a British alliance by exposing the American plots of France, and now (early in 1802) Edward Thornton reminded Hawkesbury that "experience" seemed to "have sanctioned the opinion" that if Canada had been allowed to remain in the hands of France there would have been no American Revolution. A return to French imperial ambitions in North America would force the United States into a "straiter connection with Great Britain." [9] "To the President as well as to other leading characters" in the United States Thornton even began to talk of his "satisfaction at the cordiality and friendship which the simple vicinity of France must necessarily produce" between the United States and Great Britain. He told these leaders of the "irreconcilable hatred between France and England"—

[8] Thornton to Hawkesbury, No. 25, May 30, 1803, in F. O. (5), 38.

[9] *Idem* to *idem*, No. 3, January 26, 1802, *loc. cit.*, 35.

a hatred so intense that "whoever becomes an enemy of the former, acquires by that act alone the friendship of Great Britain." "I am almost persuaded," wrote Thornton after an interview with Jefferson, "that they would accept" the Floridas and Louisiana from England "at every risk of involving themselves in war with France and Spain, in concurrence with that power." But Thornton doubted whether the seizure of Louisiana and its transfer to the United States would be wise. "Considered exclusively on the side of our relations with the United States," said Thornton, "without regarding its possible effect on the British possessions in the American Seas, the most desirable state of things seems to be that France should become mistress of Louisiana, because her influence in the United States would be by that act lost forever" and a permanent "bond of unity and amity" thereby created between England and her American kinsmen.[10]

The British government hardly knew what position to take. Rufus King's importunities were not sufficient to persuade English diplomats to oppose the acquisition of Louisiana by France. Neither did they encourage, approve, or acquiesce in this transfer. They said nothing about the matter during the negotiations which led to the Treaty of Amiens (August, 1802). Nor did they take any positive action to advance the ambitions of the United States.[11] Was this the wisest

[10] Thornton to Hawkesbury, March 9 and May 30, 1803, F. O. (5), 38.

[11] Hawkesbury to King, May 7, 1802, in *Life and Correspondence of Rufus King*, IV, 123. See also *op. cit., passim*.

course? In the spring of 1803 the British ministry hesitated, and then chose the lesser of the two evils, or rather attempted to reconcile itself to the possession of Louisiana by the United States. Around the first of April, when King told Addington that the United States expected some day to annex Louisiana, the prime minister said: "If you can obtain it well, but if not, we ought to prevent its going into the hands of France, tho' you may be assured . . . that nothing shall be done injurious to the interest of the United States." [12] When he finally notified Lord Hawkesbury that France had ceded the province to the United States, King ventured to comment: "I flatter myself that this communication will be received with satisfaction." It apparently was. The Foreign Secretary replied (May 19, 1803): "Having laid before the King your letter of the 15th of this month, in which you inform me [of the treaty by which France has ceded Louisiana to the United States], . . . I have received his Majesty's commands to express to you the pleasure with which his Majesty has received this intelligence. . . ." [13]

Thus the English government acquiesced in the addition of Louisiana to the territorial domain of the United States—and half regretted that there had been no other way out of the dilemma. American leaders developed such exaggerated pretensions with reference to boundaries! They contended that on the east the province extended to the Perdido; on the west, to the

[12] *The Life and Correspondence of Rufus King*, IV, 241.

[13] *Ibid.*, IV, 262-263.

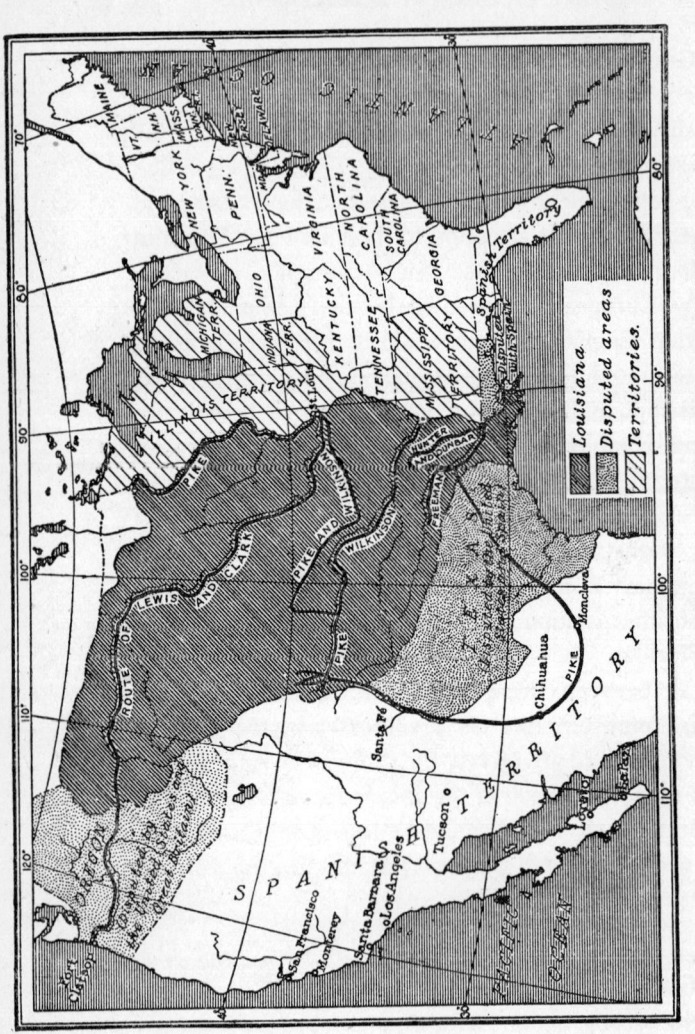

THE LOUISIANA PURCHASE AND DISPUTED BOUNDARIES

(From Bolton's *History of the Americas*)

Rio Grande and Santa Fé; on the north, that all that was not Canada was Louisiana, which meant that the British were to be shut off from the navigation of the Mississippi.[14]

For some time after 1803, however, the British government gave little attention to these issues. They did not loom large in comparison with other problems, mainly European, confronted by the Cabinet. It is true that English diplomats said nothing which might be interpreted as an acquiescence in the cloture of the Mississippi to England or in the enlarged boundaries of Louisiana. It is true that Anthony Merry, English minister at Washington, before the outbreak of hostilities between England and Spain in the latter part of 1804, industriously reported the attempts made by the Spanish minister in the United States to secure British interposition to defeat American designs upon the Floridas. It is true also that after the beginning of war between these European Powers, the same English minister, like his predecessor in the case of Chisholm, heard attentively the projects of Aaron Burr to set up a new nation in the Mississippi Valley and on the Gulf Coast, which would be less hostile to Britain than was the United States. But the English foreign secretary remained silent.[15]

[14] Anthony Merry to Hawkesbury, Jan. 16, and March 1, 1804, F. O. (5), 41.

[15] *Idem* to *idem*, No. 23, March 13, 1804, *loc. cit.*; *idem* to *idem*, Aug. 6, 1804, *passim*, F. O. (5), 42; Walter F. McCaleb, *The Aaron Burr Conspiracy* (New York, 1903), 20-23, *passim*.

II. THE ANGLO-SPANISH ALLIANCE AND AMERICAN EXPANSION INTO THE FLORIDAS

It was not until the Spanish nation rose against Napoleon in the summer of 1808 that the English government began to evince deeper concern regarding the plans of the United States to obtain territory at the expense of Spain's American possessions. And thereafter this concern never abated until Napoleon was sent as an exile to Elba. The attempts of Great Britain to interfere assumed a more critical aspect because of the growing hostility between England and the United States, and it is by no means certain that British interposition served the interests of Spain. Indeed, it appears that American desire for Spanish territory was intensified by the suspicion that Britain looked with covetous eyes upon the Floridas—a suspicion which persisted from the time of the Blount Conspiracy until 1819.

Between 1808 and 1812 the English ministers in Washington made several inquiries and remonstrances. The first of these occurred in 1809. On May 18 of that year the Spanish ambassador in London called Foreign Secretary Canning's attention to military movements and preparations in the United States. Having received news that General James Wilkinson was on the point of embarking from Wilmington for New Orleans with four thousand troops, and that the raising of fifty thousand volunteers was being warmly debated in the United States Congress, the ambassador feared the United States was preparing some hostile plan against the possessions of Spain. He therefore requested Canning to make inquiries through the British minister at Washington and check the project.[16]

Canning replied that Britain was just on the point of sending out a new minister (Francis Jackson) to the United States and that this official would be instructed "to make diligent inquiry into the circumstances . . . ; and in the event that . . . the American Government persevere in their hostile demonstrations against the Spanish territories in North America, to make the strongest representations upon the subject." [17]

Jackson was accordingly directed, in case he found the United States cherishing intentions of attack upon Spain's settlements, to make the "strongest representations," avoiding a severe tone but not disguising "the deep and lively interest which His Majesty takes in everything that relates to Spain." His Majesty's government stood ready to mediate in the disagreements of Spain and the United States and could not "see with indifference any attack upon" Spain's interests.[18]

Soon after his arrival in Washington Jackson conferred with Secretary of State John S. Smith and obtained a disavowal of hostile intentions against Spain. Smith said that the troops had been sent to

[16] Juan Ruíz de Apodaca to Canning, May 18, 1809, F. O. (72, Spain), 84.

[17] Canning to Apodaca, June 6, 1809, *loc. cit.*

[18] Canning to Jackson, No. 7, July 1, 1809, F. O. (5), 64.

New Orleans to quell certain local disorders and that they never exceeded two thousand.[19]

Before the close of the next year the Foreign Office was disturbed by an apparently groundless rumor that the United States was negotiating with the viceroy of Mexico for the cession of the Floridas. The news was communicated both to the Spanish Ambassador Apodaca and to the British ambassador in Madrid. The note to Apodaca reveals Britain's friendly disposition toward Spain. "As it appears ... that the negotiation has been carried on without the sanction of the Spanish Govt., His Majesty's Govt. have conceived that they were bound by the duties of the Alliance so happily existing between Great Britain and His Catholic Majesty as well as by the common ties of Amity and Good Faith to make the same known to Admiral Apodaca...."[20]

Fears based upon a more solid foundation were aroused late in 1810. In September the settlers around Baton Rouge, consisting mainly of American immigrants, had declared themselves independent of Spain, and in October they had asked the United States to occupy West Florida, a request which was immediately granted. J. P. Morier, then in charge of the British legation at Washington, suspected the connivance of the American government in the proceedings of the insurgents. Negotiations having failed, the

[19] Jackson to Canning, No. 10, October 18, 1809, F. O. (5), 64.

[20] The Marquis of Wellesley to Apodaca, September 27, 1810, F. O. (72), 101.

United States was beginning to adopt more drastic plans, he thought.

Morier became suspicious in November and sought an interview with Secretary Smith early the following month. At the same time he wrote to Admiral Rowley, commander of the British squadron in the Caribbean, suggesting that Rowley urge the captain general of Cuba to send reinforcements to Pensacola. During the interview between the American secretary of state and the British *chargé*, Smith curtly informed Morier that the Florida question was a matter which exclusively concerned the United States and Spain. Morier was highly irritated and advised his government to occupy Pensacola in order to prevent it from falling into the hands of the United States.[21]

When Morier read President Madison's annual message (December 5) boldly announcing that United States troops had occupied West Florida and defending the step, his irritation rose still higher. He immediately sent in a protest. "I deem it to be a duty incumbent on me, considering the strict and close alliance which subsists between His Majesty's Government and that of Spain, to express ... the deep regret with which I have seen that part of the President's message to Congress, in which the determination ... to take possession of West Florida is avowed," said Morier. He characterized the act as one of "open hostility against Spain," declared that England could not "see

[21] Morier to Wellesley, Nov. 1 and Dec. 3, 1810, F. O. (5), 70.

with indifference any attack upon" Spain's "interests in America," and demanded an immediate explanation. When this was not forthcoming at once he pressed the matter upon Smith, and was soon informed (December 28, 1810) that no explanation to Great Britain seemed necessary, that Spain was the "only Power known to the United States in the transaction," but that the minister of the United States in London had been authorized to communicate with the British government regarding the affairs.[22] President Madison then proceeded to use Morier's protest for the purpose of frightening Congress into granting permission to occupy, under certain contingencies, the whole of the Floridas![23]

Apparently Morier, in spite of his rebuff, had still more interviews. At any rate, on January 12 he wrote angrily of the "Iniquitous Transactions" which had wrested West Florida from Spain and of the arguments used to justify them. "Fearful that their endeavours to screw the Article of the Treaty of St. Ildefonso into all the shapes best suiting their purpose might not sufficiently establish the Title," said Morier, "these immaculate Republicans very quietly reconcile the usurpation on the principle of self defence, because they are not quite sure that Spain will maintain a Neutrality in case of a war between this Country and England or France, and because, after the Perfidy of

[22] *American State Papers, Foreign Relations*, III, 400-401.

[23] *Ibid.*, III, 394-395.

Destiny of Spanish Borderlands

Nations in Europe, they ought not to be so squeamish on this side the Atlantic." [24]

By this time Morier had learned that Congress was deliberating in secret sessions with reference to the Floridas and had become convinced that plans for the occupation of the entire region were under way. He expected these aggressive measures of the United States to lead to war with Spain, in which England would probably participate on the side of the latter, and he made certain suggestions relative to this prospect. The seizure of New Orleans by the British would so distress the Western settlers that they would be encouraged "to revolt from the Union," he declared. South Carolina, Georgia, and the Mississippi Territory were extremely "vulnerable," owing to the large number of slaves. The Spaniards might send to this region the black troops at Havana "to assist them in asserting their independence." Moreover, "the best point of retaliation for Spain would be in Louisiana from Mexico." [25] These suggestions were not soon forgotten by the British government, at any rate, not many of them.

Meanwhile, the United States proceeded with its drastic projects. Morier was not mistaken in his suspicions. On January 15, 1811, Congress resolved with reference to the Floridas that the United States could not, "without serious inquietude, see any part of the said territory pass into the hands of any foreign

[24] Morier to Wellesley, No. 4, Jan. 12, 1811, F. O. (5), 74.

[25] *Idem* to *Idem*, No. 11, Jan. 24, 1811, *loc. cit.*

Power." Congress, at the same time, authorized the president to take possession of East Florida — peaceably, if it could be done by an arrangement with the Spanish authorities, or by use of more forceful measures, if these should become necessary in order to prevent the region from falling into the hands of "any foreign government" (meaning Great Britain).[26] By the spring of 1812 all of West Florida, except Mobile, and a good portion of East Florida were in the hands of American soldiers.[27]

But Morier was spared the pain of a close view of this "usurpation." He was superseded early in 1811 by Augustus John Foster, who came out with full instructions. The head of the British Foreign Office did not mince words. He complained that the promise made by Smith to Morier late in December, 1810, that United States Minister William Pinkney would give explanations regarding West Florida, had not been fulfilled. "If . . . you shall find on your arrival at Washington, that America still perseveres to claim by Menaces and active demonstrations the military occupation of West Florida, you will present to the Secretary of State the Solemn Protest of His Royal Highness . . . against an attempt so contrary to every principle of public justice, faith and National Honour, and so injurious to the alliance subsisting between His Majesty and the Spanish Nation." Furthermore: "If

[26] U. S., *Statutes at Large*, III, 471.

[27] Julius W. Pratt, *Expansionists of 1812* (New York, 1925), 74 ff.

any attempt should be made to occupy East Florida you will instantly remonstrate against such a proceeding, for which it will not be possible to allege even the slightest pretexts." There were, however, a few words of caution. Foster was directed to "abstain from any hostile or menacing language." Great Britain could not "view Such Proceedings ... without regret and pain; but it is [was] not a necessary consequence of those sentiments, that this Government should proceed to vindicate the rights of Spain by force of arms." Conduct on this point would have to be determined by "future considerations," and the "ultimate decision ... in a matter of such serious Importance" must not be compromised.[28]

Thus equipped, Foster set out for his post. It was probably on the first day of July, 1811, that he had his initial interview on the question with James Monroe, now secretary of state. Discussion was first directed to West Florida. Monroe justified its military occupation on various grounds: American citizens and commerce had suffered at the hands of Spain; the United States had acquired title to the country by the purchase of Louisiana; geographical necessity dictated its acquisition; humanitarian considerations urged the occupation in order to protect the Spanish troops and officials from the bloody ire of the insurgents! "It was with real pain," said Foster, "that I was forced to listen to arguments of the most profligate nature, such as, that other nations were not so scrupulous, that the

[28] Wellesley to Foster, No. 3, April 10, 1811, F. O. (5), 75.

United States showed sufficient forbearance in not assisting the Insurgents of South America and looking to their own interest in the present situation of that Country." The question of East Florida was then taken up. Foster managed to obtain definite knowledge of the action of Congress on the fifteenth of the previous January. Was the shameless procedure in West Florida now to be repeated in East Florida? Monroe made no answer, but Foster inferred from his manner and countenance that it was.[29] On the next day Foster sent in a written protest against the action of the United States in West Florida, and six days later Monroe replied, saying nothing of geographical necessity and the political immorality of Europe, but employing all the other arguments which he had used in the conference of July 1.[30]

During the hot summer of 1811 Foster gradually accumulated evidence of the aggressive sentiments of the American Cabinet. The secretary of war frankly told him that he thought East Florida should be occupied and the reasons for the action given afterwards. A little later Monroe informed Foster that this was what the United States would probably do at the proper time.[31] Foster was greatly agitated. Should not some British official in the West Indies be authorized to offer aid to the Spanish authorities in Florida

[29] Foster to Wellesley, No. 3, July 5, 1811, F. O. (5), 76.

[30] *American State Papers, Foreign Relations*, III, 542-543.

[31] Foster to Wellesley, No. 9, July 18, 1811, and No. 12, Aug. 5, 1811, F. O. (5), 76.

Destiny of Spanish Borderlands

"in a very public manner?" Let it appear as the "spontaneous act of the individual English Governor or Admiral." This would cause timid men to reflect before "involving themselves in the risk of a war with such a power as Great Britain." [32]

Foster's prayer for the authorization of a menace was not answered, and early in September he sent in another written remonstrance against the procedure of Americans in East Florida, particularly that of George Mathews, an agent whom the State Department had sent out early in 1811 to obtain the peaceful deposit of the province into the hands of the United States. "I conceive it to be my duty," said Foster, "in consideration of the alliance subsisting between Spain and Great Britain, and the interests of His Majesty's subjects in the West India islands, so deeply involved in the security of East Florida, . . . to lose no time in calling upon you for an explanation. . . ." [33] Monroe took the document and went away to look over his Virginia crops. Foster fumed and fretted.

When Monroe returned, a conference of a "very serious nature" took place. Monroe took time for only a brief apology for the delay in answering Foster's last note. "He then began to inveigh very warmly against the interference of Great Britain with respect to East Florida, telling me [Foster] in very plain language that he had been of the opinion that the United States

---

[32] *Idem* to *Idem*, No. 12, Aug. 5, 1811, *loc. cit.*

[33] *American State Papers*, III, 543-544. On the authority and activities of Mathews, see Pratt, *op. cit.*, *passim*.

should have seized on that country long ago, and have held it as a pledge for payment of the debt due by Spain to this Country and claimed as compensation for illegal captures. He said this Government had abstained latterly from doing so but through tenderness for the situation of Spain, a feeling . . . rather diminished by the conduct of Great Britain. He told me that it had long been thought here that we meant to seize on Florida for ourselves, and that in my note there was an expression . . . which increased that suspicion." [34] Monroe also declared that the United States could not permit "any foreign power to take possession of East Florida." Foster denied that Great Britain entertained any such designs. "Mr. Monroe still maintained his former position, and grew not a little warm." He complained of Foster's two notes of protest and said he had evidence that Great Britain meant to assist Spain to subdue her colonies. "I thought," continued Foster, "I could discover an expectation and a wish that we should resist the attempt to seize Florida. . . . I asked him if they would proceed to take it without regard for any consequences, he hastily interrupted me, and assuming a serious countenance, said they were prepared for any consequences whatever."

Foster had brandished his threat and received his answer. He had, moreover, already (September 13) written Admiral Sawyer, of the West India Squadron, urging him to support the Spanish governor of St. Augustine by the dispatch of supplies and the occa-

[34] Namely, the portion quoted above.

sional appearance of British naval forces off Amelia Island.[35] With this he let the matter rest until near the first of the following April, when Monroe disavowed the activities of Mathews and informed Foster that this agent would be recalled.[36] Apparently Monroe had given the British menace a sober second thought.

But the "Expansionists of 1812" still kept an anxious eye upon the Floridas. West Florida was formally annexed in the spring and summer of 1812. Mathews was dismissed, but his commission was given first to Governor D. B. Mitchell of Georgia and later to Major-General Thomas Pinckney.[37] By this time the war with Great Britain had already begun.

III. LOUISIANA, THE FLORIDAS, AND THE WAR OF 1812

The war was caused largely by other issues, but neither the Floridas nor even Louisiana could be ignored. Some of the "War Hawks," when urging the combat, cherished eager anticipations of territorial conquests to the south. In this they were disappointed, for a fatal sectionalism prevented Congress from granting the permission which was deemed necessary.[38]

---

[35] Foster to Wellesley, No. 17, September 18, 1811, and enclosures, *loc. cit.*

[36] *Idem* to *Idem*, No. 21, April 2, 1812, and April 23, 1812, F. O. (5), 85.

[37] Pratt, *op. cit.*, 113, 124, 211; Cox, *The West Florida Controversy* (Baltimore, 1918), *passim*.

[38] Pratt, *op. cit.*, 150-152, 226-229.

Then, late in 1814, the British government began hostile operations on the Gulf coast. There could be no peace for the Floridas until they rested securely under the shelter of the American flag.

In the late summer of 1813, when a promise of Russian mediation appeared, Count Fernán Núñez, Spanish ambassador in London, implored Lord Castlereagh, British foreign secretary, to demand of the United States not only the recognition of Ferdinand VII — which it had steadfastly refused[39] — but also the evacuation of the Floridas and the restitution of all the territory taken by the Americans since the French invaded the Spanish peninsula. Castlereagh forthwith assured him that the rights and interests of Ferdinand would be upheld as well as "the Independence and the Integrity of the Spanish Monarchy."

The Russian attempt at mediation failed, and in July, 1814, Núñez made another overture. He represented to Castlereagh the earnest wish of the Spanish sovereign to "put himself in concert" with the Prince Regent of England "as well for forcing . . . the United States to a Peace as for treating thereupon." His Catholic Majesty was eager to "unite his forces with Great Britain in order to restrain" the United States. Castlereagh reminded Núñez of the previous efforts of England in behalf of Spain's interests in America,

[39] The refusal of the United States to recognize the minister of Ferdinand VII in Washington led this official to make British diplomats the medium of protests against American activities in the Floridas.

Destiny of Spanish Borderlands

assured him that these would be renewed when diplomatic relations with the United States should be resumed, and tactfully declined the offer.[40]

Castlereagh fulfilled his promise. An important project of the war with the United States was an attack upon its southern coast with the view of restoring not only the Floridas but also Louisiana to Spain. No movement of the contest proved more Quixotic and yet few objects were pursued with more tenacity.

Officers of the British navy were most eager for the drive against the South. Early in May, 1814, Captain H. Pigot anchored His Majesty's Ship *Orpheus* near the mouth of the Apalachicola and sent emissaries out into the wilderness in search of the Indians. Several Creek chiefs and interpreters were soon assembled on board the *Orpheus* and assured of the great interest of England in their welfare. Pigot left Captain George Woodbine and two assistants to train the warriors, and Woodbine was also appointed agent to the Creek Nation. Pigot then departed with the conviction that nearly 4,000 Indians in the Southwest were ready to join Britain in the common struggle with the United States. He was also convinced that the Negroes of Georgia would come over in great numbers to the English and the Indians. Admiral Alexander Cochrane, who was

---

[40] Núñez to Castlereagh, Aug. 23, 1813, F. O. (72), 149; *idem* to *idem*, July 6, 1814, F. O. (72), 165; Castlereagh to Núñez, August 28, 1913, F. O. (72), 149; *idem* to *idem*, July 30, 1814, F. O. (72), 165.

eager to give the Yankees a "complete drubbing" and wrest the command of the Mississippi from them, jubilantly forwarded the report to the War Office. "I have not a doubt in my mind," said Cochrane, "that three thousand British troops landed at Mobile where they would be joined by all the Indians, with the disaffected French and Spaniards, would drive the Americans out of Louisiana and the Floridas."[41]

Indeed, Cochrane was so enthusiastic about the project that he could hardly wait for instructions. Late in July he sent Major Nicolls and a detachment of four officers, one surgeon, eleven non-commissioned officers, and ninety-seven privates, supplied with two howitzers, a fieldpiece, and three hundred suits of clothing, to the Mobile district. Nicolls was also equipped with printed proclamations for circulation among the Negroes. The blacks were offered free lands in the British West Indies at the end of the war and assured that when it closed they would not be delivered to their former masters.[42] Cochrane then sent full accounts of his views and activities to the War Office and the Admiralty.

The Admiralty immediately approved of his conduct and promised that his plans should be given every consideration. The War Office, less optimistic than Coch-

---

[41] British Public Record Office, Foreign Office, Admiralty, Classification No. I, volume 506. Cochrane to John Wilson Croker, June 20, 1814, and enclosures; Cochrane to Bathurst, July 14, 1814, War Office, Classification No. 1, volume 141.

[42] Cochrane to Croker, July 14, 1814, Adm. (1), 506.

rane, looked about for a commander to take charge of the army of invasion.

Major-General Ross, who at this very time was leading—though the War Office did not then know it—an attack upon Washington, was picked for the task. The plan was to seize Louisiana and the Floridas and restore them to Spain. More than six thousand, instead of a mere three thousand, troops and marines were to be sent over. The seizure of the Floridas by the United States was pronounced an "usurpation," but the partiality of the inhabitants of Louisiana for Great Britain was not confidently accepted. They might desire to establish an independent state, and the English government preferred that they should be encouraged to declare for a return to Spanish authority, but since the British government was unwilling to give a pledge that either their independence or their restitution to Spain would be made a *sine qua non* of peace with the United States, the most that it could hope for with any degree of confidence was that these settlers would acquiesce in the temporary occupation of New Orleans.

It appears certain both from the instructions to Major-General Ross and from the supplementary instructions given to Sir Edward Pakenham, who was appointed to this command when the death of Ross became known in England, that Great Britain had no intention of permanent acquisitions in the region. The purpose of the expedition in the general strategy of the war was declared to be twofold: (1) to obtain control of the mouth of the Mississippi and deprive the back settlements of their approach to the sea; (2) "to occupy some important and valuable Possession, by the restoration of which we may improve the conditions of Peace, or which may entitle us to exact its cession as the price of Peace." This apparently did not mean, however, that Britain intended anything more than to serve as the medium of transmission to Spain. "You will discountenance any proposition of the Inhabitants to place themselves under the Dominion of Great Britain. . . ." Such were the orders given to Ross; and they were transmitted without modification to Pakenham. Whether the regions occupied should be used as a base for further operations against the South was left to the discretion of the officers on the ground. They were cautioned, however, not to encourage a Negro insurrection.[43] It was hoped, too, that a diversion in this region might serve to protect Canada.[44]

These, then, were the purposes of the invasion. Its failure and the reasons therefor are well known. Andrew Jackson and the loyalty of the Westerners were the imponderables which shattered British projects. The noted victory over Pakenham was not known, however, until the peace negotiations which had begun several months before had resulted in the Treaty of Ghent.

[43] Bathurst to Ross, Sept. 6, 1814, W. O. (6), 2; *idem* to Pakenham, Oct. 24, 1814, *loc. cit.*

[44] War Office Memorandum of 1814, *loc. cit.*

Destiny of Spanish Borderlands

The place of Louisiana and the Floridas in these negotiations has not been sufficiently emphasized. Not only did the expectation of news that these provinces had been taken cause the British peace commissioners to act with greater deliberation; discussion of the regions frequently occurred during all of the important conferences which led to the treaty.

Secretary of State Monroe expected from the outset that the Floridas would become the subject of a diplomatic contest. In instructing the commissioners (April 27, 1813) appointed to negotiate under Russian mediation, he had suggested that they might "perhaps find it advantageous" to inform the English diplomats that the United States had a "right to West Florida by cession from France, and a claim to East Florida as an indemnity for spoliations." A few days before he penned these instructions, he had been compelled by the attitude of Congress to order the withdrawal of United States forces from East Florida, but he had done so very reluctantly; and he now reminded the commissioners that the "law authorizing the President to take possession of East Florida in case any attempt should be made by any foreign power to occupy it is [was] still in force." He also suggested that it would be "proper" for them to bear in mind the "object of that law." [45]

A few days later Monroe was disturbed by the report from Cádiz that the Spanish Regency had sold

---

[45] *The Writings of Albert Gallatin* (Henry Adams, ed., Philadelphia, 1879), I, 539-541.

both provinces to the British government, "and that it had done so under a belief that we had or should soon get possession of it." "My firm belief," the secretary wrote, "is that if we were possessed of both it would facilitate your negotiations in favor of impressment and every other object. . . ." [46]

Thus Monroe was still eager to round out the territorial domain of the United States by annexations to the south, still hoping for an excuse to take East Florida. Apprehensions of British designs would appear to have furnished sufficient excuse for this, but the occupation of Mobile by Jackson late in 1814 was the extent of American encroachment during the war with the English.

The direct negotiations which began with England at Ghent in August, 1814, had not proceeded far until the English commissioners injected not only the Florida issue but also that of Louisiana. In the absence of certain news that the British had taken the Gulf coast, however, this issue could only be used as a bluff; and as such it was mainly employed. It was hoped that a strong suggestion of England's unwillingness to acquiesce in America's title to these regions would frighten the American commissioners into concessions on other matters, particularly in respect to the Canadian boundary.

In this latter connection the question was first brought into the discussion. The British diplomats asserted that adjustments in that boundary and exclu-

[46] Monroe to Albert Gallatin, May 6, 1813, *ibid.*, I, 543-544.

sive military possession of the Great Lakes were necessary as a precautionary measure against an American aggressiveness but "too clearly manifested by their progressive occupation of the Indian territories, by the acquisition of Louisiana, by the more recent attempt to wrest by force of arms from a nation in amity the two Floridas, and, lastly, by the avowed intention of permanently annexing the Canadas to the United States."[47] The American response hinted at British aggressions all around the world, suggested that the manner of acquiring territory from Spain and the Indians was none of England's business, and yet attempted to justify the conduct of the United States toward Spain.[48]

A few days later the British countered in more pointed terms. They declared that the purchase of Louisiana from France had been "against the known conditions on which it had been ceded by Spain to that country" and they spoke of the "hostile seizure of a great part of the Floridas under the pretence of a dispute respecting the boundary."[49] These charges struck fire. The American ministers indignantly retorted that the observation regarding Louisiana seemed very extraordinary, "as the cession of that province to

[47] The British to the American Ministers, September 4, 1814, *American State Papers, Foreign Relations*, III, 713-714.

[48] The American to the British Ministers, Sept. 9, 1814, *ibid.*, III, 715.

[49] The British to the American Ministers, Sept. 19, 1814, *ibid.*, III, 718.

the United States was, at the time, communicated to the British Government, who expressed their entire satisfaction with it, and as it has [had] subsequently received the solemn sanction of Spain herself." They further declared that "whenever the transactions of the United States in relation to the boundaries of Louisiana and Florida shall be a proper subject of discussion, they will be found not only susceptible of complete justification, but still demonstrate the moderation and forbearance of the American Government." [50]

Thus, despite the reluctance of the American commissioners, these territories were being forced into the negotiations. And they were soon to become important topics in the discussion. After the official reports of the taking of Washington reached the British Cabinet, they considered the employment of the bluff to the limit. Preparations for the expedition against the southern coast of North America were under way, but perhaps the United States could be frightened to submission without this menace. Louisiana and, especially, the Floridas furnished the instrument. Prime Minister Liverpool thought that the Florida transaction should be characterized as "one of the most immoral acts recorded in the history of any country." [51]

The language of the new note to the American commissioners at Ghent was not quite so severe, but

[50] The American to the British Ministers, Sept. 26, 1814, *ibid.*, III, 719.

[51] Frank A. Updike, *The Diplomacy of the War of 1812* (Baltimore, 1915) 274.

DESTINY OF SPANISH BORDERLANDS

it was stronger than any that had previously been used. In 1803 the British government had indeed expressed satisfaction that Louisiana had passed to the hands of the United States instead of remaining in those of the French enemy. "But the conditions under which France had acquired Louisiana from Spain were not communicated; the refusal of Spain to consent to its alienation was not known; the protest of her ambassador had not been made; and many other circumstances attending the transaction . . . were, as there is good reason to believe, industriously concealed."[52] As for "the hostile seizure of a great part of the Floridas," it had been done "under the most frivolous pretences" and "the occasion and circumstances under which that unwarrantable act of aggression took place have given rise throughout Europe to but one sentiment. . . ."[53]

This sharp characterization of the conduct of the United States with reference to the Floridas, the Americans did not deign to answer. They felt it was time to drop the subject. Nor did the British return to the charges. The commissioners of the United States came once more to the defence of their right

---

[52] This is probably an insinuation that the Louisiana cession involved an informal alliance between the United States and France—an idea which, further supported by the fact that American diplomats sought French aid in order to acquire West Florida, persisted for ten years.

[53] The British to the American Ministers, Oct. 8, 1814, *American State Papers, Foreign Relations*, III, 721.

to retain Louisiana, however;[54] and with this defence the question of title was dropped.

Arguments were now directed to the northern boundary of Louisiana, mainly with the view, on the part of the British, of securing the right to navigate the Mississippi and of gaining some advantage in Oregon. But the Americans were aware of these English designs. They also suspected that the British were trying to involve them in difficulties with Spain and, hence, managed to keep the subject of the Louisiana boundary out of the treaty which was finally signed on December 24, 1814.[55] At an earlier period they might have welcomed Spanish hostilities, but it was different now. What with an English expedition threatening New Orleans and the South, with Napoleon at Elba, and British diplomats dictating European settlements at Vienna, it was no time to provoke a break with Spain.

IV. THE FLORIDA QUESTION AND THE LOUISIANA BOUNDARY (1815-1821)

Between Great Britain and the United States the Florida issue, after 1814, was largely an aftermath of the war, and Louisiana came into the discussion because its boundaries were closely related to that issue. Some of the British agents who had operated on the Gulf coast during the struggle and probably supposed that their government wished to make per-

[54] In the note of October 13, *ibid.*, III, 723.

[55] *Ibid.*, III, 733, *passim*.

Destiny of Spanish Borderlands

manent acquisitions in the region, were very reluctant to abandon their projects. Their activities kept the United States government uneasy and furnished a ready means of arousing a popular desire to acquire East Florida by force if necessary.

Major Nicolls and George Woodbine, and their associates and successors, among whom were Robert C. Ambrister, Alexander Arbuthnot, and Gregor McGregor, had not only kept the Florida border in ferment but at one time (1817) some of them had actually occupied Galveston and Amelia Island. For the duration of the war the activities of Nicolls, Woodbine, and Ambrister had been authorized by the British government and directed by such higher officials as Sir George Cockburn and Alexander Cochrane. Negroes, pirates, and others of pro-British sentiment had rallied around the British flag. Moreover, Indians to the number of about four thousand had come over to the British side.[56]

The latter became an important consideration. To the British government, their rights became a point of honor, and the following language in the ninth article of the Treaty of Ghent was designed to protect them: "The United States of America engage to put an end, immediately after the ratification of the present treaty, to hostilities with all the tribes or nations of Indians with whom they may be at war at the time

---

[56] Nicolls to J. P. Morier, Sept. 25 and 29, 1815, W. O. (1), 143; Cochrane to Bathurst, March 12, 1816, and enclosures, *ibid.*, 144.

of such ratification; and forthwith to restore to such tribes or nations, respectively, all the possessions, rights and privileges which they may have enjoyed or been entitled to in one thousand eight hundred and eleven. . . ."[57] To the English military agents on the ground, relations with the natives not only involved a point of honor but a matter of commerce as well as a means of preparation for a future war with the United States. With these ends in view they had assembled the principal Indian chiefs early in 1815, before the arrival of news that the Treaty of Ghent had been signed, and had drawn up a treaty of alliance. Major Nicolls, accompanied by some of the chiefs, carried this document to England, and Admiral Cochrane wrote the secretary of state a strong letter urging the formation of such an alliance. He maintained that both honor and strategy demanded the step. He said that General Jackson had trumped up, late in 1814, "a sort of Treaty[58] with about two hundred Fugitive Indians," but that at the very time "most, if not all, of the Chiefs were in the vicinity of Apalachicola" with Admiral Sir George Cockburn "preparing to invade the back part of Georgia." Such a pact was therefore a mere farce, but the United States were determined to employ it as a pretext in order to prevent Article IX of the Treaty of Ghent from compelling the restitution of their lands. Moreover, the United States still cherished designs on Canada and an alliance with the southwestern Indians

[57] W. M. Malloy, *Treaties*, I, 618.

[58] This was the Treaty of Fort Jackson, Aug. 9, 1814.

"would operate more in favor of the Canadas than double their number of troops sent to that Country from home." [59]

By the summer of 1815 the United States had become alarmed at the procedure of Major Nicolls. Monroe sent a note of protest to *Chargé* Anthony St. John Baker [60] and on September 14, John Quincy Adams, now minister at the Court of St. James's, interviewed Bathurst on the matter. "Why," said Lord Bathurst, "to tell you the truth, Colonel Nicolls is, I believe, a man of activity and spirit, but a very wild fellow. He did make, and send over to me, a treaty offensive and defensive with the Indians, and he is now come over here, and has brought over some of those Indians. I sent for answer that he had no authority whatever to make a treaty offensive and defensive with the Indians, and that the Government would make no such treaty. . . . The Indians are here in great distress, indeed, but we shall only furnish them with the means of returning home, and advise them to make their terms with the United States as well as they can." [61] Baker at Washington was at the same time instructed to disavow the procedure of Nicolls,[62] and he did so both in an interview (December 7) and in a

[59] Letter cited in note 56, *antea*.

[60] Baker to Bathurst, No. 22, July 15, 1815, F. O. (5), 107.

[61] *Memoirs* (Charles Francis Adams, ed., Philadelphia, 1874), III, 271.

[62] Bathurst to Baker, No. 11, September, 1815, F. O. (5), 105.

formal note (December 15).[63] But both Monroe and Adams forgot these disavowals, as the sequel will show.

While in the midst of these discussions relative to Nicolls, Monroe received reports of a more alarming nature. They alleged that England had obtained from Spain not only the Floridas but Louisiana as well. Adams was immediately instructed to make inquiries, to remonstrate against the cession of Louisiana and West Florida, and to offer to purchase East Florida from the British.[64]

Late in January Adams brought the subject to the attention of Foreign Secretary Castlereagh. Discussion appears to have centered on the Floridas. Adams said that he had been pleased by Bathurst's disavowal of the Nicolls treaty, but that the United States had "received strong and confident intimations from various quarters that there had been a cession of Florida by Spain to Great Britain." "There is not and never has been the slightest foundation for it whatsoever," said Castlereagh. "It never has been even mentioned." "Your Lordship knows that such rumors have been long in circulation, and that the fact has been positively and very circumstantially asserted in your own public journals," remarked Adams. "Yes, but our public

[63] Baker to Bathurst, No. 39, Dec. 8, 1815, *ibid.*, 107; Baker to Monroe, December 15, 1815, *ibid.*, 112.

[64] Monroe to Adams, Dec. 10, 1815, William R. Manning, *Diplomatic Correspondence of the United States Concerning the Independence of the Latin-American Nations* I, 17-18.

Destiny of Spanish Borderlands 59

journals are *so* addicted to *lying*," replied Castlereagh. "No; if it is supposed that we have any little trickish policy of thrusting ourselves in there between you and Spain, we are very much misunderstood indeed. You shall find nothing little or shabby in our policy. We have no desire to add an inch of ground to our territories in any part of the world. . . . Military positions may have been taken by us during the war of places which you had taken from Spain, but we never intended to keep them. Do you only observe the same moderation. If we should find you hereafter pursuing a system of encroachment upon your neighbors, what we might do *defensively* is another consideration." Castlereagh then went on to refer to the close alliance between England and Spain.[65]

Here, then, was a disavowal and a threat. Adams straightway forgot the disavowal. To the threat he soon countered in an effective manner. Conservative British statesmen, who hoped for a reconciliation between the Spanish monarch and his revolting colonies in America or else the establishment of independent Bourbon monarchies in them, were given an intimation that the United States might forwith recognize republics in that region.[66] As for the unauthorized procedure of Englishmen in the Floridas — this would become very useful whenever the United States government desired popular support for a menacing attitude toward Spain, and the American public would not

[65] Adams, *Memoirs*, III, 289-290.
[66] *Ibid.*, III, 292, *passim*.

be told that these activities of Englishmen were unauthorized. The Floridas must be obtained and Adams and Monroe were growing impatient.

Castlereagh may have chuckled over the warning which he gave Adams in January, 1816, but the laugh was on Castlereagh. In a moment of exultation the British statesman had told the Spanish ambassador what he had said to Adams. The Spanish ambassador never forgot it. Nor did the Spanish government. When the United States began to press its claims and demands in the summer of 1817, Spain asked the "efficacious coöperation of the English Govt. and its decided mediation, and support,"[67] and in this connection Ambassador Francisco Campuzano said: "I am persuaded that the decided intervention of the English Govt. in this business, the moment that the United States shall be fully aware of it, will be sufficient to moderate their pretensions and limit their exorbitant demands." These demands included, according to Campuzano, not only the Floridas but Texas to the Rio Bravo and an outlet on the Pacific. He contended that British interests would certainly be injured if the United States acquired Florida.[68] And he urged the matter again and again.[69]

The British Cabinet had some misgivings [70] but was

[67] Spanish Minister of Foreign Affairs to Wellesley, June 22, 1817, F. O. (72), 203.

[68] Campuzano to Castlereagh, July 12, 1817, *ibid.*

[69] Namely, in notes of August 13 and Spetember 4, *loc. cit.*

[70] *Cf.* Castlereagh to Arthur Wellesley, April 14 and May 27, 1817, *ibid.*, 196.

Destiny of Spanish Borderlands

not entirely unwilling to intervene. Early in June, when Adams was on the point of leaving for Washington where he was to become secretary of state, Castlereagh opened the subject, pretending that he did so on his "own individual" initiative. Adams said that he did not know how President Monroe would view the matter. Adams also recalled that the English commissioners at Ghent had held an opinion "unfavorable to the United States."[71] He might have reminded Castlereagh of his threat of 1816, but he did not. He might also have reminded him of the severe language used by Morier and Foster in 1810 and 1811, but again he did not.

A few days later Adams and Castlereagh had their final interview, and once more the Florida question was brought up. Castlereagh and Adams examined a map of North America. Castlereagh inquired what would be the objection to establishing the Mississippi as a boundary, provided Spain should agree to cede the Floridas. Adams pointed to the vast extension of Louisiana to the west of the river and said, "that would be the objection." He also remarked that the matter could easily be settled if only Spain would be "rational." Castlereagh then "said, smiling, that he must admit Spain was not the easiest of parties to concede, and he might say the same of the United States." Adams "answered, in the same tone, that there could be no better judge of stubbornness and

---

[71] *Memoirs*, III, 550.

compliance, than a party so very easy and accommodating as Great Britain."

The suspicious New Englander then went home to his diary. Castlereagh's "project of offering the mediation of Great Britain to settle the differences between the United States and Spain surprised me much, after what had passed at Ghent. But his plan of bounding us by the Mississippi was exactly what I should have expected from a British mediator." [72] Thus stands the record. Adams would not forget.

But Castlereagh had entered upon these final conferences with the intention of cultivating friendly relations with the United States, and he supposed that his efforts had not been ineffective. He later wrote Sir Charles Bagot that Adams had told him he was going home "with a desire to promote a friendly intercourse with this country." [73] Perhaps so, but not with any serious sentiment in favor of admitting British mediation in the Florida issue.

Yet it was upon this fragile foundation that Castlereagh based the hope that British interposition would be accepted.[74] Nor was it without the urge of weighty considerations that Castlereagh ventured to act upon this slender hope. European Powers were threatening to detach Spain from English influence and important

[72] *Ibid.*, III, 560.

[73] Castlereagh to Bagot, Private and Confidential, Nov. 10, 1817, F. O. (5), 120.

[74] *Ibid.*

DESTINY OF SPANISH BORDERLANDS 63

commercial negotiations with the Spanish nation had to be looked after.[75] It was a tedious affair.

Castlereagh waited until Adams was securely established in the State Department. Then he drew up careful and elaborate instructions for Bagot. He said that the British government was willing to undertake mediation only on condition that it was "equally at the desire of both parties interested." If Bagot should find the United States disinclined to submit the differences with Spain to a formal mediation, he was not to press the matter.[76] The Spanish diplomats had been trying to prevail upon the Prince Regent of England "to make their cause his own," or at any rate "to press his Intervention somewhat in a tone of Menace." The English government was not going to allow itself to be drawn into such a position. It was not indifferent to the mode of settlement which might be adopted; it was still less indifferent to the calamitous consequences of a rupture between Spain and the United States; but nothing must be done to thwart the endeavors of the English government "to preserve and even improve" friendly relations with the United States.

This, then, was the crux of the matter. The United States must not be offended, and yet there was reluctance to abandon the negotiation to its fate. The United States might pursue a very aggressive course toward Spain if it were allowed to feel that all of the Euro-

[75] *See* Arthur Wellesley to Castlereagh, No. 88, July 14, 1817, and *passim*, F. O. (72), 199.

[76] Castlereagh to Bagot, No. 23, Nov. 10, 1817, F. O. (5), 120.

pean powers were indifferent. On the other hand, if the United States really desired to settle the difficulties without a rupture with Spain, perhaps it might welcome British good offices in order to overcome Spanish obstinacy. But Spain must not be permitted to expect too much of British interposition. The particular interest which England had in the result of these discussions must not be over-rated. Spanish diplomats had tried to give the United States the impression that the Floridas could not be ceded without England's consent, basing this assumption upon the Treaty of Utrecht;[77] but that treaty was no longer in force. These diplomats had also urged that British interests in America would be imperiled by the cessions which the United States was demanding of Spain. There was some ground for this contention, but the position of the British government for the present must not be mistaken. "Were Great Britain to look to its own Interest alone, and were that interest worth asserting at the present moment, at the hazard of being embroiled with the United States, there can be no question that we have an obvious Motive for desiring, that the Spaniards should continue to be Our Neighbours in East Florida, rather than Our West India Possessions should be so closely approached by the Territory of the United States; — but this is a consideration that we are not prepared to bring forward in the discussion

[77] This treaty contained a pledge that Spain would not alienate any of its American possessions without the consent of England.

at the present moment, in bar to a Settlement between Spain and North America. . . ."

This was the way Castlereagh looked at the matter now. He was not willing to follow up the threat of January, 1816, and it was causing him some uneasiness. "You will find in one of the Spanish notes," he wrote Bagot, "an assumption that I had declared to the Spanish Ambassador in London that the British Govt. would forcibly oppose any extension of the Limits of the United States, on the side of Mexico." "This is a convenient, but not a true statement," said Castlereagh. He then went on to state exactly what did happen. "Some time since there was a report prevalent that Gt. Britain was about to acquire the Floridas from Spain. Mr. Adams adverted to this report cursorily in a conversation, which gave me the opportunity to disavow the story, and I added that I could . . . assure him that so long as the United States forebore to encroach upon neighboring States Gt. Britain would wholly abstain from seeking any possession of that description. That if the United States set the example, I could not answer for what might in such case be the line of Policy to which this Country might be driven. . . . I repeated this conversation some time after to the Spanish Ambassador, stating it as a hint which I had given to the American Govt. which might be of some use. This is converted into an assurance given to the Spanish Ambassador; whereas it was in truth nothing more than a warning to America, if she did not wish to see us on her Southern Boundary, not to provoke any change in our existing Policy, which was wholly to abstain from acquisitions in that quarter." [78]

But Castlereagh was not in a mood for warnings and guaranties in November, 1817. "The avowed and true policy of Great Britain ... in the existing state of the world" was "to appease Controversy, and to secure, if possible, for all states a long interval of Repose." Spain must accordingly prepare herself to purchase peace by the cession of the Floridas and endeavour to "secure, on the side of Mexico, the best frontier that Circumstances will admit of her obtaining in exchange for so serious a concession on her part." [79]

Britain's attitude toward the United States was unusually friendly at this time. Peace and harmony were uppermost in the minds of English statesmen of the conservative school who still shuddered at the thought of what French radicalism and pugnacity had unleashed in Europe less than three decades before. The United States must not be provoked into the republican extravagance of championing Liberty, Equality, and Fraternity in Spanish America.[80]

Near the last days of January, 1818, Bagot cautiously approached Adams with an offer of mediation in the difficulties with Spain. Adams had slight inten-

[78] Castlereagh to Bagot, Private and Secret, Nov. 11, 1817, F. O. (5), 120.

[79] *Idem* to *idem, Most Private and Secret*, Nov. 10, 1817, *loc. cit.*

[80] The possibility of American recognition and support of the Spanish colonies had been causing uneasiness since 1810.

tion of accepting, and the other members of the Cabinet still less. The ground for a refusal had already been prepared. For months the newspapers had been carrying on an agitation regarding the activities of Gregor McGregor and other Englishmen in the Floridas, and the *National Intelligencer*, the official journal of Adams's own party, had just published the old protests of Morier and Foster.[81] It might have published Baker's disavowal of December 10, 1815, but it did not. It might have published Castlereagh's more explicit disavowal of January, 1816, but again it did not. Public opinion having thus been stirred against England, Adams could inform Bagot, on February 3, that he and Monroe were convinced of the "good faith, the friendship, and the impartiality" of the English government, but that the attitude of the people must be considered! In the United States the opinion of the executive government was of "little weight" unless backed by "popular" approval, and England's former sentiments against the claims of the United States "were in the recollection and the hands of everyone." It would be difficult to convince the public that these sentiments had undergone a change. If the mediation should result in compromise, the irritation of the American people would be directed not only against Monroe's administration but also against Great Britain. The very interposition of England would, in fact, cause popular irritation and "check" the "amicable feelings which were daily arising towards Great

[81] *Cf.* the issue of January 26, 1818.

Britain" and which it was the earnest wish of Adams to "cherish and improve." Adams also complained of Spain's attempt to disturb the harmony between the United States and Great Britain by the suggestion of this mediation.[82]

Thus the attempt at mediation failed, and the English government said no more of it. It was not to be shaken from its resolution not to support Spain at the risk of a war with the United States. Not even the drastic action of a military officer in the Floridas, justified, if not even connived at, by the American government, could effect this. Andrew Jackson's execution of Ambrister and Arbuthnot in April, 1818, brought about a critical situation in the relations of the United States and England, but the British Cabinet saved the day. The British public and many members of Parliament were furious and Adams's delay in giving explanations must have been irritating. The Spanish ambassador in London, with obvious intent, descanted on the extravagant demands of the United States for Texas, a part of New Mexico, and a passage to the Pacific, to say nothing of the two Floridas. Surely, he said, Britain's interests would be adversely affected by such a concession. Moreover, he declared that it was plain from the notes of Adams to the Spanish government that the United States stood opposed to all the great political principles of Europe. And, besides, there was Castlereagh's statement of 1816,

[82] Bagot to Castlereagh, Nos. 14 and 15, Feb. 8, 1818, F. O. (5), 130; Adams, *Memoirs*, IV, 48-52.

that England might be driven by American aggressions to change its friendly attitude toward the United States. Now was the time for the English government to adopt its policy of active opposition to the expansion of the United States![83] The situation in England was indeed tense, and "war might have been produced by holding up a finger." But Castlereagh, standing firmly by his resolution, cautioned Bagot to take no action without instructions, and finally (January 2, 1819) directed him not to make any official representations whatever. Jackson's proceedings were "harsh and unwarrantable," but "the unfortunate sufferers . . . had been engaged in unauthorized practices of such a description as to have deprived them of any Claim on their own Govt. for interference on their behalf."[84]

A few weeks later Adams and Luís de Onis signed a treaty ceding the Floridas to the United States and fixing the western boundary of Louisiana at the Sabine. It would appear that none but the blind could have failed to see the futility of all hope of British aid in the attempt to reduce American demands. And yet for almost two years Spain seems to have clung to this

[83] The Duke of San Carlos to Castlereagh, July 23, 1818, F. O. (72), 216.

[84] Castlereagh to Bagot, Jan. 2, 1819, F. O. (5), 141; *idem* to *idem*, Aug. 18 and 31, 1818, *ibid.*, 129.

On Jackson's activities in Florida and the correspondence between the United States and Spain, *see* John Spencer Bassett, *The Life of Andrew Jackson* (New York, 1925), 233 ff.; H. B. Fuller, *The Purchase of Florida* (Cleveland, 1906), *passim*.

hope. In the end the British government not only refused to support Spain but even went out of its way to urge the ratification of the Adams-Onis agreement. In doing so it was motivated by the oft-avowed desire for peace as well as by a fear that the United States would immediately recognize the new governments of Spanish America and attempt to extend its boundaries farther toward the west.[85]

Thus British opposition to our acquisition of the Floridas, like their opposition to our acquisition of Louisiana, was toned down by larger considerations in other spheres. Both annexations were acquiesced in reluctantly as the choice between two evils. What would happen when American territorial ambitions should be directed toward Texas and Cuba?

[85] These statements regarding the later phase of the question are based upon the correspondence between Castlereagh and Ambassador Arthur Wellesley, too bulky to cite in detail. *See* F. O. (72), 222, 224, 225, 226.

CHAPTER III

TEXAS AND CUBA

For the beginning of British opposition to the designs of the United States, alleged or real, upon Texas and Cuba, one must go back as far as the year 1809. In its relation to Texas, the opposition passed through two phases: the defense of Spanish interests and the championship of Mexico against Yankee encroachments. In respect to Cuba, it amounted to a constant championship of Spain, which continued to hold the island throughout the period. In the case of both regions, an immediate national interest of England was thought to be involved in the possible extension of the boundaries of the United States along the Gulf coast and into the Caribbean. So far as England was concerned, there existed no desire to acquire either area. The United States, on the other hand, looked forward to the acquisition of both; but, for the period under consideration, the desire was not imperative. Each Power suspected the purposes of the other, and in attempting to resist them intensified the suspicion. In the United States there was an even deeper conviction than in England of the peril involved in the possession of Texas and, especially, Cuba by a great rival maritime power, particularly if that power cherished anti-slavery sentiments.

I. CUBA AND TEXAS (1809-1820)

As early as November, 1805, President Jefferson had told the British minister that the United States might seize Cuba in case of a war with Spain. "In the Event of Hostilities he considered that East and West Florida and successively the Island of Cuba, the possession of which was necessary to the Defense of Louisiana and Florida, . . . would be an easy conquest" for the United States. So Anthony Merry reported in 1805.[1] In August, 1807, Jefferson returned to the idea, including northern Mexico in the theatre of activities. "I had rather have war against Spain than not, if we go to war against England," wrote Jefferson. He then suggested that "our Southern defensive force can [could] take the Floridas, volunteers for a Mexican army will [would] flock to our standards, and . . . probably Cuba would add itself to our confederation."[2] Again, in 1809, when Napoleon seemed on the point of extending his rule to Latin America, Jefferson wrote Madison that the Emperor would give us the Floridas and perhaps also "consent to our receiving Cuba into our Union, to prevent our aid to Mexico and the other provinces." This would be enough for the time being. "We should then have only the north to include in our Confederacy, which

[1] Merry to Mulgrave, No. 45, November 3, 1805, F. O. (5), 45.

[2] As quoted in W. S. Robertson, *Francisco de Miranda* (Washington, 1908), 395.

would be of course in the first war." He did not indicate what he meant by the "north."

It was probably these larger schemes, as well as the Floridas, that Ambassador Apodaca had in mind when he appealed to Great Britain in May, 1809. At any rate, Luís de Onis was alarmed a few months later by the situation on the Mexican border, and Minister Francis Jackson noted that there were many persons in the United States who believed that in case of a war with Spain prospects of booty in Mexico would make it easy to assemble an army with the view of invading that country.[4] Moreover, Canning's instructions to Jackson (1809) were broad enough to include all of the overseas possessions of Spain[5] and the discussions of the English ministers in Washington embraced the entire northern portion of the Spanish empire in America.

In June, 1809, when Envoy D. M. Erskine and Secretary of State Smith were discussing French activities in Spanish America and the fate of the Spanish colonies, Erskine managed to elicit assurances from Smith with reference to the immediate intentions of the United States. "He assured me," reported Erskine, "that the Rumours and Suspicions which had been so extensively spread that this Government were carrying on various Intrigues for the purpose of ob-

[3] As quoted by John H. Latané, *The Diplomatic Relations of the United States and Spanish America* (Baltimore, 1900), 90.

[4] Jackson to Canning, No. 7, Nov. 9, 1809, F. O. (5), 64.

[5] *See antea*, Ch. II, note 17.

taining Possessions of some of the Spanish Colonies on this Continent, were totally unfounded; that their opinions were unanimously against engaging in any such schemes, well knowing (as he said) that they had it not in their Power to afford any real Protection to those Colonies, and it was not for the interest of the United States to extend their Territory . . . at Present. He said that General Wilkinson never had been authorized to receive any Proposals whatever from the people of Cuba"; he had only gone there in order to assure the Spanish authorities that the sending of United States troops to New Orleans had not been with hostile intent. From another reliable source Erskine had learned that the principal inhabitants of Cuba had asked for annexation or a protectorate, but that the United States had refused to comply.[6]

In the following October, when Jackson inquired about the troops at New Orleans, he also asked if they were "intended for hostile operations against Spanish America."[7] Evidently these British agents were thinking of Cuba and Texas, as well as the Floridas.

During the next eight years the Cuban question was shoved aside by the growing absorption in the Florida issue, but Texas was not forgotten. Evidence of the

[6] Erskine to Canning, No. 25, June 7, 1809, F. O. (5), 63.

There was a slight equivocation here. Wilkinson had been sent to Cuba in order to ascertain the political aspirations of the Cuban people and assure them of American friendship. (*Cf.* Henry Adams, *The History of the United States*, IV, 340; Jefferson, *Writings* (Memorial edition), XII, 176).

[7] Jackson to Canning, No. 10, Oct. 18, 1809, F. O. (5), 64.

Texas and Cuba 75

persistence of American interest continued to reveal itself, filibusters kept the border in agitation, and the expansionists frequently referred to northern Mexico in their utterance.[8] Just before the outbreak of the War of 1812 Minister Foster "made a verbal representation at the request of the Spanish Minister on the subject of the bands of robbers who are [were] said to invest the country between the Sabine and the River Hondo in what is called the Neutral Territory." Secretary of State Monroe admitted that the governor of the Territory of Orleans had called upon the commander of the national troops to disperse these bands, but said that this official had declined on the ground that he lacked orders. Monroe also remarked that Governor Claiborne would probably advance against the outlaws with the territorial militia.[9]

It has already been pointed out that one phase of the strategy of the War of 1812 was the restitution of Louisiana to Spain and the confinement of the United States to the east of the Mississippi. It has likewise been suggested that this was one of the ideas brought forward during the early stages of the British effort to mediate between the United States and Spain (1816-1817). In this manner protection was sought for northern Mexico.

It should also be noted that the Texas question was included in the Castlereagh-Adams conference of January, 1816. Although the discussion at that time

[8] Pratt, *Expansionists of 1812*, passim.

[9] Foster to Wellesley, No. 21, April 2, 1812, F. O. (5), 85.

related mainly to the Floridas, Texas was not entirely lost from view. Castlereagh's disavowal included all Spanish America, and when he told the Spanish ambassador about the warning he had given Adams, the Spanish ambassador inferred that the British government "would forcibly oppose any extension of the limits of the United States, on the side of Mexico." Moreover, Adams had felt called upon to declare that his government "had no views of an ambitious nature on ... Mexico, that they merely looked to a settlement of Boundaries ... consistent with mutual Interest and what ... they were entitled to claim." [10]

During the next three years both Texas and Cuba were connected with the Florida negotiations. English diplomacy exerted itself to persuade Spain to give up the Floridas in order to secure the best possible boundary on the west, urging that this was a very important consideration.[11] Although the Cuban question came up late in 1817 from a slightly different angle,[12] rumor soon alleged that England desired to get possession of the island in order to restore the balance which would be disturbed when Florida passed to the United States. Reports to this effect came in from

[10] Castlereagh to Bagot, Private and Secret, Nov. 11, 1817, F. O. (5), 120.

[11] Wellesley to Castlereagh, No. 88, Aug. 6, 1819, F. O. (72), 225; *idem* to *idem*, Private, of July 6, 1819, *loc. cit.*

[12] It was reported that Cuba was to be ceded to England in order to cancel the debt incurred by the British defense of Spain against Napoleon. (Latané, *The Diplomatic Relations of the United States and Spanish America*, 91.)

Texas and Cuba

many quarters. The English press raised a "clamor, charging ambition and rapacity upon the United States"[13] and demanding Cuba as an offset. The French minister at Washington came to Adams in alarm; the Saxon minister in London made inquiries of Richard Rush;[14] United States *Chargé* Alexander H. Everett wrote from Brussels in regard to the report.[15] Adams was not inclined to believe the rumors, but he noted in his *Memoirs* that there had been "some mysterious negotiation between Spain and England about Cuba, the secret of which is not unfolded." [16]

Adams was right. There had been secret negotiations, but they related to the suppression of the slave trade and the pirates, not to the cession of Cuba to England.[17] Moreover, Rush was given assurances both by the English ministry and the Spanish ambassador in London that the cession of Cuba to England was not being considered, but it was many years before either the Americans or the British were at ease over Cuba's fate.

---

[13] Richard Rush, *Memoranda of a Residence at the Court of London* (Philadelphia, 1845), 58.

[14] *Ibid.*, 112.

[15] Manning, *Diplomatic Correspondence*, III, 1712.

[16] Adams, *Memoirs*, IV, 367-368.

[17] Castlereagh to Wellesley, January 31, 1819, F. O. (72), 222; *idem* to *idem*, April 17, 1820, *loc. cit.*, 233.

II. MUTUAL SUSPICIONS REGARDING CUBA (1822-1827)

Previous lecturers on the Shaw Foundation[18] have so ably dealt with the Cuban question that no more than a brief summary, designed to place the matter in its general setting of British opposition to the southward expansion of the United States, is necessary at this time. The mutual apprehensions of the period now under review were mainly occasioned by the policies of the two Powers with reference to privateers and slavery. Both the United States and England adopted measures to defend their commerce from the privateers which lurked in Cuban waters. England also made attempts to suppress the slave trade, while the main interest on this score in the United States arose in connection with the danger which an insurrection in Cuba, particularly if it should lead to a change in the status of the Negro slaves, would involve for the Southern States. Moreover, the issue was further complicated by the fear of French designs and the possibility that Colombia and Mexico would dispatch a liberating army to the region. Neither England nor the United States — and this was particularly true of the former — seriously considered the annexation of the island at this juncture. Each tried to defeat the alleged ambitions of the other by mutual disavowals and the sending of war vessels to the Caribbean. Pressure was also exerted upon Colombia,

[18] Namely, Latané, *op. cit.*; William R. Manning, *Early Diplomatic Relations between the United States and Mexico* (Baltimore, 1916).

Mexico, and Spain, and a guaranty of Cuba to Spain was discussed but never agreed upon. Cuba was becoming the "Turkey of trans-Atlantic politics." [19]

Deep anxiety regarding the fate of Cuba was felt both in the United States and England late in 1822 and in 1823. Diplomatic agents sent in alarming reports, war vessels moved suspiciously in the Caribbean, cabinets discussed the matter with serious faces. Both Powers were equally alarmed.

In July, 1822, Henry Theo Kilbee, who had been sent out to Havana in 1819 in connection with England's endeavor to suppress the slave trade, pointed out the critical state of affairs and the "prevailing suspicions" of American designs. Stratford Canning, British minister to the United States, was instructed to make inquiries and report.[20] In November, George Canning, now foreign secretary, drew up a memorandum on the subject of piratical raids on English commerce and American ambitions. He argued that, "The possession by the United States of both shores of the channel, through which our Jamaica trade must pass, would . . . amount to a suspension of that trade, and to a consequent total ruin of a great portion of the West Indian interests." He urged that the ships and harbors of Cuba and Porto Rico be held responsible for the depredations upon British trade in the region. Let

[19] Quoted by J. M. Callahan, *Cuba and International Relations* (Baltimore, 1898), 140.

[20] George Canning to Stratford Canning, No. 7, October 11, 1822, F. O. (5), 165.

the English squadron in the West Indies be devoted to that purpose. Let it be employed also to keep the Americans in check, for "whatever they might do in the absence of an English squadron, [they] would hardly venture in the face of one to assume the military occupation" of Cuba.[21] The squadron was so employed, and in December marines were landed in the island in order to suppress bands of privateers.[22] At the same time Stratford Canning was given further instructions. He was authorized to declare that England had no intention of permanently occupying Cuba. He was also directed to make inquiries regarding American purposes, but cautioned not to ask direct questions or impute aggressive designs, lest the very charge suggest the evil "which it deprecates." [23]

In the fall of 1822, the American Cabinet was also considering the fate of Cuba. A secret agent had come from Havana to ask annexation and British designs were feared. The whole question was carefully gone over and Adams has preserved an account of the conferences. "Mr. Calhoun has a most ardent desire that the island of Cuba should become a part of the United States, and says that Mr. Jefferson has the same. There are two dangers to be averted by that event: one, that the island should fall into the hands of Great Britain; the other, that it should be revolutionized by

[21] As quoted in Latané, *op. cit.*, 93-94.

[22] George Canning to Stratford Canning, No. 13, Dec. 7, 1822, F. O. (5), 165.

[23] *Ibid.*

the negroes. Calhoun says Mr. Jefferson told him two years ago that we ought, at the first possible opportunity, to take Cuba, even though at the cost of a war with England; but as we are not now prepared for this, and as our great object must be to gain time, he thought we should answer this [Cuban] overture by dissuading them from their present purpose, and urging them to adhere at present to their connection with Spain." Adams disagreed with Calhoun. He thought it best, he said, "to give them no advice whatever; to say that the Executive of the United States is not competent to promise them admission as a State in the Union; and that if it were, the proposal is of a nature which our relations of amity with Spain would not permit us to countenance." To advise the Cubans to remain loyal to the Mother Country "would expose them to be transferred to Great Britain," either by the revolutionary government of Spain as the price of English aid against the Holy Alliance or by Ferdinand in consideration for support in the consummation of a counter-revolution. Furthermore: "As to taking Cuba at the cost of a war with Great Britain, it would be well to inquire, before undertaking such a war, how it would be likely to terminate; ... for the present, and for a long time to come, I held it for certain that a war with Great Britain for Cuba would result in her possession of that island, and not ours." The excitement of W. H. Crawford was only equalled by that of Calhoun. The French minister in Washington had told him that his government "knew for a certainty" that England "had been for two years negotiating with Spain for the island of Cuba, and had offered ... for it Gibraltar and a large sum of money; that there was a British Agent living at the Havana in great splendor and with profuse expense."[24] Crawford thought it would be a "great misfortune" if England should "get possession of the island." President Monroe was of the opinion that an "intelligent Agent" should be sent to Havana.

Adams had his way. The Cuban delegate was answered as he had suggested.[25] No drastic measures were adopted. An agent was not sent to Cuba, but John Forsyth, United States minister to Spain, was instructed to make investigations and in case he found negotiations in progress for a cession of Cuba to England, to declare that the United States desired to see Cuba remain in the hands of Spain.[26]

These mutual suspicions continued all through the year 1823. Reports which came to the United States were not particularly alarming, but, on the other hand, they were not entirely reassuring. Returning from a visit to Mexico and stopping for a few days in Cuba on his way to the United States, Joel R. Poinsett wrote of the importance of the island and the advisability of preventing its seizure by any of the great Powers of

[24] Perhaps this rumor related to Kilbee.

[25] Adams, *Memoirs*, VI, 70-74, 111-112.

[26] Manning, *Early Diplomatic Relations between the United States and Mexico*, 92, note 3.

Europe.[27] From Madrid came reports that no negotiations for the cession of Cuba were under way, but there were no explicit assurances that England did not desire the acquisition.[28] From England came newspapers which frankly advocated the seizure of Cuba in order to prevent it from falling into the hands of the United States.[29] Then more Cabinet discussions occurred in March and April. "Calhoun for war with England, *if* she means to take Cuba. Thompson [Secretary of the Navy] for urging the Cubans to declare themselves independent, *if* they can maintain their independence, and that this nation will not, and could not, prevent by war the British from obtaining possession of Cuba, if they attempt to take it," while Monroe urges "a mutual promise not to take Cuba"— a step opposed by Calhoun and Adams.[30] Meanwhile, English and American men of war move back and forth in the vicinity of the island, ominously, and Adams soon sends instructions to Hugh Nelson, the minister to Spain, remarking on the law of gravity, comparing Cuba to a ripening apple, and urging that for the present it was best for the fruit to remain on the Spanish tree.[31]

[27] Poinsett, *Notes on Mexico* (Philadelphia, 1824), 209-223.

[28] Manning, *Diplomatic Correspondence*, III, 225 ff.

[29] Latané, *op. cit.*, 96.

[30] Adams, *Memoirs*, VI, 138-139.

[31] Adams to Nelson, April 28, 1823, *American State Papers, Foreign Relations*, V, 408 ff.; and see also, for further apprehensions, Adams, *Writings* (W. C. Ford, ed.), VII, 379 ff.

In England apprehensions were equally grave and perhaps more justified. In January Stratford Canning noted the "strong feelings of jealousy excited" by the landing of English marines in Cuba. They were certainly remarkable, he thought. He also summarized a letter from the British consul at Norfolk, where an American squadron was fitting out with the view of chasing the Cuban pirates. The consul thought the United States was in search of a "pretext for securing a more permanent footing in Cuba." [32] A little later Canning reported discussions in American newspapers relating to the advisability of seizing Cuba in order "to prevent so formidable an increase of British power." [33] At about the same time a British army officer urged the annexation of Cuba in order to forestall France and the United States and as compensation for the annexation of the Floridas by the latter and the growing influence of the former in Spain.[34]

The Cuban question had thus become very critical and Canning probably had the island in mind when he approached Richard Rush, in the summer of 1823, on the Spanish problem and the procedure of France and the Neo-Holy Alliance. At any rate, his proposal that

[32] Stratford Canning to George Canning, No. 3, Jan. 1, and No. 15, Jan. 22, 1823, F. O. (5), 175.

[33] As quoted in Manning, *Early Diplomatic Relations between the United States and Mexico*, 95.

[34] Colonel de Lacy Evans to Canning, April 9, 1823, E. J. Stapleton, *Official Correspondence of George Canning* (London, 1887), I, 116.

Texas and Cuba

each Power should declare that "it aimed not at the possession of any portion of" the Spanish colonies would certainly have applied to Cuba. Such a declaration would have tended to tie the hands of each nation, and American statesmen did not fail to note the fact. Madison suspiciously inquired whether the disclaimer would apply to Cuba and Porto Rico[35] and Adams was sure that Canning's "object was to obtain by a sudden movement a premature commitment . . . against any transfer of the island . . . to France, or the acquisition of it by ourselves." [36] For this and other reasons Canning's overture was rejected; and the head of the Foreign Office turned to Spain, offering to guarantee Spain's possession of Cuba on condition that the Spanish government extend recognition to its revolting colonies.[37] But again he was disappointed.

The apprehensions of the two Powers died down in 1824, but blazed forth again in 1825. At this time it was the mysterious proceedings of the French fleet in the West Indies and threats of a combined Colombian-Mexican expedition against the island that occasioned alarm. On the part of the United States there was little suspicion of English designs at this particular juncture, but on at least one occasion Canning did not fail to reveal his distrust of the United States.

[35] As quoted in Manning, *Early Diplomatic Relations between the United States and Mexico*, 98.

[36] Adams, *Memoirs*, VI, 188.

[37] Canning to Wellesley, No. 14, Secret, April 2, 1824, F. O. (72), 284.

For the crisis which France and the two Spanish-American states threatened to provoke, each Anglo-Saxon Power had its own particular remedy. The United States, unwilling to allow Cuba to fall into the hands of Colombia or Mexico, proposed to hold them in restraint while urging Spain to save the island by granting recognition to the new governments in Spanish America. In recommending this policy to Spain the aid of the other European powers was to be invoked. With reference to France no vigorous protest appears to have been made until the crisis had passed, although it was intimated both to France and to the Russian government, perhaps with the view that the news would be passed on to France, that the United States could not see with indifference the island transferred to any European Power. When all immediate danger was over, France was then informed that the United States would "not consent to the occupation of those islands [namely, Cuba and Porto Rico] by any other European power than Spain, under any contingency whatever." [38]

Canning, on the other hand, was more or less indifferent to the projects of the Spanish-American states. If Cuba could not be retained by Spain, he preferred that it should become "independent, either singly or in connection with Mexico." "But what cannot or must not be," he wrote to the English ambassador in Paris, "is that any great maritime power should get posses-

[38] Manning, *op. cit.*, 117 ff.; Temperley, *The Foreign Policy of Canning* (London, 1925), 170-171.

Texas and Cuba

sion of it."[39] But the movements of France made Canning angry, and he at once demanded and obtained explanations and a disavowal of aggressive intentions. In doing so, however, he represented the United States as in agreement with England in opposing French ambitions in the West Indies, and this may have given added force to his demands. But toward Clay's project of joint mediation between Spain and Spanish America in the interest of Cuban security he assumed an attitude of suspicious cynicism. He declared that it was sure to prove ineffective and, moreover, he suspected that it concealed a hidden aggressive purpose, for "the Yankees," he said, "may be just the rogues that we have always hitherto taken them to be, but which I was willing to hope they might have resolved to be no longer."[40] Canning's own plan for the permanent solution of the Cuban problem was a tripartite guaranty of the island to Spain,[41] but France and the United States declined to accept the proposal. Twice in three years he was rebuffed by the United States in his attempt to deal with the Cuban issue.

Soon afterwards certain diplomats of the United States began to regret it. Conflicting interests and

---

[39] Canning to Granville, June 21, 1825, Stapleton, *Official Correspondence of Canning*, I, 276.

[40] Canning to Liverpool, Aug. 6, 1825, *ibid.*, I, 283.

[41] Manning, *Diplomatic Correspondence*, III, 1557-1569. The proposal was made on August 7, 1825. On October 26, 1825, Minister Rufus King was instructed to reject it. (*Ibid.*, I, 261-262.)

policies in Portugal brought England and Spain to the verge of war late in 1826, and as the crisis approached, Canning began to consider an attack upon Cuba. "God forbid war," he wrote Liverpool in October, "but if Spain will have it, ought we not to think of the Havannah? Where else can we strike a blow? and what other blow would be so effectual?" [42] Albert Gallatin, then minister at the Court of St. James's, became uneasy. He discussed the matter with the Mexican *chargé*, who favored Cuban independence under the joint guaranty of England and the American states. He also sought reassurances from Canning, hinting at the desire to discuss some such guaranty as the Mexican *chargé* had suggested. But Canning was piqued and non-committal. Gallatin then lamented the failure of the United States to accept the tripartite proposal of the previous year. "There would certainly have been an advantage," he wrote Clay, "in signing the agreement proposed by Mr. Canning, . . . not with the view he suggested in reference to Spain, but for the purpose of binding Great Britain." [43]

By the end of the first week in February, however, the Anglo-Spanish crisis appears to have passed, although details of an alleged English project to seize Cuba continued to be revealed at Madrid. It was reported in August, 1827, for instance, that English emissaries had been sent to Cuba, in the early part of

[42] Canning to Liverpool, Oct. 6, 1826, Stapleton, *op. cit.*, II, 144.

[43] Manning, *Diplomatic Correspondence*, III, 1583, *passim*.

Texas and Cuba

the year, in order to examine its defences and instigate a revolt, which was to be followed by an insurgent invitation to the British to take possession of the island. The project, however, if it ever existed, was "in a great measure personal to Mr. Canning" and came to an end with his death.[44]

At precisely the same time English statesmen were disturbed by rumors of American plots to revolutionize Cuba. In July, 1827, Minister Charles R. Vaughan reported from Washington that a correspondence between the bishop of Baltimore, the governor of Cuba, Poinsett, and certain Mexicans was in progress. Vaughan's letter was sent to Richard Pakenham, British minister in Mexico, who was instructed to ascertain the object of the correspondence and to transmit the information at his earliest opportunity.[45] Pakenham's investigations convinced him of the existence of a revolutionary party in Cuba and that an appeal had been made to the Mexican government for aid, but he could not determine whether the United States was involved in the insurgent movement.[46] From Washington Vaughan wrote (January 20, 1828) that he had been unable to discover evidence that the United States was in communication with the Cuban revolutionary

[44] *Ibid.*, III, 2146-2154.

[45] The Foreign Office to Pakenham, No. 6, Secret, August 18, 1827, F. O. (50, Mexico), 33.

[46] Pakenham to Dudley, No. 80, Secret, Dec. 2, 1827, *loc. cit.*, 36.

party "in the expectation that the Island may ultimately fall under their protection."[47]

There was good reason for this failure; for, as a matter of fact, the United States did not at that time cherish any such design. On the contrary, it was anxious to maintain the *status quo*. In the spring of 1827 Daniel P. Cook had been sent to Cuba as a confidential agent, but not with the view of fomenting an insurrection. He was instructed to ascertain the disposition of the inhabitants toward Mexico, Colombia, Spain, and Great Britain, as well as "the Spanish means of resistance" to a British attack upon Havana, but he was directed to "keep aloof from, and entirely unconnected with, any of the parties within the Island." "It does not enter into the policy or views of the Government of the United States," said Clay, "to give any stimulus or countenance to insurrectionary movements, if such be contemplated by any portion of its inhabitants."[48] In Madrid, Everett, the United States minister, used even stronger language in speaking to what appeared to be an agent of the Cuban *insurrectos* (December, 1827), informing him that the efforts of the United States would be employed in support of the Spanish authorities in the island.[49] The time for negotiations for the annexation of Cuba to the United States had not yet arrived.

[47] To Dudley, No. 6, F. O. (5), 236.

[48] Manning, *Diplomatic Correspondence*, I, 282-284.

[49] *Ibid.*, III, 2150-2151.

III. BRITISH AGENTS AND THE TEXAS ISSUE (1823-1830)

But it was different in the case of Texas. Some of the Western leaders had been opposed to fixing the western boundary of the United States at the Sabine and much delay had occurred in establishing the line of demarcation. In the fall of 1823 Adams had had Texas as well as Cuba in mind in rejecting Canning's proposals to Rush.[50] By the summer of 1825 the Adams administration had formed the resolution to push the limits of the United States toward the Rio Grande. Moreover, emigrants from the United States were crossing the border into Texas by the thousand.

The English government, less alarmed than in the case of Cuba, did not issue specific instructions on the matter during the period now under discussion, but its previous attitude and the conduct of its agents leave no doubt of its opposition to the further expansion of the United States in this direction. These agents exercised the utmost vigilance and did what they could in a diplomatic way to defeat American projects.

English statesmen had no thought of adding Texas to the Empire, but American expansionists sometimes pretended to fear this danger. A single illustration of this last point must suffice. On August 18, 1829, when Andrew Jackson was preparing for another attempt

[50] Calhoun thought Rush should be given "discretionary power" to make the joint declaration "even if it should pledge us not to take Cuba or . . . Texas." Adams expected the inhabitants of these countries to declare for annexation to the United States, and, hence, opposed the joint declaration (*Memoirs*, VI, 177-178).

to revise the southwestern boundary, the Nashville *Republican and Gazette* presented five arguments in favor of the acquisition of Texas. The argument most emphasized was the one which maintained that the region must be kept out of the "hands of those who would be more troublesome than its present proprietors." Mexico was bankrupt; Britain was its creditor. "It is unnecessary," said the writer, "to inform those at all acquainted with the pride and all-grasping rapacity of the British character, that they would consider the live oak and sugar lands of Texas worth any sacrifice of blood and treasure. . . . Our Government has manifested its policy in relation to Cuba, namely, that it shall not change hands. The same policy will certainly extend to Texas, communicating with us by land and water, and in the heart of 20 or 30 tribes of Indians. We are, it is to be hoped, by this time sufficiently convinced of the necessity of keeping the British and Indians asunder." But this is getting ahead of the story, and we must turn back to 1823.

Patrick Mackie, who had gone to Mexico as a sort of unofficial secret agent of George Canning early in 1823, did not fail to notice conditions on the international border. He reported with evident delight General Victoria's alleged hostility toward the Yankees. Mackie wrote that Victoria, in expressing his sentiments regarding the United States, "represented them as an ambitious people always ready to encroach upon their Neighbours without a spark of good Faith; and added, that He was well aware of their Aggressions

Texas and Cuba

on the side of Louisiana, and that as soon as arrangements could be made with Great Britain, he would immediately adopt the necessary means to check them." [51] What Mackie did to stimulate these suspicions and resolutions he does not say, but it is certain that an agent who had gone to Mexico with the avowed purpose of counteracting alleged aggressive "designs" of the United States, would say nothing which would allay the General's distrust.[52]

The commission which Canning dispatched to Mexico late in 1823 likewise expressed no little alarm regarding Texas. They wrote on January 18, 1824. "The Americans have already commenced the colonization of the Province . . . , although not belonging to them, and are eagerly encouraging the construction of Roads which may facilitate the communication between Louisiana and the Northern Mexican Provinces." [53]

But it was Henry George Ward, British *chargé d'affaires* in Mexico from May, 1825, to April, 1827, who became most excited over the fate of Texas. On September 6, of the former year, he wrote that he had "more than once alluded" to the migration of American backwoodsmen" to Texas in the course of "conversations with M. Alaman and Esteva [members of the Mexican Cabinet]," and had urged upon them the importance of putting a stop to the evil "at the very

---

[51] Mackie to Canning, London, Nov. 20, 1823, F. O. (50), 1.

[52] The correspondence relative to the Mackie mission will be found in F. O. (50), I.

[53] F. O. (50), 4.

commencement." [54] On November 7, following, he went over the whole affair with President Victoria, laying before him a map containing the location of all of the American settlements, and a detailed report on Texas, which accused Poinsett of endeavoring to influence the Mexican Congress to take the matter out of the executive's hands by relinquishing control over the public lands to the several states. Ward suggested that the subject ought to be given immediate attention. At the end of a long interview, the Mexican president came to the conclusion that a commission should be sent to Texas at once in order to report upon the situation.[55] Soon afterwards Ward heard that General Mier y Terán had been offered the headship of this commission.[56] Aware that Terán was strongly antiAmerican and fearing that he might decline the offer on account of pique over his failure to obtain appointment as minister to England, Ward hurried to the General and persuaded him to accept the position. "I have little doubt that the affair will now be very speedily arranged," exulted the British *chargé*. "The President has given General Terán the manuscript

[54] Ward to Canning, F. O. (50), 14.

[55] *Idem* to *idem, loc. cit.*

[56] In fact Ward appears to have been instrumental in persuading the Mexican chief executive to appoint Terán. "It was partly at my instigation that the Countess [Regla] interfered in favor of General Terán, and it was principally owing to her exertions that General Victoria ['s] dislike to him was overcome." (Ward to Canning, *Separate and Private*, March 25, 1826, F. O. (50), 20.)

map of Texas which I left with him. . . . If General Terán goes to the frontier, there will be no occasion for any further interference on our part, as he will, I know, send in a report which will open the eyes of the congress, and make them fully aware of the danger with which they are threatened." [57]

Time was to reveal, however, that Ward was far too jubilant. Terán's appointment was indeed soon ratified by the Mexican chambers, but there was much delay in fixing his salary and general allowance and still further delay in completing the equipment of the commission. It was not until November 10, 1827, that he left the City of Mexico, and it was March 1, 1828, when he arrived at San Antonio de Bexar. Meanwhile the British *chargé* suffered great anxiety respecting the fate of Texas.

Early in December, 1825, Ward was much agitated by a rumor that Poinsett was negotiating for a vast tract of land which would "give the Americans complete possession of the Gulph of Mexico, from the Floridas, to within a little distance of Sota la Marina, and Tampico." "I have . . . seen both the President and Mr. Esteva upon the subject, and done my utmost to make them sensible of the imminence of the danger with which they are threatened," wrote Ward. At the same time, he complained of the difficulty of making Victoria "or any Mexican sensible, either of the value of Time, or of the necessity of applying an immediate

[57] Ward to Canning, No. 54, November 15, 1825, *loc. cit.*, XV.

remedy to an evil of so rapid a growth." That Ward's anxiety was not confined solely to the welfare of Mexico is evident from his contention that "His Majesty's Government can never see with indifference the whole Northern coast of the Gulph of Mexico, and the best ports which this country possesses on the Atlantic side, ... fall into the hands of the Americans, who would thus acquire the means, in the event of a rupture with England, of destroying our whole trade with the Gulph." [58]

Nor did the British agent confine his efforts to goading the Mexican government to action. Early in 1826, he lent his aid to two projects designed to counteract the influence of the American settlers along the northern frontier of Mexico. Due largely to Ward's efforts, General A. G. Wavell, an English subject, obtained a large grant south of the Red River and east of the Sabine, with the express purpose of colonizing it with Europeans and cutting the American line of communications. At about the same time, Ward composed a petition for another Englishman, J. D. Hunter, who sought permission to settle upon the international frontier some thirty thousand Indians. Speaking of the latter project, the British envoy remarked: "Hunter having assured me that they are well able to comply with their engagements, and determined to resist all encroachments on the part of the Americans, ... I thought that a better opportunity would not easily be

[58] *Idem* to *idem*, No. 64, Dec. 10, 1825, *ibid*.

found of opposing a formidable obstacle to the designs of the United States upon Texas." [59]

When, late in 1826, Ward perused a copy of the recently signed commercial treaty between Mexico and the United States he was worried because it contained no article defining the boundary. In fact, he intimated that he would have interfered if he had not been misinformed about the matter. Now that the treaty had been signed, however, he declared that he would not oppose its ratification. Indeed, there was now no need of opposition. Ward had already, as he himself said, done everything he could to bring the Mexican government to a realization of the danger of losing Texas. Once thoroughly aroused, apprehension with respect to this region was all that was required, as the sequel proved, to defeat the commercial agreement. For two reasons, both of them connected with the Texas issue, the Mexican Congress refused to ratify the agreement. Ward must share a portion of the responsibility for its defeat.[60]

The Texas question seems not to have caused Ward any more uneasiness until the early days of February, 1827, when he received news of the so-called "Freedonian Revolt." He was sure he detected Yankee intrigue back of this uprising of American immigrants

[59] *Idem* to *idem*, Nos. 18 to 20, March 18, 1826, *loc. cit.*, XX. Wavell's project failed. Hunter later (1827) proved disloyal to Mexico and was killed during the "Freedonian Rebellion."

[60] *Idem* to *idem*, No. 83, July 11, 1826; No. 103, Sept. 9, 1826; No. 123, Oct. 20, 1826, F. O. (50), vols. 22, 23, and 24, respectively.

and Indians on the Texas frontier. He declared that "a more flagrant violation of territorial Rights has certainly not frequently occurred, in the History, either of the Old or New World"—words which remind one of what Liverpool had said of American procedure in the Floridas more than a decade before. Ward feared that the declaration of independence which, according to reports, the Freedonians had promulgated, would prove to be the first act in a drama that would end in the incorporation of the whole region between the Sabine and the Rio Grande into the American Union and the realization thereby of the "great object" of Poinsett's mission to Mexico. He noted with evident satisfaction, however, that the Mexican government had determined to send an army into Texas at once. "It is possible," he wrote hopefully, "that this display of vigor in the first instance may terminate the affair at once; and with a view to this I urged the President strongly not to underestimate the importance of the contest, nor to imagine that in these adventures, — because they were adventurers, he would find a contemptible enemy: — I told him that they were Men reckless of danger, — excellent Marksmen, and so perfectly acquainted with the Country, that they would be able to meet upon their own ground, more than double their number of Regular Troops; — In short, that too much caution could not be displayed, until a Force was assembled, sufficient to bear down all opposition." [61]

[61] *Idem* to *idem*, *Confidentials* of Feb. 17 and 21, 1827, *ibid.*, 31.

In the course of the interview between Ward and the Mexican chief executive, the latter intimated that he intended, through the Mexican minister in London, to make "some communication" to the British government regarding the designs of the United States upon Texas. Ward appeared to be anxious to forestall such application unless the danger should prove real. He accordingly returned to England, whither he had been recalled largely because of financial extravagance, by way of New York, where he consulted with Vaughan. He found the latter confident that the United States had not "connived at the conduct of the New Settlers" in Texas [62] and "decidedly of the opinion" that both the American executive and the American Congress accepted the boundary "as fixed by the Treaty of Onis." This Ward communicated to President Victoria. At the same time he wrote Canning, apologizing for bringing the matter before him "prematurely." [63]

Thus ended Ward's Mexican mission, but not the currents of suspicion which he had set in motion during his residence. These continued to flow and had far-reaching results. Ward had spared no effort in stimulating Mexican apprehensions with respect to the ambitions of the United States and the menace of the

[62] Vaughan to Canning, No. 7, Feb. 25, 1827, F. O. (5), 233.

[63] Ward to *idem*, Separate and Private, June 20, 1827, F. O. (50), 32. For a thorough discussion of the "Freedonian Rebellion," see E. C. Barker, *Stephen F. Austin* (Dallas, 1925), Ch. VII.

American "backwoodsmen" in Texas. He had expressed his conviction "both publicly and privately, that the Great End of Mr. Poinsett's Mission" was to "embroil Mexico in a Civil War, and to facilitate, by doing so, the Acquisition of the Provinces to the North of the Rio Bravo, by the United States." [64] Such suspicions, once implanted in the Mexican mind, could not be rooted out by any private letters to the Mexican chief executive. Ward had been instrumental in causing the Victoria administration to send to Texas a commission headed by Terán, of whose unfriendly attitude toward the American settlers he was well aware. He had spread propaganda tending to convince the Mexican reading public of the greed and perfidy of their neighbor. The effect of these acts was irrevocable.

The sequel of Ward's machinations may be read in the reports of Terán and in the Mexican regulations based upon them. Soon after arriving in Texas, this commissioner began to compose alarming accounts of conditions in the province. From Nacogdoches, on June 30, 1828, he wrote: "The whole population here is a mixture of strange and incoherent parts without parallel in our federation: numerous tribes of Indians ... ; colonists of another people, more progressive and better informed than the Mexican inhabitants, but also more shrewd and unruly; among these foreigners are fugitives from justice, honest laborers, vagabonds and criminals, but honorable and dishonorable alike travel

[64] *Idem* to *idem*, Private, March 31, 1827, *ibid.*, 31.

with their constitutions in their pockets, demanding the privileges, authority and offices which such a constitution guarantees. The most of them have slaves, and these slaves are beginning to learn the favorable intent of the Mexican law toward their unfortunate condition and are becoming restless under their yoke, and the masters, in an effort to retain them, are making that yoke even heavier; they extract their teeth, set on the dogs to tear them in pieces, the most lenient being he who but flogs his slaves until they are flayed. . . ." Terán then went on to assert that the American immigrants held the Mexicans of the frontier in contempt and to predict a growing antagonism between the two groups. "I am warning you to take timely measures," he concluded, "Texas could throw the whole nation into revolution."[65]

Somewhat later, after he had become commander of the northeastern frontier, Terán sent the War Department a vehement denunciation of American methods of expansion. "They begin," said Terán, "by assuming rights, as in Texas, which it is impossible to sustain in a serious discussion, making ridiculous pretensions based on historical incidents which no one admits — such as the voyage of La Salle, which was an absurd fiasco, but serves as a basis of their claim to Texas. Such extravagant claims as these are now being presented for the first time to the public by dissembling

[65] As quoted by Alleine Howren, "Causes and Origin of the Decree of April 6, 1830," in *The Southwestern Historical Quarterly*, XVI (1913), 395-398.

writers;[66] the efforts that others make to submit proofs and reasons are by these men employed in reiteration . . . in order to attract the attention of their fellow-countrymen, not to the justice of the claim, but to the profit to be gained from admitting it. At this stage, it is alleged that there is a national demand for the step which the government meditates. In the meantime, the territory against which these machinations are directed, and which has usually remained unsettled, begins to be visited by adventurers and *empresarios;* some of these take up their residence in the country, pretending that their location has no bearing upon their government's claim or the boundary disputes; shortly, some of these forerunners develop an interest which complicates the political administration of the coveted territory; complaints, even threats, begin to be heard, working on the loyalty of the legitimate settlers, discrediting the efficiency of the existing authority . . . ; and the matter having arrived at this stage —which is precisely that of Texas at this moment— diplomatic manoeuvres begin. . . . He who consents to or does not oppose the loss of Texas is an execrable traitor who ought to be punished with death. . . ."[67]

In a subsequent letter written under Terán's direction the United States was accused of collusion in the

[66] This was not the first time the claims to Texas had been presented in the newspapers of the United States, but a lively agitation for the annexation of the province was then (1829) being carried on.

[67] *The Southwestern Historical Quarterly*, XVI, 400.

Texas and Cuba

Freedonian uprising of 1826-27. "General Terán does not doubt," says the despatch, "that the United States will carry out its project of possessing Texas at the first opportunity . . . ; either they would incite the population of Texas to revolt, as they tried to do in 1826 at Nacogdoches, or else force would be used to support these pretended claims. . . ." The writer then proceeded to outline a plan for checkmating the influence of the American settlers in Texas and binding the region more closely to the central government. The encouragement of European and Mexican settlers, the establishment of a coastwise trade, and the increase of the army, were the most important recommendations. The letter then concluded: "General Terán thinks it not impossible that the government of the United States of the North, on perceiving a firm determination on our part to hold our own and to support and improve Texas, will begin to carry on its work openly; therefore it may be expedient to act quickly and place ourselves on the defensive as soon as possible. . . ." In transmitting this report, Terán's aide asked whether England might not be induced to make some declaration against American designs on Texas. Ward's attitude had not been forgotten![68]

The official under whose eager scrutiny these reports eventually fell was none other than Lucas Alamán, of whose pro-British sentiments Joel R. Poinsett had often complained. Several upheavals in Mexican politics had brought him for the third time to the head-

[68] *Ibid.*, 407-408, 412.

ship of the Mexican foreign office. Early in February, 1830, he transmitted his now famous report to Congress. It was mainly a reiteration of the charges and suggestions of Terán, with two or three recommendations relating to colonization legislation added. Nor was the suggestion regarding Britain overlooked. Alamán had urged this upon Congress even before he presented the main report.[69] On April 6, the Mexican Congress accepted his recommendations virtually as presented.[70] At last the Texans were to be taken in hand, and this at the very time when their tariff exemptions had expired and they were beginning to feel the weight of a revenue system more "abomnable" than that of 1828 in the United States. Moreover, the official who was designated to carry out all these measures was that same Mier y Terán who owed his connection with Texas affairs largely to Henry George Ward! Events now moved with all the inexorableness of fate toward the Texas revolution. For precipitating this event it is fair to assume that the British *chargé* was partially responsible.

[69] Alamán had made a preliminary statement to Congress on January 14, 1830. The more famous report was dated February 8. It may be found translated into English in *House Ex. Doc.* No. 351, 25 Cong., 2 Sess., 312 ff.

British influence may be seen even in this latter report, for Alamán remarks: "Some of them [i. e. of the Americans] have said that Providence had marked out Rio Bravo as the natural boundary of those States, which has induced an English writer to reproach them with an attempt to make Providence the author of their usurpations. . . ."

[70] For a careful discussion of the origin of this law, see Howren *op. et loc. cit.*

Meanwhile, Richard Pakenham, who had succeeded Ward as *chargé d'affaires* early in 1827, had little to say regarding the Texas question. In November, of that year, he refused to intervene in behalf of the Irishman, Powers, who had asked his aid in order to secure confirmation by the Mexican government of his title to certain Texas lands.[71] In May, 1829, he remarked that General Guerrero, who had recently become chief executive of Mexico, was supposed to be very friendly toward Poinsett. He thought that Poinsett might therefore take advantage of the situation in order to obtain Texas. He believed, however, that the executive would encounter "strenuous opposition" if he made an attempt to alienate this province, and, immediately afterwards, he expressed doubt as to whether Guerrero was really favorably disposed toward the American minister.[72] Again, early in 1830, he suspected that the United States was determined "by fair means or foul" to get possession of Texas. He had derived the impression from Alamán, the Mexican press, and a letter which he had seen from a Frenchman living in Louisiana.[73]

But the apprehensions of the British government, if it had any, were allayed by Vaughan who, somewhat disturbed by the Texas agitation in the American

[71] Pakenham to Dudley, No. 74, Nov. 26, 1827, F. O. (50), 36.

[72] *Idem* to Aberdeen, No. 50, May 3, 1829, and No. 52, of the same date, F. O. (50), 54.

[73] *Idem* to *idem*, No. 7, January 9, 1830; No. 23, March 5, 1830; *Separate and Secret*, March 5, 1830, all in F. O. (50), 60.

press in 1829, had interviewed the secretary of state, Van Buren, regarding the matter. The conference took place in March, 1830, and Van Buren assured Vaughan that the United States cherished neither any ill will towards Mexico nor a wish to acquire any part of Texas by any means whatever. The clever New York politician also alluded to the "ascendancy" of British influence in Mexico and expressed the hope that it would be used to remove all unfounded suspicions regarding the United States.[74] In this manner, apparently, the English government was placed at ease regarding the Texas issue. It probably did not know that for five years American agents in Mexico had had instructions to buy as much of the province as they could![75]

[74] Vaughan to Aberdeen, No. 46, Sept. 12, 1829, and No. 56, Oct. 12, 1829, F. O. (5), 249; *idem* to *idem*, No. 15, March 30, 1830, F. O. (5), 259.

On September 20, 1829, Vaughan reported that Jackson's enemies were saying that he intended to purchase Texas. He said that the "Middle and Northeastern States" were expected to oppose any increase of influence of the Southern States. He also pointed out that "the public discussions which must take place in order to obtain the consent of Congress . . . and to find means of payment will [would] give ample time for any Representation which it may [might] be deemed advisable to make."

[75] See Manning, *Early Diplomatic Relations between the United States and Mexico*, Ch. IX.

CHAPTER IV

THE ANTAGONISM OF CANNING AND ADAMS; RIVALRY IN SOUTHERN SOUTH AMERICA

Discussion of the territorial aspect of Anglo-American rivalry as related to Hispanic America has led to a violation of chronological sequence. It is time to return to the economic and political clashes of the two Powers with reference to the new states.

I. A MORE ENERGETIC ERA

Their rivalries entered a more energetic era with the rejection of Canning's proposal of a joint declaration against European interference in the former Spanish colonies, the promulgation of the Monroe Doctrine, and the arrival in Spanish America of the consuls and diplomats of England and the new ministers from the United States. The contest continued, however, to be both political and economic, although these interests were closely related and often difficult to separate.

In the matter of investments the competition was of little importance. Citizens of the United States had little to invest outside of their own country. They put some capital into the mines of Mexico, secured a canal concession in Central America, and made two or three unsuccessful attempts to market the government loans of Chile, Rio de la Plata, and Mexico;[1] but, in general, the British were left with an open field.

And the British rushed in with great eagerness to possess the old Spanish mines and subscribe to the government loans. During the years 1824 and 1825 they organized mining companies capitalized at over £14,000,000 and absorbed government loans amounting to more than £20,000,000. Nothing like this enthusiasm had occurred in the whole history of English finance. It amounted to a "mania" which ended in a panic.[2]

Commercial rivalry was keener. So far as commodities were concerned, there was little competition: Americans were selling mainly the products of the farm; Englishmen, mainly those of the factory. In the matter of shipping, however, it was different, for both the British and the Yankees were eager to participate in the carrying trade of infant nations without merchant marines, and each was suspicious of the other, in spite of repeated mutual disavowals of any intention to seek special concessions either in shipping or in trade.

Moreover, they were rival sea powers, with a clear conception of the potential bearing of the Hispanic-

---

[1] Henry Clay Evans, *Chile and Its Relations with the United States* (Durham, 1927), 39; Manning, *Dip. Cor.* I, 348 ff.; Aberdeen to Vaughan, No. 6, April 22, 1829, and John Backhouse to *idem*, F. O. (5), 247.

[2] Great Britain, Parliament, *Accounts and Papers* (1844), VII, 352 ff.

American states upon the issue of the contest. The United States, with its policy of isolation, viewed commercial questions from the vantage ground of a neutral. In Europe's wars Yankee statesmen were determined not to participate. If the hostile nations must fight, the United States would furnish them with supplies, building up its trade and shipping at their expense; that is, provided the old navigation system could be broken down and the rights of neutrals maintained at the maximum. England, on the contrary, viewed commercial questions from the angle of a great belligerent sea power whose security and prosperity depended almost entirely upon the domination of the ocean. Hispanic America might very well furnish the weight which would tip the balance in favor of the one party or the other.

Lord Liverpool, British Prime Minister from 1812 to 1827, stated this issue very clearly late in 1824. To him the most "formidable" phase of the Spanish-American question was this very matter of sea power. "The great and favourite object of the policy of" Britain, "for more than four centuries," he said, "has been to foster and encourage our navigation, as the sure basis of our maritime power. In this branch of national industry the people of the United States are become more formidable rivals to us than any nation which has ever yet existed.... The views and policy of the North Americans seem mainly directed toward supplanting us in navigation in every quarter of the globe, but more particularly in the seas contiguous to America.

"Let us recollect that as their commercial marine is augmented, their military marine must proportionately increase. And it cannot be doubted that, if we provoke the new states of America to give a decided preference in their ports to the people of the United States over ourselves, the navigation of these extensive dominions will be lost to us, and it will, in great measure, be transferred to our rivals."

Liverpool appears to have been truly alarmed. On December 8, 1824, he wrote to the Duke of Wellington: "I am conscientiously convinced that if we allow these new states to consolidate their system and their policy with the United States of America, it will in a very few years prove fatal to our greatness, if not endanger our safety." [3]

---

[3] Yonge, *Liverpool*, II, 301-303, III, 305.

The attitude of the United States, at this period, toward British sea power hardly needs illustration. The following paragraph from Clay's instructions to the delegates sent to the Panama Congress is worth quoting in this connection, however:

"At all times there has existed more inequality in the distribution among nations of maritime than of territorial power. In almost every age some one has had the complete mastery on the ocean, and this superiority has been occasionally so great as to more than counterbalance the combined maritime force of all other nations. . . . When a single nation finds itself possessed of a power anywhere which no one, nor all the other nations, can successfully check . . . , the consequences are too sadly unfolded in the pages of history. . . . If the superiority be on the ocean, the excesses in the abuses of that power become intolerable." (*International American Conference*, IV, 113, *passim.*)

Of course, England is the power which Clay had in mind.

From this viewpoint, then, the rivalry of the two powers represented a continuation of the contest which had begun decades before and was left unsettled by the War of 1812 and the Treaty of Ghent. Liverpool probably overestimated the maritime ambitions of the United States, but the conviction was about as important as the fact. The clash of maritime policies and principles was the cloud that overhung the sky during the years now under consideration. The main issues were politico-economic and related to maritime laws, blockades, contraband lists, the definition of "national" vessels, and the perpetuation of the colonial system.

This last point, perhaps, requires special emphasis. The word *colony* brought to American minds a train of unpleasant associations. To them it signified the old colonial system instituted by Spain and Portugal and followed in large measure by all the colonizing nations. Certain American statesmen feared that the English government, which was in fact beginning to abandon the monopolistic idea, might attempt to apply the old exclusive principles to Hispanic America, and they felt that this must be vigorously opposed.

So far as purely political questions were concerned, only two, as already noted, were a source of antagonism. The United States favored democratic republics and, except for Canada and a few other colonies, a complete political separation of the Old World from the New. England, on the other hand, was partial to conservative, though constitutional, monarchies and desired to bring Europe and the Americas into a common sphere of political action. But there were factors which relieved the situation. Both rivals stood for the rule of non-intervention in the domestic affairs of other nations and neither favored a crusade in behalf of its own peculiar political system. Individuals— business men and minor diplomats — might become, as before, the missionaries of one system or the other, but the governments were not likely to be involved. And the peril of the antagonism between the policy of isolation and the attempt to use the New World in order to adjust the balance of the Old would depend upon conditions in Europe and America, the importance of the Hispanic-American states, and the distance which the two rivals could, or would, go in support of their clashing political policies.

II. CANNING VERSUS ADAMS

Any examination of the jealous competition of the two Powers during the period now under consideration must begin with the opposing views of George Canning and John Quincy Adams, who were in charge of their respective foreign offices. Fortunately, expressions of the attitudes of these two men are not difficult to find. Each frequently revealed suspicions of the other, and mainly for the same reasons.

Of Canning's preference for monarchies in the New World there can be no doubt. In the notable Polignac interviews of October, 1823, he admitted that monarchies for Spanish America were desirable, but remarked that there were difficulties in the way.[4] Seven weeks later he told the London representatives of the leading European states that there was ground to hope that "monarchic and aristocratic principles" would be strengthened in Mexico, Peru, and Chile.[5] He was willing to delay the recognition of Mexico and Colombia in order to see if they would set up monarchies. He instructed the British commission sent to the former to encourage the establishment of a monarchy if he found leaders favorably disposed toward that institution, while the agents dispatched to the latter were directed to avoid the term "republic" in the treaty which they were authorized to sign.[6] He attached "great importance" to the continuation of a monarchy in Brazil, declaring that monarchy in that country and Mexico "would cure the evils of universal democracy" in America. He mediated in the difficulties of Portugal and Brazil on the one hand, and of Rio de la Plata and Brazil on the other, mainly with the view of preserving that form of government.[7]

Yet there was a limit to Canning's efforts in support of the monarchical principle, for a too active encouragement would constitute a violation of the rule of non-intervention. He would not prevent the establish-

[4] Temperley, *The Foreign Policy of Canning*, 117.

[5] *Ibid.*, 139.

[6] *Ibid.*, 158; Canning to Hervey, No. 5, Oct. 10, 1823, F. O. (50), 3; *idem* to Campbell, Private, Jan., 1825, F. O. (18, Colombia), 11.

[7] Temperley, *The Foreign Policy of Canning*, 138, 129, *passim*.

ment of monarchy by a hasty recognition of republics; he would promote it when proposed by the Spanish Americans themselves; he would strengthen it where it prevailed; but he would do nothing more.[8]

A further motive back of Canning's attitude was his desire to counteract the influence of the United States, whose alleged designs, as he supposed, could be more easily realized under a republican régime. This is very evident in the views he expressed with reference to British recognition of the new states and other matters in 1824 and 1825. "Sooner or later we shall probably have to contend with the combined maritime power of France and the United States. The disposition of the new States is at present highly favourable to England. If we take advantage of that disposition we may establish through our influence with them a fair counterpoise to that combined maritime power. Let us not, then, throw the present golden opportunity away. . . ." "I believe we now have the opportunity (but it may not last long) of opposing a powerful barrier to the influence of the U. S. . . .; but if we hesitate much longer . . . all the new States will be led to conclude that we reject their friendship upon principle, as of a dangerous and revolutionary character, and will be driven to throw themselves under the protection of the U. S. as the only means of security."[9] So ran the cabinet memoranda for which Canning was largely responsible. A little later, after his recognition

[8] *Ibid.*, 139, note 2, and *passim*.
[9] *Ibid.*, 145, 553.

policy had been carried, he wrote Granville: "The deed is done, the nail is driven. Spanish America is free; and if we do not mismanage our affairs sadly, *she is English.*" [10] He also told one of his political friends that the "great danger of the time" was that the world would be divided into European and American, monarchical and republican, with the United States at the head of the republican group.[11] Finally, to give only one more illustration, he wrote Vaughan on February 18, 1826, that "The avowed pretension of the United States to put themselves at the head of the confedaracy of all the Americas, and to sway that confederacy against Europe (Great Britain included), is [was] *not* a pretension identified with our interests, or one that we can [could] countenance or tolerate." [12]

Thus Canning expressed his policy clearly and emphatically. He was opposed to the doctrine of the two spheres, he feared the political and maritime principles and ambitions of the United States, and, as possible means of counteracting American views and aspirations, he looked with favor upon the establishment of New World monarchies and finally urged the recognition of the new states.[13] That his jealousy of

[10] Temperley, "The Later American Policy of George Canning." *Am. Historical Rev.*, X (1906), 796.

[11] *Ibid.*, *The Foreign Policy of Canning*, 158.

[12] F. O. (5), 209. The despatch is slightly misquoted by Temperley, *op. cit.*, 158.

[13] Of course there were other reasons for recognition, but this one was important.

Yankee commercial competition was not so clearly expressed may be due to Adams's repeated disavowal of exclusive commercial aims. That they would be opposed if they appeared may fairly be assumed.

The views of Adams, accepted and probably sometimes modified, and even formulated by Monroe and Clay,[14] were expressed with equal emphasis. To Adams, the colonial system meant commercial exclusion and, with reference to England, the effects of that system had long been felt in the restrictions placed upon American trade with the West Indies. Near the close of 1822, in a significant conference with Stratford Canning, British minister at Washington, Adams bluntly stated his dislike for the "old exclusive and excluding" colonial policy. He declared that it had originated in papal bulls and the employment of the "sword of injustice." "Spain had set the example. She had forbidden foreigners from setting a foot in her Colonies, upon pain of death, and the other colonizing states of Europe had imitated the exclusion, though not the rigor of the penalty. . . . The whole system of modern colonization was an abuse of government, and it was time that it should come to an end." [15]

This politico-commercial angle of the question was the important consideration in Adams's connection with the Monroe Doctrine; and, in Adams's mind, that

[14] *Cf.* Dexter Perkins, *The Monroe Doctrine* (Cambridge, 1927), *passim.*

[15] *Memoirs*, VI, 104.

Doctrine was directed as much against England as any other Power. Opposition to commercial monopoly was the main motive back of the non-colonization section. In a letter of July 22, 1823, to Rush, who then represented the United States at London, Adams placed the policy of Russia in the Northwest in its more general setting. He remonstrated against the "application of colonial principles of exclusion" to any part of the American continents.[16] Furthermore, in urging the promulgation of the Monroe Doctrine as a whole, he returned to the same idea. "If," argued Adams, "the Holy Allies should subdue Spanish America, however they might at first set up the standard of Spain, the ultimate result of their undertaking would be to recolonize them [it], partitioned out among themselves. Russia might take California, Peru, Chile; France, Mexico — where we know she has been intriguing to get a monarchy under a Prince of the House of Bourbon, as well as at Buenos Ayres. And Great Britain, as her last resort, if she could not resist the course of things, would at least take the island of Cuba for her share of the scramble. . . . The danger, therefore, was brought to our own doors, and I thought we could not too soon take our stand to repel it." Adams then added another suggestion, even more significant for our present study. "Suppose," said he, "the Holy Allies should attack South America, and Great Britain should resist them alone and without our cooperation. I thought this not an improbable con-

[16] Perkins, *op. cit.*, 18.

tingency, and I believed in such a struggle the allies would be defeated and Great Britain would be victorious, by her command of the sea. But, as the independence of the South Americans would then be only protected by the guarantee of Great Britain, it would throw them completely into her arms, and in the result make them her Colonies instead of those of Spain. My opinion was, therefore, that we must act promptly and decisively." [17]

Thus Adams feared that Great Britain, under certain contingencies, might take possession of a part or even the whole of the Spanish colonies, and he was prepared to resist mainly because this augmentation of British dominions would prolong "the old exclusive and excluding Colonial system" which he hoped would not "much longer endure anywhere." Of course, this was not the only motive which led Adams to advocate the message of Monroe — Russia and the other "Holy Allies" were also feared — but it was *one* motive, and it had an important bearing upon the relations of the two Powers in reference to Hispanic-American issues. The commercial policy of England was disliked, watched, and opposed.

Adams likewise resented the maritime rules and pretensions of England. This phase of the struggle needs no illustration. It is only necessary, in order to be convinced of his attitude on these issues, to recall that Adams had spent many years contesting British views on impressment, the right of search, and the

[17] *Memoirs*, VI, 207-208.

rights of neutrals in general. The instructions transmitted to the agents sent to the new governments of Hispanic America and the treaties negotiated with the new states will reveal the determination and success with which he resisted England's policy in these matters. The War of 1812 was continued in the realm of diplomacy.

Neither do Adams's purely political views relating to Hispanic America call for extensive comment. The doctrine of the two spheres so much resented by Canning was the doctrine of Adams perhaps more than of any other man. When others favored joint action with England or the championship of Greek independence, it was Adams who insisted that the United States should "make an American cause, and adhere inflexibly to that."[18] President Monroe accordingly announced the doctrine of American isolation in a formal message to Congress. With reference to democratic partisanship, it must be admitted that Adams was not so ardent a democrat as Clay or Monroe, nor so profoundly influenced by political idealism in formulating a policy with reference to Spanish America. He desired that the Spanish colonies should become independent largely because he wished that they should *cease to be colonies*.[19] Yet Monroe's message, which Adams approved and helped to write, set forth the antagonism between republican and monarchical

[18] Adams, *Memoirs*, VI, 197 ff.; Perkins, *The Monroe Doctrine*, 9, *passim*.

[19] Perkins, *op. cit.*, 45.

forms, and Adams was ready to transmit to Russia a lecture on the virtues of the democratic republican system.[20] Moreover, the instructions given to the first ministers sent to the Spanish-American states were filled with sentiments favorable to the same system. They may have been in part the work of Monroe and Clay, but there is no reason to suppose that they were not largely the product of Adams's own mind.

At any rate, these instructions expressed the policy of the government of the United States and, as such, deserve more attention than they have received. To Caesar A. Rodney, minister to Buenos Aires, Adams outlined his policy as follows:

"Mr. Rivadavia, the Minister of Foreign Relations, and the most effective member of the Government, is represented as Republican in principle, of solid talents, stern integrity, and faithfully devoted to the cause of order, as well as of Liberty — It is with infinite difficulty and in conflict with repeated conspiracies that he has been able to maintain himself hitherto, and the hope may be entertained that the principles of which he is the supporter will ultimately surmount all the obstacles with which they are contending, and that a Constitution emanating from the people and deliberately adopted by them will lay the foundations of their happiness, and prosperity on their only possible basis, the enjoyment of equal rights. . . . To promote this object so far as friendly counsel may be acceptable to the Government existing there, will be among the in-

[20] *Ibid.*, 86-89, 95, note 66.

teresting objects of your Mission.... With relation to *Europe* there is perceived to be only one object, in which the interests and wishes of the United States can be the same as those of the Southern American Nations, and that is that they should all be governed by Republican Institutions, politically and commercially independent of Europe....

"The foundation of our municipal Institutions is equal rights. The basis of all our intercourse with foreign powers is Reciprocity. We have not demanded, nor would we have accepted special privileges of any kind in return for an acknowledgment of Independence. But that which we have not desired and would not have accepted for ourselves, we have a right to insist ought not to be granted to others. Recognition is in its nature, not a subject of equivalent; it is claimable of right or not at all. You will therefore strenuously maintain the right of the United States to be treated in every respect on the footing of the most favoured; or as it is more properly expressed, the most friendly nation ...; and should you negotiate a Treaty of Commerce you will make that principle the foundation of all its provisions...."[21]

Similar views were set forth in the instructions to Richard C. Anderson, who was sent as minister to Colombia. It was a *republican* government to which he was being accredited and a *chargé d'affaires* of the "Republic of Colombia" had already been received by

[21] Adams to Rodney, May 17, 1823, as quoted in Manning, *Diplomatic Correspondence*, I, 186 ff.

President Monroe. Any and all attempts "to concert a general system of popular representation for the government of the several independent States which are floating from the wreck of Spanish power in America, the United States will still cheer . . . with their approbation, and speed with their good wishes. . . . The European alliance of Emperors and Kings have assumed, as the foundation of human society, the doctrine of unalienable *allegiance*. Our doctrine is founded upon the principle of unalienable *right*. The European allies, therefore, have viewed the *cause* of the South Americans as rebellion against their lawful sovereign. We have considered it as the assertion of natural right. They have invariably shown their disapprobation of the revolution, and their wishes for the restoration of the Spanish power. We have as constantly favored the standard of independence and of America. . . ." Moreover: "The political systems of Europe are founded upon partial rights and *exclusive* privileges. The colonial system had no other basis. . . ." But the United States favored no such monopolistic system; it desired to negotiate a treaty of commerce and navigation *"upon the bases of reciprocal utility and perfect equality."* [22]

The instructions later given to Joel R. Poinsett, when he was appointed minister to Mexico, were not essentially different in tone. In fact, they were in many respects only an enlarged edition of the instruc-

[22] Adams to Anderson, May 27, 1823, quoted in *ibid.*, I, 192 ff.

tions to Anderson, a copy of which was enclosed.[23] Of similar import, likewise, were the instructions given the ministers to the other new states. They were all authorized to encourage the consolidation of the *republican* system, freedom of competition in commerce, and the resistance of European interference in their affairs.[24] They were also instructed to embody in treaties the views of the United States regarding maritime law and neutrals' rights.[25]

So there was a real antagonism between the Hispanic-American policies of Adams and Canning. Although it is true that portions of the various instructions of Adams (and Clay) were written more for Continental Europe than England, Britain was often included in the general references to European Powers; and in their politico-commercial phase they were designed specifically for England. It is well to be reminded, however, that in some respects both Adams and Canning were tilting at windmills. Canning never sought exclusive commercial privileges in Spanish America, nor was he disposed to carry his encouragement of monarchies beyond the limits prescribed by his other policy of non-intervention. Similarly, Adams never seriously considered the organization of an American league of nations headed by the

[23] Clay to Poinsett, March 26, 1825, U. S. Inst., X, 225 ff.

[24] Adams to Heman Allen, Nov. 23, 1823, *ibid.*, X, 129 ff.; Clay to James Cooley, Nov. 6, 1826, and April 15, 1828, *ibid.*, XI, 176 ff., XII, 89 ff.

[25] *Post*, Ch. VIII.

United States any more than he or Clay contemplated the support of democratic republics beyond the giving of friendly advice and counsel.

With regard to the immediate successors of Adams and Canning in the conduct of the foreign policy of the two nations, little needs to be said. In neither case did important modifications occur. There were in both instances a little more indifference and a little less suspicion, but, in the main, the precedents of Adams and Canning were followed.[26]

What of the execution of these opposing policies and the clashes of the agents chosen to carry them out? To this larger phase of the subject attention must now be directed. Friction was most intense in Argentina and Mexico,[27] but numerous encounters occurred in Brazil, Central America, Chile, and the regions where Bolívar held sway.

III. FRICTION IN CHILE AND BRAZIL

The British consuls in Chile — there were no diplomatic representatives prior to 1830 — revealed little or no jealousy of the United States. In the Spanish-American policy of Canning and his successors the small state of the South Pacific was not of prime importance. Due largely to the turbulent condition of its politics it was not even recognized by England during the era now under consideration.

[26] *Post*, 291 ff.

[27] *Post*, Ch. VII.

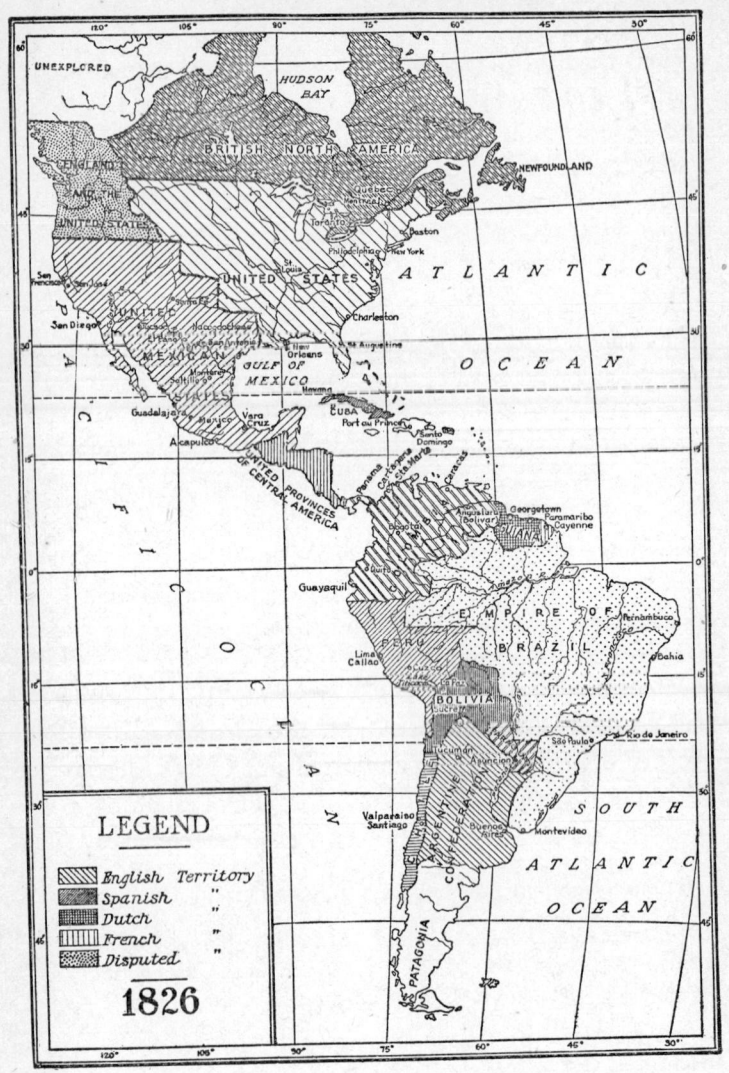

THE AMERICAS AFTER HISPANIC-AMERICAN INDEPENDENCE (1826)

(From Bolton's *History of the Americas*)

Yet, English trade and investments were not unimportant and English influence was powerful in this little country. In the summer of 1824 Canning was "styled, even in the Senate, by all of the officers of State, The Redeemer of Chile." [28] The refusal of Great Britain to extend recognition caused some irritation later, but this did not seriously affect British economic interests. The Chilean government loan was floated in London; British capital operated the most important mines; the average value of British commerce amounted to more than four million dollars annually; British commercial houses were in all the ports, their agents living with Chilean wives; and even the constitution of 1831 was as much English as Yankee.[29] Sometimes the capitalists complained of lack of protection or failure to receive dividends on their government bonds, but this was due more to political disorders than to Chilean hostility.[30]

With the United States it was different. Its citizens had no funds to invest abroad; its annual trade never reached $200,000 in value; and in spite of Chile's early adoption of its political principles and appreciation of its early recognition, its prestige was never equal to

[28] Consul Nugent to Canning, No. 4, July 30, 1824, F. O. (16), 1.

[29] *Idem* to *idem*, No. 20, March 17, 1825, *loc. cit.*; G. B., Parliament, *Accts. and Papers*, XXXIV, p. 207; Evans, *Chile and its Relations with the U. S.*, 39-40.

[30] J. Backhouse to Nugent, May 19, 1827, and Nugent to Backhouse, Oct. 1, 1827, F. O. (16), 6.

that of Great Britain.[31] American agents sensed the situation and did not fail to complain.

Heman Allen, the first minister of the United States, complimented Chile on the adoption of a republican form of government and expressed the ardent wish that it might be preserved. "Oh! never may it be said, of this rising Republic," exclaimed Allen in the peroration of his presentation address, "she *once* was free, she *once* was happy, she *once* was independent." He later warned the foreign minister "against considering the arrival of the British consuls as an act of recognition" and pointed out the fact that Canning had refused late in 1823 to accede to the American request that the new states of Spanish America be acknowledged as independent.[32]

This early expression of jealousy of British influence was frequently reiterated during the three years which Allen spent in Valparaiso. "This new government feels that it has recognition from us," he wrote in 1825. "It now gives its favors to England and France so as to obtain recognition from them."[33] When he learned that the British government had been invited to attend the Panama Congress he was greatly alarmed. "The preponderating influence of England,

[31] Henry Clay Evans, *Chile and its Relations with the United States*, Ch. III; W. S. Robertson, *Hispanic-American Relations of the United States*, 197, 421.

[32] Allen to Adams, April 29, 1824, Manning, *Dip. Cor.*, II, 1092 ff.

[33] Quoted by Evans, *op. cit.*, 41. *Cf.* Manning, *op. cit.*, II, 1105.

in the affairs of these countries is already seen and felt in almost every department; to the monopoly of their commerce and riches, she is already looking with a most steadfast eye, and if she is now permitted to become a member of this proposed alliance it does appear to me, that the destiny of the new states, is at once placed in her hands, and that with all their boasted independence, they are *de facto* her colonies." [34] Allen accordingly attempted to dissuade Chile from attending the congress. But his efforts were unavailing; only lack of money kept the Chilean delegates away.[35]

Samuel Larned, Allen's successor, revealed no such decided apprehensions, but he did not fail to note British "commercial jealousy," nor did he neglect to point out, at an earlier period, how the English-Mexican treaty of April 6, 1825, had put into Chilean heads ideas which were destined to interfere with American negotiations on the same subject.[36] The British agents in Mexico had admitted a stipulation reserving to the Mexican government the privilege of granting special advantages to the new states of Spanish origin.[37] Larned attempted to prevent Chile from granting any such stipulation, but the sequel would reveal that Chilean diplomats were to insist upon placing it in the commercial agreement with the United States. Yet

[34] Manning, *Dip. Cor.*, II, 1112.
[35] Evans, *Chile*, 40.
[36] Manning, *op. cit.*, II, 1122, 1129.
[37] *Post*, Ch. VII.

it must be admitted that political disorders, monopolistic predilections, and religious intolerance, as well as this partiality for the sister states of Spanish origin, were responsible for the postponement of the commercial treaty with the United States beyond the period now under review.[38]

In Brazil, the jealousies were mutual but somewhat mild, particularly on the side of the British. In fact, Englishmen had no very good reason to be jealous. The House of Braganza had been under English domination for centuries, and this House was ruling in Brazil. Under the treaty of 1810 the English had been granted special privileges in commerce and they were in no hurry to give them up in the negotiations which were begun with the independent state of Brazil in 1825. In fact, Canning preferred to retain the "signal commercial concessions" of 1810 until a complete settlement between Portugal and its former colony had been effected, and was even prepared to demand special favors in the proposed new agreement.[39] If he did not seek advantages in Spanish America where England had legally received none before, he did not lightly give them up in Brazil, where they had been enjoyed for years. If a headstrong agent (Charles Stuart) rashly negotiated a commercial agreement surrendering some of these privileges as well as certain maritime contentions of the English nations, the agent

[38] Evans, *Chile*, 32 ff.

[39] Canning to Stuart, No. 31, October 10, 1825, and *passim*, F. O. (13), 2, 6 ff.

SOUTHERN SOUTH AMERICA

was not only scolded for a course which favored the United States and the countries of northern Europe; he was recalled and another more cautious minister sent out to take his place.[40]

Aside from commercial considerations, the main concern of the British government with regard to Brazil was to preserve monarchical institutions from both internal and external dangers and thereby to prevent the separation of the Old World from the New. British agents were frequently reminded of these purposes[41] and constant efforts were made to accomplish them. Not only did English diplomacy endeavor to remove the difficulties which arose between the mother country and its former colony and to mediate in the dispute which occurred between Brazil and Buenos Aires over the eastern bank of the Rio de la Plata; British agents also offered advice to the Brazilian government on matters of domestic policy and carefully guarded English prestige.[42]

In the main, British diplomacy was successful. Trade increased from approximately $20,000,000 in 1825 to almost $30,000,000 in 1830; by 1829 British bankers had invested £6,000,000 in Brazilian govern-

[40] Canning to Stuart, No. 2, Jan. 12, and No. 5, Feb. 2, 1826, *loc. cit.*

[41] *Cf.* Canning to Chamberlain, Dec. 8, 1823, and Jan. 9, 1824, F. O. (63), 257, 275; *idem* to Ponsonby (who was to pass through Rio on his way to Buenos Aires), Jan. 28 and March 18, 1826, F. O. (6), 12.

[42] *Cf.* Temperley, *The Foreign Policy of Canning*, 189 ff.; also *post*, 143-149.

ment bonds at fifteen to twenty-five per cent below par and offered them in the London market; and the British were putting their money freely and profitably into the Brazilian mines. Moreover, the monarchy was firmly established in Brazil, Britain had secured a favorable commercial treaty, and, despite frequent irritations, British prestige was about as great as could be desired.[43]

Except for the unfavorable progress of events in the basin of the River Plate, there was little room for complaint or jealousy of the United States. And yet this jealousy at times appeared. Perhaps it may be observed in Consul-General Chamberlain's report upon the way in which the news that the United States had recognized the independence of Brazil was received at Rio. He said that a general salute was fired (August 27, 1824), but there were no illuminations;[44] and United States Consul Condy Raguet suspected that a little envy had been excited "in consequence of the apprehension, that we should take the lead in a matter, so important to Great Britain in a commercial point of view."[45] Jealously certainly appeared several months later when Chamberlain's attempt to take precedence over Raguet at the Brazilian court brought a letter of protest from Raguet and a notification

[43] Great Britain, Parliament, *Accounts and Papers*, 1831-1832, VI, 587; XXXIV, 207; 1844, VII, 352; Chamberlain to Canning, Oct. 27, 1825, F. O. (13), 10.

[44] Chamberlain to Canning, August 28, 1824, F. O. (63), 278.

[45] Raguet to Adams, Sept. 12, 1824, Manning, *Dip. Cor.*, II, 804.

from the Brazilian foreign secretary that Chamberlain must "assume" his proper place.[46]

Moreover, Chamberlain's successor, Arthur Aston, was by no means pleased with the terms of the United States-Brazilian commercial treaty of 1828. He objected particularly and quite naturally to its support of the rights of neutrals and its restrictions upon the application of blockades.[47] In these respects it was directly opposed to the principles maintained by England.

But these demonstrations of British jealousy are milder than were those of American diplomats. Condy Raguet, first as consul and later as *chargé,* watched the development of British policy with envious apprehension. In August, 1824, he was alarmed at the prospect of British mediation in the dispute between Dom Pedro I and his father. He declared that if "under the influence of England" Portugal should grant recognition to Brazil, the British would certainly "intrigue for some advantages in favor of" their commerce.[48] In October, he urged the advantage of acknowledging Brazil *"before any other nation."* This, he contended, "would give us an influence which otherwise we never can possess" and enable us "to assume a stand which every exertion will be used to prevent by England and France, who are desirous to see

[46] Chamberlain to Canning, May 25, 1826, F. O. (13), 26.

[47] Aston to Aberdeen, No. 4, July 11, 1829, F. O. (13), 62.

[48] Manning, *Dip. Cor.*, II, 802-803.

Brazil, as ever heretofore, direct her eyes to Europe and not to North America." [49] When he learned (July, 1825) that Sir Charles Stuart, whom the English government had sent out to negotiate a settlement between Portugal and Brazil, had also been given instructions to secure a commercial treaty, he expressed further alarm. "The English merchants rely with great confidence," he reported, "upon the continuance of the duty upon their products at its present rate of 15 per cent, and should that be accorded, they will no doubt use their influence, and solicit that of their Government, to prevent other nations from being equally favored." [50]

The United States government shared Raguet's uneasiness on the commercial issue. "Great Britain will, no doubt," wrote Clay, "seek to secure with the new Government, the same extraordinary advantages as those which her Commerce has so long enjoyed with Portugal—advantages which have placed Portugal almost in a condition of a colony or dependence of Great Britain." Raguet was instructed to resist such concessions; "the President is altogether unprepared to see any European State, which has come tardily and warily to the acknowledgment of Brazil, running off with commercial advantages . . . denied to an earlier and more uncalculating friend," [51] said Clay.

[49] *Ibid.*, II, 807.

[50] Condy Raguet to Clay, July 30, 1825, *ibid.*, II, 826.

[51] Clay to Raguet, April 14, 1825, *ibid.*, I, 237-238.

Raguet and his government were justified in their apprehensions, as we have already noted. But Raguet was embarrassed by delay in receiving his credentials as *chargé d'affaires* and kept more or less in ignorance of the movements of Stuart, and hence was not in a position for effective opposition. Although Stuart's treaty was rejected for reasons already noted, the old agreement of 1810 was continued in force pending further negotiations. And by the time these had gotten under way, Raguet found himself involved in a bitter dispute with the Brazilian government over alleged depredations committed upon American commerce in connection with the blockade of Buenos Aires.[52]

In the course of this dispute, he had his sensibilities somewhat wounded by the proffered mediation of Stuart's successor, Robert Gordon. This ambassador felt that a break between the United States and Brazil might result in serious injury to the interests of England, and accordingly offered to smooth away the difficulties. But in his letter to Raguet, he expressed the opinion that Raguet's demand for passports was not justified. This aroused the ire of the American *chargé*. He reciprocated Gordon's polite assurances of personal esteem, but bluntly told him that he did not have full information on the disagreements in question and declined his good offices, giving a full statement of his attitude. "As to your kind and amicable offer of mediation," wrote Raguet, "I am

---

[52] Gordon to Canning, June 15 and August 18, 1827 (F. O. (13), 38), gives an account of British commercial negotiations.

extremely sorry that I am under obligation . . . to decline it—first, because I have no overture to make, as being the Representative of the injured party—secondly, because . . . the interests involved in any discussion would necessarily depend upon points connected with the Doctrines of Blockade and maritime rights, upon which a difference of opinion exists between . . . Great Britain and . . . the United States; and, thirdly, because I have reason to believe it to be the sentiment of my Govt. that a misunderstanding between it and any other American Power, if referred at all, should be referred for adjustment to a third American Power."[53]

Having thus delivered a lecture on the American view regarding blockade, maritime rights, and the relation of the two worlds, Raguet sailed away. His government disapproved of his demand for passports, but it could not have conscientiously condemned his broadside to Gordon, for it was an accurate expression of Adams's position.[54]

Raguet's place was soon taken by William Tudor, who was equally disturbed by European influences and equally alert to counteract them. He negotiated a commercial treaty embodying American principles[55] and did what he could to uphold the American cause.

[53] Gordon to Canning, April 3, 1827, and to Raguet, March 17, 1827; Raguet to Gordon, March 18, 1827, all in F. O. (13), 37.

[54] *Antea*, 116-123.

[55] See Malloy, *Treaties*, I, 133 ff.

In the spring of 1829, he surveyed the history of the last few years and summarized his work. "The principal Sovreigns [sic] of Europe had followed with a degree of natural predilection, the transfer of one of their companions, to the establishment of the only monarchy on this Continent. England of course, was the first to extend her ancient connection with the House of Braganza...; and to obtain favours for her trade and manufactures in this extensive region. France followed after a time to establish a rivalship in the same objects, and to prevent the influence of England from being as predominant in Brazil, as it had long been in Portugal." Other commercial powers soon took a similar course. "These connections with the Sovreigns of Europe, and the habitual dislike and enmity between the two races of Spanish and Portuguese origin, were naturally calculated to increase a vague kind of prejudice or indifference towards the republics of America; and were in danger" of making the Emperor "lose sight of the true policy, that is essential to his position, and the interests of his Empire, and to create [of creating] an erroneous preference for European ... connections. It was highly necessary to inculcate here, that the policy of this Empire, should rise above such considerations; that political institutions and forms could not change the direction of such circumstances as were inseparably united with geographical position. That the system of America should necessarily be a liberal one after being so long the victim of European monopoly ... ; that the

Colonial system and navigation laws of the old Continent, were radically injurious and offensive to every American Government, and to none more so than Brazil; that the whole was now emancipated from Foreign domination, in which memorable event the United States had taken the lead . . . ; and that a tacit understanding between the United States and Brazil, in which all the other states would join, must infallibly in a few years, destroy the last vestiges of the Colonial system, of which portions were still perversely and unwisely maintained by some of the European States. I have dwelt on these topics on all suitable occasions, and I believe not without effect; the United States are certainly regarded more favorably than any other Foreign Power, by the Brazilians generally." [56]

On the whole this last statement was perhaps true then, as it has been since 1825, and particularly true of the comparative places held by the United States and England in the affections of the Brazilian government and people. American trade, with an average annual value of more than $4,000,000, was more important than its trade with any other South American country, though, of course, it was many times less than the Brazilian trade of Great Britain.[57] There had been friction over the blockade, but England had had diffi-

[56] Tudor to the Secretary of State, April 18, 1829, Manning, *Dip. Cor.*, II, 867-868.

[57] Robertson, *Hisp.-Am. Rels. of the U. S.*, 197, 419; G. B., Parliament, *Accts. and Papers* (1830), XVII, 253, (1831-1832), XXXIV, 207.

culties on the same score and, owing to its position upon maritime matters, had aroused equal hostility in Brazil without obtaining satisfactory results. The United States had already secured indemnity for the injuries to its commerce, but Britain had not; and for the next two years English naval officers assumed an attitude as irritating as it was menacing.[58] But more of this anon.[59]

IV. JEALOUSIES IN THE LA PLATA AREA

In Buenos Aires, more decided antipathies were revealed. The envious irritations of the former decade continued unabated. The important issues related to commerce and the war between Brazil and the Buenos Aires government over the lower eastern bank of the River Plate, but questions of prestige and political forms and attitudes were also involved.

The diplomatic representative of the United States during almost the entire period was John M. Forbes, a democratic firebrand. When Minister Caesar A. Rodney reached Buenos Aires late in 1823, after a

[58] British correspondence on this matter is too bulky to permit detailed citation, but see the following: Dudley to Gordon, No. 32, Nov. 10, 1827, F. O. (13), 35; *idem* to *idem*, No. 10, March 24, and No. 16, April 5, 1828, F. O. (13), 46; Aberdeen to Ponsonby, Nos. 5 and 6, Oct. 29 and Nov. 10, 1828, F. O. (13), 49; *idem* to Aston, Nos. 18 and 21, Oct. 6 and Dec. 22, 1830, F. O. (13), 70.

On the side of the United States I have had access to a thorough study which is being prepared by Professor L. F. Hill on Brazilian-American relations, as well as to the manuscript sources.

[59] *Post*, 143 ff.

long and tedious voyage, his health was greatly impaired. During the next few months he was seldom out of bed. He arose late in the following May in order to attend an official reception; early in June he gave a grand ball, and the next morning was found dead. Had he lived, it may be that personal friction between British and American agents would have been reduced to the minimum, for Woodbine Parish, the talented, and tactful young *chargé* who was in control of the English legation almost continuously down to 1832, spoke of Rodney in most cordial terms.[60] But it was different with Forbes conducting American diplomacy. Suspicious and volatile, patriotic and energetic, he was a constant source of uneasiness and irritation both to Parish and to Lord Ponsonby, who spent almost two years (1826-1828) in an attempt to negotiate a peace between the United Provinces of the River Plate and Brazil. And in the end Forbes seems to have succeeded only in rendering British negotiations more difficult while accomplishing little for his own government.

Before Rodney's arrival, Forbes had already begun to complain of the character and disposition of the people of the La Plata region. He declared that he was losing daily "somewhat" of his faith in their

[60] "His [Rodney's] amiable manners made him very popular here and his loss will be very generally felt." Parish to Canning, No. 27, June 20, 1824, F. O. (6), 3.

For a brief sketch of Parish's career, *see* the English *Dictionary of National Biography*.

capacity for "perfect republican liberty." He then added: "I see to my great mortification so much idolatry for everything European and such an indifference, bordering on hatred, towards the North Americans (whose model of Government is the only one which they ought to emulate) that I am quite disgusted...." [61] Forbes had also noticed many evidences of the government's "partiality for the English," and on April 30, 1823, he gave one instance of it. "On the 4th of July very soon after our recognition of this Country was made known ... our national anniversary was kept by our Countrymen here. Salutes were fired from an American Merchantman, Morning, Noon, and Evening, our flag was publickly exhibited joined with that of this Country. On that occasion all that was done by the Government ... was to run up their Flag for an instant at noon, fire a single gun and lower their flag. On the 23rd [of April] the English celebrated their King's birth day and the flag of the Government was kept flying all day and at Sun set a regular salute of eleven guns was fired from the Fort, and all this, without any british official representation or any salute fired on their part." Worse still: at a dinner given in honor of the occasion the foreign minister, acting as chief executive, gave a toast which was published in the official gazette. It ran as follows: "To the most wise Government, the English. To the

---

[61] Forbes to Adams, March 2, 1823, Manning, *Dip. Cor.*, I, 617-618. Forbes had been in Buenos Aires since October, 1820.

most moral and enlightened Nation,—England." [62] No wonder Forbes was envious!

Confronted by such an attitude, Forbes could not expect a warm reception for Rodney upon the latter's arrival in December, 1823; and no agreeable surprise awaited him, for "the ... popular demonstrations were excessively cold," and Forbes had no doubt that the attitude was due to the "Government in concert with the two great parties which now [then] influence [influenced] their Councils, The old Spaniards and the English." [63] In a speech to Congress, wherein a survey of the political history of the last year was given, not one word was said about United States recognition or the arrival of an American minister!

How different was the reception of the British consul—Parish first came out in that capacity—three months later! All was cordiality and enthusiasm and Canning's letter to the foreign secretary was published in the papers without taking time to obtain Parish's consent. Moreover, assurances were given that no political changes would be inaugurated in opposition to the British government or without its knowledge and consent. English prestige and English capital, invested in the public debt and the most valuable properties of the region, were talking. There were three thousand British residents in Buenos Aires.[64] The

[62] *Idem* to *idem*, April 30, 1823, *ibid.*, I, 621.

[63] *Idem* to *idem*, Jan. 3, 1824, *ibid.*, I, 631.

[64] Parish to Canning, April 7, 12, and 25, 1824, F. O. (6), 3.

politicians were grateful for all that Englishmen had done.

As soon as the first indications of national unity and stability appeared—perhaps even before—Parish began negotiations upon a commercial treaty and rumors of English recognition were in the air. Forbes was extremely uneasy. He sent to the minister of foreign relations a protest and a reminder. He pointed out that "the liberal system of commercial reciprocity, now extending its benign influence to most of the Nations of Europe, had its origin in the legislation of the United States of America." The United States had not demanded any price for the recognition of the new states of the Western Hemisphere and it did not intend to ask any special concessions, but it did expect and would insist upon most favored nation treatment in matters of commerce. The government of Buenos Aires had promised that and the promise must be kept.[65] Some of the American residents were equally alarmed and equally demonstrative.

But these protests, mostly beside the point, had little effect. On February 2, 1825, Parish's treaty of amity and commerce was signed, and on February 19 it was ratified at Buenos Aires. It did not stipulate any special concessions to English commerce—none were asked—but it contained everything else which either

[65] Forbes to García, Dec. 6, 1824, Manning, *Dip. Cor.*, I, 642-643.

Parish or Canning could desire.[66] Yet, Parish did not fail to note the American attitude. He wrote Canning on the day before the agreement was ratified: "There has been a great deal of intrigue against our Treaty here amongst the foreigners but principally set going by the Yankees who have been working in every way upon the ignorance of these people in such matters. ... The American Chargé ... has not confined himself to private insinuations but has addressed a note to the Government upon the subject."

Parish knew what had been done, because the Argentine foreign minister had given him a copy of Forbes's remonstrance! The British consul then continued: "Their great object [that of the Americans] has been to defeat the negotiations by persuading the natives that Great Britain is only working for her own Benefit, and will certainly humbug them. That a Treaty is no recognition, and that the United States are their only sincere friends;—and ought to have the first place in their estimation.—They are very much out of humour at the Result." [67]

The English had scored their first victory. They had their treaty of commerce, and the Americans not only had none, but were at that very time being injured by a decree forbidding the importation of flour, the chief commodity in the Yankee trade. In the year

[66] *Cf.* Canning to Parish, No. 4, May 24, 1825, F. O. (6), 7. A copy of the treaty may be consulted in *British and Foreign State Papers*, XIII.

[67] Parish to Canning, Feb. 18, 1825, F. O. (6), 8.

1825 the commerce of Great Britain with the United Provinces of the Rio de la Plata was valued at approximately six million dollars; that of the United States, a little over one million. By 1830 the figures had reached eight million for the English, while they were less than two for the Yankees; and still Forbes had obtained no treaty. Nor does it appear that his failure was due to British influence, whatever he himself may have thought.[68]

The other important question which engaged the attention of the rival diplomats both in Brazil and the Argentine was the dispute between these two states over the area that eventually became the Republic of

---

[68] For the figures on trade, see the authorities cited in note 57 of this chapter.

With all of his hostility for the British, Forbes appears to have considered Clay mainly responsible for the failure of the United States to obtain a satisfactory treaty of commerce and navigation. In his instructions to Forbes, Clay expressed a preference for reciprocity over the most-favored-nation principle and for reciprocal national legislation rather than an international agreement. The negotiation of a treaty was suggested but not pressed (Clay to Forbes, April 14, 1825, *U. S.* Insts. to Ministers, X, 258).

On March 25, 1829, Forbes wrote: "While on the subject of . . . the invidious preference which the English have secured by their treaty, it is my duty to state that . . . the formal official offer was made by the Minister to conclude a treaty with the United States on precisely the same bases . . . ; and there never has been a period when, if I had been duly instructed and empowered, I could not have made a transcript of that treaty . . . , or even have made better terms for the United States. Should the people now in power maintain themselves, I am very confident that we could obtain a treaty on our own terms." (B. A. Desp., III.)

Uruguay. While this issue had an important economic aspect—hostilities between Brazil and Buenos Aires were very injurious to commerce and investments—it also involved the security of the Brazilian monarch and the whole question of the proper relation between Europe and the Americas. If England could successfully mediate in the dispute and obtain a permanent settlement of the status of the contested region, Emperor Dom Pedro would be saved from the menace of a republican crusade and the new states of America taught to look to the Old World for arbitration. In a word, the matter furnished Canning an opportunity to protect monarchy from republican hostility and deliver a blow at the Yankee doctrine of the two spheres.[69]

The British diplomats who undertook the negotiation were Robert Gordon, at Rio, and Viscount John Ponsonby, at Buenos Aires, and, later, also at Rio. Critically watching and sometimes even opposing them, were Raguet and Tudor, in Brazil, and Forbes, in the Argentine. Their efforts extended over a period of more than two years.

The problem was a difficult one. The dispute had been inherited from the colonial era and there had been intermittent fighting since 1814 between Brazil and its more or less independent Spanish neighbors.[70]

[69] Temperley, *The Foreign Policy of Canning*, 182-184.

[70] In F. O. (97), 76, will be found an excellent *Memorandum* of the proceedings with reference to the region from 1810 to 1824.

Late in 1825, hostilities began in earnest and Brazil blockaded the ports of the United Provinces of Rio de la Plata. Soon afterwards the English attempt at pacification began.

The American agents were suspicious from the outset. They feared that England was seeking to establish a protectorate or even to get possession of the Banda Oriental (Eastern Bank).[71] Forbes was particularly apprehensive and hostile. Moreover, he was partial towards Buenos Aires. Referring to the possible basis of British mediation, he wrote as early as June 21, 1826: "It is said to be what I have often predicted it would be; nothing short of the erection of a neutral and independent Government in the Banda Oriental, *under the guarantee of England*. This arrangement would probably lead to the making a free port of Montevideo; and, without this last wholly inadmissible idea, it would only create a *Colony in disguise.*" Forbes thought that such a project would meet with decided opposition on the part of the Buenos Aires government. He had talked to Don Ignacio Núñez, who had important connections with the ministry and had once been secretary of the Argentine legation in England. Forbes does not reveal the views which he expressed to Núñez, but he does relate what Núñez thought of England and Europe. "He returned [from London]," said Forbes, "quite cured of his previous strong predilection in favor of Great Britain.

[71] The views of Raguet may be ascertained by consulting Manning, *Dip. Cor.*, II, 853, *passim*.

Mr. Núñez has repeatedly declared to me his perfect conviction that the South American States had nothing to expect from the European Powers but duplicity and contempt: that their only means of safety were a perfect and most cordial union of American feelings and American resources...."[72] And one may be sure that Forbes did nothing to discourage this attitude.

A few months later the American *chargé* wrote: "My opinion is still unaltered, that the British have an occult wish to see this Government so reduced and desponding, and the Province of Banda Oriental so disgusted by inglorious suffering, as to consent to the cherished project of an independence, guaranteed by Great Britain, or, in other words, a *Colony in disguise*."[73] Soon afterwards he reported: "I had yesterday a long and agreable [*sic*] Conference with the President, rendered interesting to him by the communication, on my part, of some important news from Rio. I consider this struggle between Brazil and this Republic as of the highest general interest in its consequences to the liberty and happiness of *all America*, and I cannot dissemble a lively sympathy in the fortunes of the Republican party to the question. This sentiment gains for me the friendship (perhaps momentary) of this Government, and I hope will not be disapproved by my own."[74]

[72] *Ibid.*, I, 654-655.

[73] To Clay, Aug. 3, 1826, *ibid.*, I, 656.

[74] To *idem*, Sept. 5, 1826, *ibid.*, I, 657.

Forbes's sentiment was not "disapproved" by his own government; for, although his interference had not been specifically authorized by Adams, the instructions given to Rodney at the time he set out for Buenos Aires had expressed the hope that "the inhabitants of the Oriental Band" would decide to join their neighbor to the west, thereby "re-uniting under one free and Republican Government the scattered fragments of the old Vice-royalty of La Plata."[75] Nor were Forbes's sympathies different from those of the majority of his countrymen. In fact, the press of the United States was so hostile to Brazil and England that both Canning and the Brazilian minister in Washington noticed the fact with bitterness.[76]

Canning, on his part, was one of the first British diplomats to perceive the situation. The miscarriage of his plans regarding southeastern South America was one of the failures of his career. He had expected difficulties in dealing with the Spanish-Americans who, like the Spaniards, were "impatient of foreign advice" and suspicious of "gratuitous service"; he had foreseen that his suggestion regarding the neutralization of Banda Oriental might "excite a jealousy of some design favourable to British Interests"; and now, late in 1826, he remarked that this jealousy had been "openly inculcated by the publick press of North

---

[75] Manning, *Dip. Cor.*, I, 190.

[76] *See* Manning, *op. cit.*, II, 862, for the protest of the Brazilian *chargé d'affaires*.

America, and no doubt secretly by their diplomatic Agents." [77]

Early in 1828 the secret got out, for Ponsonby reported in high indignation that Forbes had been opposing the surrender of the Eastern Bank by Buenos Aires. But he also revealed something of his own jealousy when he added: "The North Americans generally hold the same language: perhaps they are prompted to it by the advantages they derive from being the only or chief persons who supply this city in its state of Blockade." [78] Here indeed was where the shoe was pinching. The United States, which had always stood for a narrow definition of blockade and the broadest possible definition of neutral rights, had protested actively, vigorously, and effectively against Brazil's blockade of the Rio de la Plata. England's exertions had always been in the interest of belligerent sea powers and its government could not now remonstrate without a guilty feeling of inconsistency.[79]

[77] Canning to Ponsonby, No. 21, Nov. 27, 1826, F. O. (6), 13.

[78] Ponsonby to Dudley, April 5, 1828, F. O. (6), 22.

[79] England's position was clearly seen by Canning from the beginning. Early in 1826 Forbes had protested against the Brazilian blockade and asked Parish to coöperate. Parish had declined and Canning had approved his action. "It is not for this country," said the foreign secretary, "to stir unnecessary discussions upon abstract points of belligerent rights . . . ; nor to bring into disrepute an exercise of maritime power to which, as a belligerent, she has so often had, and must probably again have recourse." (Instructions of June 23, 1826, F. O. (6), 11.)

But defeated and injured merchants were howling in the ears of British statesmen and diplomats and something had to be done. Foreign Secretary Dudley found a way. He did not object to a wide application of the power of blockade, but he protested against its partial application. If English merchants were not allowed to pass through, neither should those of the United States be allowed to pass. He assumed a menacing attitude, informing both belligerents that peace must be made or Britain's navy would be employed to prevent the continuation of this investment of the Argentine ports. At length, early in September, 1828, a peace was signed erecting Uruguay into an independent state. By stimulating this last vigorous British effort the Yankees had been indirectly responsible for the settlement.[80]

[80] The correspondence on the later phases of the mediation is too bulky to cite in detail, but *see, inter alia,* Dudley to Gordon, No. 32, Nov. 10, 1827, F. O. (13), 35; Aberdeen to Ponsonby, No. 5, Oct. 29, 1828, F. O. (13), 49; Parish to Planta, Feb. 6, 1827, F. O. (6), 20; Dudley to Gordon, No. 26, Oct. 1, 1827, F. O. (13), 39.

CHAPTER V

RIVALRY IN NORTHERN SOUTH AMERICA

Bogotá and Lima were the main centers of diplomacy in northern South America during the period now under review, and the entire area possessed a kind of unity derived from the fact that Bolívar was the dominating personality and the political storm center. The rivalry between the United States and England was more exclusively political than in any other region, although the economic element was not totally absent.

1. CLASHES IN PERU

In Peru, there were no spirited encounters. Indeed, so far as the American agents, William Tudor, James Cooley, and Samuel Larned, were concerned, expressions of hostility and envy were less violent than elsewhere. Such antagonism as occurred between the rival diplomats arose mainly from an antithesis in political sympathies, the English being partial to Bolívar while the Americans preferred the more democratic leaders. Yet the British agents were often sarcastic and bitter.

Trade rivalry was not an important cause of friction, for neither the English nor the Americans enjoyed a commerce of any consequence. British trade with Peru, prior to 1830, never far exceeded an annual average of £500,000, and that of the United States amounted to about as many dollars.[1] Neither Power obtained a commercial treaty during the period nor made any serious attempt to do so. It was only when the British representatives in Peru considered the broader aspect of Hispanic-American affairs that they revealed decided economic jealousy of the Yankees, and, even then, it was usually expressed along with jealousy of a political nature.

Patrick Kelly, a sort of consular *attaché* at Lima, was the first of the English agents to take note of William Tudor. Kelly had just had an interview with Bolívar at Huancayo and he reported with evident pleasure that the Liberator was "much prejudiced against" the United States and France. "He [Bolívar] expressed much dissatisfaction with the Gentleman appointed by the United States to be Consul General here," said Consul Thomas Rowcroft in giving an account of the interview. He then went on to state that Bolívar's irritation was caused by Tudor's insistence in putting himself in official connection with the Spanish viceroy.[2]

A few days later, Rowcroft wrote critically of the procedure of Tudor in connection with a religious issue which had arisen. Governor José Ramón Rodil

[1] Robertson, *Hispanic-American Relations of the United States*, pp. 197, 419; G. B. Parliament, *Accounts and Papers* (1830), XVII, 253, (1831-1832), XXXIV, 207.

[2] Rowcroft to Planta, Sept. 8, 1824, F. O. (61), 3.

of the province of Lima had transmitted to the English and American agents a somewhat bitter complaint regarding the behavior of foreigners in Roman Catholic churches. Rowcroft said that he had deemed it prudent not to take any notice of the language of the note but that Tudor had chosen a different course, commenting "at some length on this" and going "a little further, as was natural for him, into the Claim for a tolerance of difference in religious persuasion. . . ." [3]

The accounts given by British agents in Peru of the numerous conferences which they had with Bolívar in 1824, 1825, and 1826, do not reveal any hostility toward the United States on their part, but the conferences themselves were replete with potentialities of friction. In all of them Bolívar evinced both a preference for the English political system and a desire for an English alliance, and so was placing himself in opposition to the favorite Yankee ideas of republicanism and New World isolation.

The first of these interviews took place between Bolívar and Captain Thomas Maling at Chorillas, Peru, in March, 1825. The substance of what the Liberator said may be ascertained from the following excerpts: "No country," said Bolívar, "is more free than England, under a well-regulated Monarchy; England is the envy of all Countries in the world, and the pattern all would wish to follow in forming a new Constitution and Government. Of all Countries South

[3] *Idem* to Canning, No. 13, Sept. 24, 1824, *loc. cit.*

America is perhaps the least fitted for Republican Governments. What does its population consist of but of Indians and Negroes who are more ignorant than the vile race of Spaniards we are just emancipated from. A country represented and governed by such people must go to ruin.

"*We must look to England for relief,* we have no other resource. And you have not only my leave but my request that you will communicate our conversation and bring the matter under the consideration of H. B. M.'s Government in any manner which seems best to you either officially or otherwise. . . . Democracy has its charms for the people, and in theory it appears plausible to have a free Government which shall exclude all hereditary distinctions, but England is again our example; how infinitely more respectable your nation is, governed by its Kings, Lords, and Commons, than that which prides itself upon an equality which holds out little temptation to exertion for the benefit of the State, indeed I question much whether the present state of things will continue very long in the United States. . . . I wish you to be well assured I am not an enemy either to Kings or to an Aristocratical Government provided they be under the necessary restraints which your Constitution imposes upon the three degrees. If we are to have a new Government let it be modelled on yours, and I am ready to give my support to any Sovereign England may give us." [4]

[4] Maling to Lord Melville, March 18-20, 1825, as quoted in Temperley, *The Foreign Policy of Canning,* 558-560.

In subsequent interviews with Charles Ricketts, Rowcroft's successor, Bolívar's discussions were little more than a repetition of what he had said to Maling, and Ricketts, like Maling, appears to have expressed to Bolívar no views of his own. In February, 1826, the Liberator said that the interests of South America "pointed to the expediency of securing the friendship of Great Britain in preference to that of any other Nation." Its prosperity depended upon commercial intercourse with England and the imitation of its institutions. For an ally he preferred England to any other country, "even more than any of the States of America." He regarded the British constitution as the "wisest, best, and most just among nations." He hoped the Powers of Europe would not feel that the South Americans were imbued with a radicalism designed to destroy monarchical governments. As for himself, he "most assuredly did not at this juncture uphold a Republican form of Government as superior to another." He believed in the principle of adaptation and was convinced that the South Americans were not prepared for the federal system which had been adopted in the United States. The Colombian constitution did not conform to the capacities of its population and should be changed. He also referred to the proposed congress to be held at Panama, remarking that he hoped it might serve to cultivate closer political relations with England and the United States and that England must not fail to send an agent. In reporting the interview Ricketts expressed warm admiration for Bolívar.[5]

Near the end of April another important conference took place. Bolívar had just had irritating difficulties with a turbulent Peruvian congress and was on the point of sending the Colombian troops which had been there for three years back to their native land, and of leaving, himself, for Colombia. Ricketts had joined with others in the attempt to persuade the Liberator to remain and Bolívar had finally consented to stay, reluctantly, as Ricketts believed. In the course of the conference Bolívar remarked that there "was no guiding Peru except by the application of the rod" and that he hesitated to undertake the task, well knowing that all military leaders had lost their renown whenever they had been vested with the uncontrolled management of civil power. He also said that his heart always beat in favor of liberty, but that his head ever leaned toward aristocracy. He declared that the African and Indian elements in the country were "ignorant, debased, profligate," totally unprepared for self-government and liberty. If they were not held in check, the white minority, "the Albocracy," as he called it, would be exterminated. This small white group was the only one with intelligence enough to run the government, and even it must be held in restraint because of its lack of experience. If the "Albocracy" should be destroyed, all would go down in chaos.

The British consul general was now even more

[5] Ricketts to Canning, *Secret*, Feb. 18, 1826, F. O. (61), 7.

sympathetic with Bolívar than formerly. "I am quite sure," he said, ". . . that had he consulted his own inclinations he would not have hesitated in retiring from the cares and annoyances attendant upon his endeavours to resist the efforts of ignorance, prejudice, and bigotry, to retard his progress; and that although he will be obliged in the adoption of rational measures to exert a degree of vigour and determination which some may construe into an undue exercise of power, his conduct will be regulated by just principles of Liberty." The Liberator was confronted, said Ricketts, with vexing problems and the "page of History" furnished no guidance, for conditions in South America were unique. So Bolívar now had dictatorial powers and Ricketts had no disposition to censure him.[6]

In July the two men had another long and intimate conference. It related mainly to the Panama Congress then in session. Nothing was said about the possible rôle of the United States in this assembly; attention was confined exclusively to the participation of England, and Bolívar unfolded his aspirations in greater detail. He expressed the "anxious hope that Great Britain would not be a silent observer of the discussions which would arise in the Congress, since he was satisfied that they could not terminate in any practical good, unless aided by your [Canning's] judicious and impartial counsels. The several States required to be upheld by the power and influence of Great Britain,

[6] *Idem* to *idem*, No. 2, April 25, 1826, *loc. cit.*

without which no security could be expected, no consistency preserved, and no social compact maintained. All would be alike subjected to destruction by disputes with each other, and by internal anarchy. Different interests were already propelling them; wars which might have been prevented unfortunately raged, as exemplified between Brazil and Buenos Aires; contending chiefs were disturbing the tranquillity of Chile; jealous and rancorous feelings were at work in some of the States, as manifested by the current papers of the day; whilst in others a spirit of rivalry was engendering factions among the several provinces; the respective classes of inhabitants began to feel that they had equal rights, and as the coloured population so far exceeded the white, the safety of the latter was threatened.

"Under the protection of Great Britain the South American States would learn the measures most advisable to adopt for their general preservation and security; disagreements would be prevented; the respective Governments would be consolidated; wholesome laws and regulations would be established; the coloured population would be kept in awe by the union which was [to be] formed; the *Albocracy* would gradually increase in power; and ere the lapse of many years each State would be relieved from all existing apprehensions.

"His Excellency felt that it was just in Great Britain not to interfere in the convulsive efforts which the people of South America had made to obtain what they considered to be their rights; he was aware also of the liberal policy which actuated you in seeking no benefit beyond what other European powers might possess; but in fact the weight and influence of Great Britain already preponderated, by her generous, friendly, and steady procedure, and by the capital advanced and the industry introduced by British subjects. The further boon sought from her, that of the preservation of the existence of the several States by her wisdom and protection, would not only prove a blessing at large . . . , but be a substantive guarantee to the European Nations, of the peace and stability of South America, and of her anxiety to receive them as friends. . . .

"His Excellency in conclusion observed that he in common with others at the head of public affairs in Colombia, Peru, and Bolivia, considered this to be the fittest moment for South America to express her anxiety to be guided by the counsels of Great Britain. . . . He could answer for her decisions being supported by the majority of the States, and he felt assured that those who might hesitate about the expediency of a foreign power regulating the proceedings of Congress, would speedily learn that benefit to all was best realized by the wisdom, impartial judgment, and generous policy of Great Britain. For his part, what he thus sought would be an additional evidence, if any were wanting after his distinct assurances to me, of his having no personal interests in view, since a congress so constituted would necessarily counteract all ambitious designs of individuals; and since the objects to which his proposition evidently pointed were, the adoption of the best means for promoting the general welfare, for maintaining each State in her own rights, and for consolidating all in one salutary coalition under the protection of Great Britain. If he were fortunate enough to obtain your approbation of the measure, he should feel that his services could no longer be required by his country, and that he should be at liberty to release himself from the cares of public life, and to enjoy that retirement which had now become necessary for his peace and happiness." [7]

Such were the proposals made by Bolívar in 1825 and 1826. Although they are a bit indefinite in detail, it appears clear that he desired to establish in South America monarchies on the English model and under English patronage, or at least to secure the support of Britain for governments composed of the small white groups in each of the states. The extent of the aid and protection which he desired is not clearly stated, but it seems reasonable to suppose that he would have accepted all that England was willing to grant.

In the latter part of 1826, the electoral college of Peru accepted the Bolivian (conservative and virtually monarchical) constitution and chose Bolívar president for life—an honor which he "reluctantly" accepted. Before the end of the year he left for Great Colombia, in order to deal with disturbances in Quito, Guayaquil, and Caracas. Before he departed he told Ricketts that he hoped to secure the adoption of the

[7] Ricketts to Canning, *Secret*, July 14, 1826, F. O. (61), 8.

Bolivian organic law in Great Colombia. Ricketts regretted his absence, for revolts soon occurred which brought men less friendly toward England to the head of affairs in Peru. Bolívar had indeed no more than gone when the minister whom he left in charge of the foreign office began to question the form of Ricketts' commission.[8]

The British consul-general evinced an unfriendly attitude toward the new leaders, while he continued his partiality for the Liberator. As early as September 15 he had declared that "faction, disorganization, ignorance, prejudices, dishonesty" were "universally disseminated," and had withdrawn a former recommendation that the Peruvian government be recognized by the negotiation of a commercial treaty.[9] In the following February he was shocked by a military insurrection which had been "followed by the destruction of a Government and a Constitution which the people so recently swore to maintain." He saw in the movement no honest striving toward liberalism, toward freedom from foreign troops and the aristocratic fundamental law imposed by Bolívar. To him the disturbances involved "a chain of political intrigue extending from Buenos Ayres to Colombia." He thought Bolívar had been justified in introducing the Bolivian constitution into Peru. It gave the people as much power as they were "fit to direct; ... it established a system of mixed Government, with a divided authority in the hands of

[8] *Idem* to *idem*, No. 3, Jan. 6, 1827, F. O. (61), 11.

[9] To Canning, F. O. (61), 8.

the Executive and the Aristocracy and Democracy of the country." As for the Colombian troops, whom the insurgents had succeeded in expelling, they had been invited into Peru, and Bolívar could not have removed them without endangering Peruvian tranquillity.[10]

In March, 1827, Ricketts reported that Manuel Vidaurre, who had recently become minister of foreign affairs, had referred to him in an insulting manner in a speech which the minister had made during a "dinner party" given by a "North American." He said he would not seek further interviews with the offending minister and begged to be allowed to return to England for his health. In May he declared that Vidaurre was very friendly with the "North Americans" for three reasons: he was a "practical republican;" his niece had married a Yankee; and he desired to form an "American continental interest, in opposition to an European interest. . . ."[11] Ricketts also stated that Vidaurre was making preparations to promote his political views, trying to build a navy, "courting North Americans and other foreigners for the purpose of raising a fund for the augmentation of the military force," seeking an alliance with Chile and Buenos Aires.

The bases of this projected alliance were of particular interest to an agent familiar with Canning's views. They were (1) the territorial integrity of each state;

[10] To *idem*, Feb. 6, 1827, F. O. (61), 11.

[11] To *idem*, No. 7, March 8, and No. 14, May 11, 1827, *loc. cit.*

(2) "the obligation of each state to have a republican form of Government;" (3) the resistance of a Monarchy or of a President *Vitalicio* in South America; and (4) the "union of their whole strength against any attempt at foreign usurpation." This project elicited from Ricketts the significant comment that a government like that of the United States could not be applied in South America, where all that could be desired was a constitution which was calculated to hold the people in restraint and promote their happiness and education. He believed that nothing better for Colombia, Peru, and Bolivia could be had than a government dominated by such military chiefs as Sucre, Bolívar, and La Mar.[12]

Soon afterwards Ricketts returned to London and near the close of the year handed to the Foreign Office a memorandum "on the importance of Great Britain settling the dispute between Brazil and Buenos Ayres, and on the Expediency of her promoting the tranquillity generally of South America." In this document hostility toward the United States, hinted at only mildly in his previous reports, comes out in an unequivocal manner. The memorandum deserves to be carefully analyzed.

Ricketts began by pointing out how the struggle between Brazil and the United Provinces of Rio de la Plata was injuring British commercial interests. Goods worth £300,000 were in deposit at Montevideo; property worth £1,500,000 was shut up in Buenos

[12] To *idem*, No. 6, May 16, 1827, *loc. cit.*

Aires; goods and ships under adjudication before the "corrupt courts of Rio" were worth another £400,000; the outstanding and, pending the war, uncollectable debts of British merchants were "enormous." The United States, on the contrary, was not suffering any great loss or inconvenience. Its merchants had traded on a cash basis; its government was resisting the blockade. For these reasons the war should be stopped. Great Britain and France should persuade the United States to join them in forcing a suspension of hostilities and in erecting Banda Oriental into an independent state under the guaranty of these three Powers.

This problem having been settled, the English government should then turn its attention to the remainder of Spanish America. "General Bolivar has a sincere desire to conciliate Gt. Britain," said Ricketts, and "the same anxiety is felt by Generals La Mar, and Sucre." Furthermore, "their plans for the prosperity of the States over which they preside are in every respect to be approved, and the prompt manifestation of our protection at this juncture will confirm our influence throughout S. America. An overture for our support has been distinctly made by Genl. Bolivar. . . ; and if we go the full length of what he seeks in behalf of Colombia, Peru, and Bolivia, we do no more than meet what is virtually desired by Brazil and Bs. Ayres, and also I may add by Chile, and equally so I believe by Mexico and Guatemala. . . .

"Our Treaties have a semblance of gain to ourselves without granting anything in return; and the consequence of our withholding the protection sought will be the destruction of our influence to the aggrandizement of the U. States; her policy is to nurse the growing disposition of many of the S. Americans to separate themselves altogether from European connection. ... A struggle against this feeling and the ascendency of the U. States is surely desirable, and the more called for considering the encouragement given to our merchants and capitalists to resort to and establish themselves in these new countries, and the immense sums which have been advanced in loans and other adventures; and I may say imperative on us with reference to the enormous advantages which would unquestionably result to our commercial interests. . . .

"If the anxious state of apprehension in which all the European powers were kept by the war of persecution which the Turks have so long pursued against the Greeks has been deemed a sufficient cause for the interference of Gt. Britain, France, and Russia, surely the plea applies in S. America. . . . [A] dreadful state of anarchy . . . exists. . . ."

Ricketts argued that a British protectorate would not be difficult to establish. "The [Bolívar] plan may at first sight appear Utopian, but South America must be viewed as differing in all respects from Europe; a population not much exceeding that of Ireland, tho' extending over a region more spacious than Europe; varying as much in habits as in colour; a fifth part of it only who can read, who govern the rest, who are split among themselves into parties, who are weak and pusillanimous, and who would be easily overawed under the system contemplated, if fixed and persevered in under the auspices of Gt. Britain. Her very name would be sufficient to check the ebullitions of faction if the impression existed that she was serious."

Ricketts then went on to suggest that France be asked to participate in the proposed protectorate of Hispanic America, predicting that she would be most willing to coöperate. He then added, significantly: "The jealousy of the U. States might be roused, but no legitimate grounds would exist of opposition to the plan suggested; any clamor against European nations interfering with the internal concerns of S. America would be illtimed if the U. States were committed and involved as . . . contemplated in effecting a settlement of the differences between Brazil and Bs. Ayres; and Gt. Britain and France would in no respect be entering into a compact like that of the Holy Alliance, as the object is not to uphold the legitimacy of Sovereigns, but to support whatever form of Govt. may be chosen by each respective State. . . ."

The consul-general concluded his memorandum with the assertion that the Spanish Americans owed their independence largely to the British and that the British should share the advantages which would ultimately result therefrom, but which might be "snatched" away if the government now retired and left these countries to "their own struggles and . . . to the too probable intrigues of the United States." He then revealed the aggressive motive back of his memorandum. "If through our efforts tranquillity be established in S. America," said Ricketts, "I am prepared to prove that our Commercial ascendancy can be secured without exciting jealousy, and that great advantages will also offer to our capitalists by working the mines of the two Perus." [13] Thus the Englishmen were to take the place of the recently expelled Spaniards in the New World and the revolutions of the nineteenth century were to mean to England what the discoveries of the fifteenth had meant to Spain!

When Ricketts set out from Lima in the late spring of 1827 he had left Thomas S. Willimott and Patrick Kelly in charge of his office with the title of "pro-consuls." Their attitude was in most respects similar to that of their former chief. Like him they praised Bolívar, spoke disapprovingly of the conduct of the agents of the United States, and favored a Bolivarian dictatorship or a monarchy.

In November, 1827, for instance, Willimott noted the "malignant" hostility of the Yankees "against" the Liberator, remarking that some of them carried their animosity "to the pitch of regretting unreservedly that where a second Caesar had arisen, there should not yet have arisen a second Brutus." [14] Two months later he declared that Bolívar was the only man in the country who possessed a "strong arm directed by a skilful head." He alone must be counted upon to

[13] This undated memorandum was found in F. O. (61), 15.

[14] To Dudley, No. 3, Nov. 17, 1827, F. O. (61), 13.

Northern South America

counteract anarchy "by what is here termed despotism." [15]

In December, 1829, he referred to another overturn which had recently occurred in the Peruvian government and led to the installation of authorities favorable to Bolívar. He also paid his respects to the *chargé* of the United States. He said that Larned was not only "exceedingly inimical to the Liberator," but that he expressed his sentiments in an "indiscreet" manner. He reported, moreover, that Larned had shown him a copy of Clay's instructions to the agents sent to Panama and that these instructions both deprecated in the most decided manner the establishment of a monarchy in any of the South American States and avowed a determination to resist the interference of any foreign power for such a purpose. These instructions provoked Willimott into an expression of his views on the subject. "My impressions," he said, "are decidedly in favor of a form of government approaching as nearly as possible to the monarchical; and I should even wish to see a monarchy established in Peru, if I knew where to select the Sovereign, and could satisfy myself that he had the means of supporting his authority." "For nothing short of this," he added, "is the country qualified; . . . stability in the government and tranquillity among the governed, will be looked for in vain under any modification of republicanism." [16]

---

[15] Willimott to Campbell, January 21, 1828, F. O. (61), No. 15.

[16] Willimott to Aberdeen, No. 2, Dec. 8, 1829, F. O. (61), 16.

A few months later the situation became very unpleasant for the English pro-consuls. Disorders increased, British property was confiscated, British subjects maltreated, and no interest was forthcoming on the Peruvian government loans. The agents could only protest and withdraw to Valparaiso, where they remained until the close of the year 1830.[17] Anarchy was interposing itself between the sons of Albion and the Spanish heritage.

We must now return to the views and procedure of the American agents in Peru. It should be noted at the outset that they were hostile neither toward Bolívar nor toward the British consuls until after the larger schemes of the Liberator became the topic of discussion, and even then they evinced little hostility toward the British.

Indeed, only two instances of critical comment against the English have been found in the entire correspondence of the American representatives. William Tudor, in noting that the British *chargé* at Bogotá had exerted his influence to prevent the resignation of Bolívar from being accepted, wrote in August, 1827, as follows: "With respect to the English agent, political sympathies may have had their effect; for I have found some English agents supporting Bolivar because he was overthrowing republican systems, which they hated; but a more substantial reason probably was, the belief that his remaining at the head [of the Colom-

[17] Willimott and Kelly to *idem*, June 21 and Oct. 22, 1830, F. O. (61), 17.

bian government], would keep the country together, and thus give a better chance of recovering the heavy debts they owe in England. Yet if it were so, it was an erroneous calculation. General Bolivar's element is war, ... and as ... long as he lives, all the resources of these countries will be expended in it." [18]

The other instance occurred in 1830 in connection with the seizure of British property by the Peruvian government and the retaliation of the British consul and naval commander. "These occurrences," said *Chargé* Larned, "have ... produced ... a strong feeling against the English. ... There can be no doubt, that the consuls and Senior Officer, have been precipitate in their measures; and that the former managed the affair with very little skill and judgment." Yet there was no exultation of triumph over a rival. Larned merely remarked that the incident would probably prove beneficial to all foreigners by inculcating a greater respect for their property rights.[19]

Thus the agents of the United States in Peru showed unusual moderation in their attitude toward England. If further proof be desired, it may be found in Larned's report on the Peruvian tariff. Certain decrees issued from time to time had discriminated against such American commodities as flour, coarse cotton fabrics, cabinet wares, and household furniture. Secretary Clay was inclined to believe that these discriminations had been dictated by British agents, but

[18] Consular Letters, Lima, I. Tudor to Clay, Aug. 9, 1827.
[19] Larned to Van Buren, May 29, 1830, Desp. Peru, I.

Larned ventured to correct the impression. He declared that the English had had little or nothing to do with the tariffs, but that, on the contrary, they represented Chilean influence and the quite natural desire of the Peruvians to protect their own simple manufacturing establishments, which were specializing in the production of these commodities.[20]

In the matter of political sympathies there was a very decided antipathy, but hostility was directed toward Bolívar and the monarchists of northern South America rather than toward the British. Bolívar's ambitions, alleged or real, with reference to the consolidation of this vast region under semi-monarchical institutions, after they had been once thoroughly suspected, lost him the friendship of every Yankee in Peru. And their unfriendliness swept them over the brink of neutrality into the general stream of opposition to these alleged schemes. A few illustrations must suffice.

Not even the British agents accused James Cooley of unneutral conduct. Yet his attitude was extremely unfriendly toward Bolívar. Cooley was amazed and grieved when he learned that the American *chargé* at Bogotá had revealed a partiality for the Liberator. He declared that the people of Peru had "certainly enough to contend with, in attempting to build up a Republican form of government out of ... a good deal

[20] Clay to Cooley Nov. 6, 1826, U. S. Inst. to Ministers, XI, 176; *idem* to Larned, Jan. 1, 1829, *ibid.*, XII, 172; Larned to Van Buren, March 5, 1830, Desp. Peru, I.

of bad material . . . not to suffer the additional embarrassment of having it supposed that we had thrown our weight into the scale of those whom they believe their enemies." [21]

A little more than a year later, Cooley expressed himself even more pointedly. "It can certainly," he said, "neither accord with our principles, our feelings, or our interests, to witness these immense regions sinking under a military government—the whole concentrated in the hands of a single ambitious and profligate individual. If we can suppose it possible that success would attend the designs which it is believed Bolivar entertains upon these countries, it is morally certain such a form would not last beyond the life of the individual who should create it. A *Continent* would then remain to be divided among the military chiefs of the Libertador, as a world was partitioned among the officers of Alexander." Moreover, "before such a power . . . can be accumulated in the hands of Bolivar disastrous and bloody wars must be waged, during which our very important and growing commerce with these Countries must be liable to constant interruptions and vexations, [their] resources . . . dissipated and destroyed, industry paralyzed, and a train of evils entailed upon them which ages may not be able to efface; and what is perhaps of more importance to us, the progress of free governments arrested and their principles brought perhaps into . . . disrepute." [22]

---

[21] Cooley to Clay, August 23, 1827, Desp. Peru, I.
[22] *Idem* to *idem*, Dec. 12, 1828, *loc. cit.*

Samuel Larned was less severe in his language, but he was nevertheless disturbed by the plans generally attributed to Bolívar. He reached Lima late in 1829, just after a pro-Bolívar revolution had brought General Augustín Gamarra to the head of the national government. He at once reported that the Liberator had monarchical partisans in all of the new states. "Upon the whole," he said, "I do conceive, that the cause of free, republican institutions was never in so great danger." [23] He declared that he had adopted the policy of strict non-interference in the domestic concerns of Chile and Peru, but, as already noted above, the British consul declared that Larned expressed his hostility to Bolívar in an "indiscreet" manner and his despatches leave no doubt as to what his disposition toward Bolívar was. He said that this powerful leader was a factor to be reckoned with all the way from Mexico to Chile, Argentina, and Brazil. His "influence" was "unrivalled" in Peru and Bolivia. One of the factions had solicited his interference in Central America and Larned doubted not that the solicitation would be granted. The same was, or would soon be, true of Mexico. And, besides, in Chile and Buenos Aires Bolívar had strong partisans and exercised a "most powerful sway." "In short, the monarchical party in all those countries" recognized him as their "Head" and looked to him for the "consummation of their plans."

Furthermore, Larned was convinced that Bolívar's

[23] Larned to Van Buren, Dec. 19, 1829, *loc. cit.*

ascendancy would certainly prove injurious to the United States, for his partisans hated everything that savored of "republicanism" and assumed that the Yankees would oppose "the establishment of their favourite system of government in these new States." Bolívar's influence, said Larned, "uniformly manifests itself inimical to the interests and good name of the United States, and their government." [24]

Such, then, were the views of Cooley and Larned. Those of William Tudor were much more passionate. Originally an ardent admirer of the eminent South American, he first began to question and then to denounce his motives and plans. It would be difficult to find in all the annals of diplomacy a more bitter indictment of any individual than is contained in the reports of this partisan of democracy.

Tudor's faith in Bolívar was first shaken early in 1826 by his high-handed methods in dealing with the Peruvian congress. "The deep hypocrisy of General Bolivar has hitherto deceived the world," said Tudor, "tho' many of his former friends have for more than a year past discovered his views and abandoned him." "With the violent dissolution of the Congress," he continued, "the mask must fall entirely, and the world will see with indignation, or with malicious delight, that he who was occupying the attention of politicians in all countries, and for whom fate by a fortunate combination of circumstances, had prepared the means for leaving one of the noblest reputations that history

[24] *Idem* to *idem*, Jan. 14 and March 8, 1830, *loc. cit.*

could record, may be handed down as one of the most grovelling of military usurpers, loaded with the execration of his cotemporaries for the calamities his conduct must bring upon them."

Tudor then expressed his faith in the Peruvian democracy in more generous language than any ever used by Jefferson himself. "Doubtless there is a great deficiency of administrative talent," he said, "because the Spaniards filled all offices almost exclusively with their own subjects, who are all dead or absent. But the people are naturally intelligent, and tho' there is a sad want both of morality and education in Peru, both may be produced. It has been remarked by all who have had occasion to observe them, that the improvement of these countries under a few years of self government, tho' impeded by factions, is great and visible. . . ." "But," he added, bitterly, "it is the fashion of tyrants and their panders to calumniate the people, as an excuse for enslaving them, as the Boa covers an animal with his slime that he may be able to swallow it." [25]

Having presented this initial denunciation of Bolívar, we may appropriately draw the veil over Tudor's subsequent more violent criticisms. It will be sufficient to point out that he thought Bolívar was hostile toward the United States and determined to extend his sway, under European protection, over all of South America. The extent to which Tudor

[25] Manning, *Dip. Cor.* III, 1792, and *passim* for Tudor's further denunciations of Bolívar.

carried his hostility into action is difficult to determine in the light of evidence now available, but it appears certain that he encouraged republicanism and national independence in Peru, probably helping the leaders to frame a federal constitution and undoubtedly persuading them to appeal to the United States and England for protection against the consolidating ambitions of Bolívar.[26] As to whether his undiplomatic conduct served the best interests of Peru and South America, few would venture to hazard an opinion; but an even smaller number would question his good intentions. His motives and the faith which sustained him are clearly revealed in the following quotation:

"It is unfortunately true, that the people of this country are ill-prepared for supporting a free government; but it is equally true, that they never will be quiet under a despotism. The spirit of the age has its influence here as elsewhere; the current may be impeded, or diverted for a time, only to resume its course

[26] The British consul reported that a federal form of government "was warmly espoused and urged by the public functionaries of the United States." (Willimott to Canning, June 21, 1827, F. O. [61], 13.) This may well have included both Tudor and Cooley, for they were both in Lima at this time. Tudor's correspondence shows that he was attending the sessions of the Peruvian Congress in the summer of 1827. Samuel Larned had lent a hand in drawing up a constitution for Chile. (Evans, *Chile*, 31.)

For Tudor's account of his urgent suggestion of an appeal to the United States and England for an interposition designed to protect the Peruvian government from the rage of Bolívar, see Tudor to Clay, Nov. 7, 1827, Consular Letters, Peru, II.

with accumulated strength and South America is destined to try at least for a long time, to establish a popular and liberal system; they may and probably will suffer many reverses and factious disturbances; but by these very events will acquire intelligence and experience, and the representative system, more or less purified, must eventually triumph." [27]

II. MUTUAL JEALOUSIES IN GREAT COLOMBIA

The jealousies of the British agents toward the United States were less pronounced in Colombia than in Peru, but the opposite was true of the attitude of the consuls and diplomats of the United States toward Britain. Trade rivalry was perhaps more keen here than elsewhere, although the competition was probably more apparent than real. Beginning with an almost equal share of about three million dollars each in 1825, the commerce of Britain dropped to less than two and one-half millions in 1830, while that of the United States fell off until in 1830 it was barely half of what it had been five years before.[28] The Yankees were selling mainly flour and coarse cotton fabrics and competing with the British only in the sale of English goods which had first to be imported into the United States before they were exported to the Colombian markets. The decline in the commerce of the two powers was due not to their competition, but to the

[27] Tudor to Clay, Aug. 9, 1827, Cons. Lets. Lima, II.

[28] See the references cited in Note 1 of this chapter.

political and financial disorders of Colombia. Perhaps the real basis for their somewhat bitter rivalry was their exaggeration of the immediate economic importance of Colombia and the political significance which they attached to the lands dominated by the personality of Bolívar. In general, it may be said that the British government and its agents hoped to see a monarchy, amenable to English political and maritime views, set up in the region, and were friendly to the Liberator, while the United States and its agents were partial to republican institutions and inclined to condemn what some of them conceived to be the monarchical aspirations of this able warrior.

The three commissioners sent out by Canning late in 1823 arrived in Bogotá early in the following March. In a short time they reported that the new state was stable and its authorities resolved to maintain its independence. Their reception was highly satisfactory and their treatment became even more so when news reached Colombia of England's intention to recognize some of the Spanish-American states. Commissioner J. P. Hamilton described the excitement occasioned by this information in vivid terms: "All the people of Bogotá are half mad with joy.... Rockets are flying in all directions, bands of musick parading the Street, and the Colombians galloping about like mad men, exclaiming 'We are now an Independent Nation!!' I have been to the Palace and met with a most cordial reception from ... the Vice President. Senor Gual, the Minister of Foreign Affairs, got me in his arms, and I really thought at one time he would have squeezed me inside out. ...."[29]

On April 5, 1825, the commissioners began the negotiation of a treaty, and just two weeks later it was brought to completion. Everything was going well. And yet during this residence of eleven months at the Colombian capital the commissioners had not failed to evince a little jealousy of the United States. Hamilton, who left soon after the middle of April to carry the treaty back to London, had merely remarked that Richard Anderson, the United States minister, picked his teeth with a fork,[30] but Colonel Campbell, who was to become *chargé d'affaires* after British recognition had been consummated by the ratification of the treaty, found more serious grounds for criticism. He was somewhat alarmed at the commercial and maritime ambitions of the United States.

By the early part of November, 1824, he had heard rumors that the minister of the United States was seeking special trade concessions. Although he did not then know that Anderson had already negotiated[31] a treaty of amity and commerce without demanding any exclusive concessions, he was nevertheless optimistic with reference to the superior prestige of England. "My own experience," he said, "and the information which I have received from other persons ... enable me to state that there is a strong feeling of

[29] Hamilton to Planta, March 8, 1825, F. O. (18), 12.
[30] *Idem* to *idem*, March 7, 1824, F. O. (18), 3.
[31] The treaty was signed on Oct. 3, 1824.

attachment towards Great Britain, and I may even venture to assert that this partiality and consideration is stronger than towards the people of the United States . . . , notwithstanding their similarity of Government and their early recognition of the present Republic of Colombia." The "name of Englishman," he said, was a "passport for a good reception in all parts of Colombia."[32]

During the first half of the following year his confidence in the efficacy of British prestige was somewhat diminished. Early in April he expressed the fear that Colombia wished to "frame a code of maritime laws distinct from those generally received in Europe"[33]— a code, in other words, which would conform to the contentions of the United States. Three months later, when he learned the terms of the United States-Colombian treaty, he expressed further uneasiness. He disliked several of its provisions and particularly the one which admitted "the principle that free flags shall make free cargoes." "According to the best information I can obtain," said Campbell, "it is the decided intention, not only of the Government of Colombia, but of all the other Governments of America, including the United States, to establish this principle among themselves." He then went on to say that this matter would probably be taken up at the projected congress at Panama.[34] This principle, if generally adopted,

[32] Campbell to Planta, Nov. 6, 1824, F. O. (18), 3.
[33] *Idem* to Canning, April 9, 1825, F. O. (18), 13.
[34] Campbell to Planta, June 9, 1825, *loc. cit.*

would indeed have constituted a potential blow at English sea power, for it would have meant that the neutral states of America could take over the carrying trade of Britain's enemies during a war and thus greatly diminish the effectiveness of British blockades. It was for this reason, as well as because of the suspicion that the United States desired to form a republican American league in opposition to the monarchies of Europe, that Campbell was somewhat alarmed in 1825. The one scheme was a threat to British sea power; the other, to British institutions; and they were both closely related.

Therefore, Campbell's main concern, after he learned that the United States had not received any exclusive commercial concessions in its treaty with Colombia, was to keep watch over the maritime and political views of England's rival kinsmen in America. From Foreign Minister Gual he soon received what he assumed to be the assurance "that the object of the Congress of Panamá was not at all to establish a Republican American Confederacy as opposed to European Monarchies, and that the Colombian Government would never interfere or attempt to influence the other new Governments in any modification" of their political forms; moreover, that Gual was eager not to give the impression of hostility to monarchical governments.[35] And from Vice-President Santander's state papers he got the impression that, after all, Colombia

[35] *Idem* to *idem*, Aug. 19, 1825, F. O. (18), 14; *idem* to Canning, No. 16, Sept. 7, 1825, *loc. cit.*

was disposed to conform to the "acknowledged Law of Nations" and by no means determined to erect "a policy altogether American." [36] Yet, near the end of the year 1825, he was a bit puzzled because of the return of Minister Plenipotentiary Anderson after the treaty of the United States with Colombia had already been ratified and proclaimed. He suspected that the reappearance of a diplomat of so high a rank indicated a design hostile to England, but he was uncertain what this could be. "As to whether or not it may be the object of the Government of the United States to form an American federation," wrote Campbell, "I will not presume to venture an opinion, but should such be the case, I do believe that neither General Bolivar, nor the Government of Colombia would willingly consent to the United States being the head of it." [37]

Less than a year later, he had his first interview with the Liberator, who had been away for many months in Bolivia and Peru. He learned that this great leader was so ardent in his admiration for England that he could find no higher compliment for the people of the United States than to call them "children of Great Britain." On November 16, Campbell gave a dinner to Bolívar, and his account of what occurred is worth quoting. "After the removal of the cloth," said Campbell, "His Excellency requested my permission to propose a toast, and after warmly dwelling on the virtues

[36] Campbell to Canning, No. 3, Jan. 4, 1826, F. O. (18), 25.

[37] *Idem* to *idem*, Separate, Dec. 19, 1825, F. O. (18), 14.

of His Majesty and the debt of gratitude due from Colombia to England, he proposed the health of the King of Great Britain, and hoped all present would join him in three times three cheers, . . . which was done with great enthusiasm. I afterwards proposed the health of Bolivar and the prosperity of Colombia. . . . General Bolivar then stood up, and after a very eloquent speech, . . . he proposed the health of Mr. Canning . . . , which was drank [sic] in the same manner. . . . He afterwards proposed the health of Mr. Adams, and in a short speech mentioned the advantages the citizens of the United States had in being English descendents, and hoped that they would continue to immitate the virtues of the Parent State."[38] Bolívar had won his man at the very outset. Campbell at once pinned his faith to the Liberator, and nothing thereafter ever succeeded in shaking his confidence in him.

These were busy days for the great South American, and he was called away to Venezuela, after a brief sojourn of only a few months, in order to quell the revolt of General José Antonio Páez. When he returned to Bogotá in September, 1827, he honored Campbell by pointing him to a seat on his right hand during a public reception of the foreign agents in the capital.[39] Bolívar spent most of the next fifteen months, namely, from September 10, 1827, to December 28, 1828, in Bogotá; and during this time Campbell

[38] Campbell to Canning, Private, Nov. 27, 1826, F. O. (18), 28.
[39] *Idem* to Dudley, No. 23, Sept. 14, 1827, F. O. (18), 42.

had frequent conferences. Although the Liberator did not discuss his political views so freely with Campbell as he had with the British agents in Peru, both he and the monarchists frequently took occasion to express their lack of faith in democracy as well as their partiality for England.

In Campbell they both found a sympathetic auditor. The British *chargé*, completely under the spell of Bolívar, praised him in unmeasured terms. He declared that he was the only leader who could accomplish the Herculean task of cleansing northern South America from political corruption, military insurgency, and popular imbecility; for Bolívar was indefatigable, unimpeachable in his integrity, disinterested, patriotic, awe-inspiring, capable of commanding the coöperation of all good men.[40] As early as February, 1828, Campbell was hoping that the Liberator would be given almost absolute political power. "The personal character and unimpeachable integrity of General Bolivar, his high sense of honor . . . ; his enlightened patriotism and his rigid impartiality in the administration of justice, will be the surest guarantee for the prosperity of Colombia." His "ambition for honest glory and for the good opinion of the world and posterity, will be the best shield against any abuse" of the power conferred upon him.[41] Such were the views of Campbell at this time.

[40] Campbell to Dudley, Private, Oct. 14, 1827, F. O. (18), 42.

[41] *Idem* to *idem*, No. 13, Feb. 10, 1828, F. O. (18), 52.

He accordingly looked with some favor upon the project of making Bolívar president for life, with the privilege of choosing a prince of some European house for his successor. By the spring of 1829 this project had gotten well under way and Campbell began to write of its prospects. "The question of the establishment of a European Prince in this Country appears to me to involve so many considerations of high importance to Great Britain," said the English *chargé*, "that it would be presumptuous in me to detail them to Your Lordship. I shall therefore limit myself to ... the following points ... — the Geographical situation of this Country, possessed of a large coast with excellent harbours on both Oceans ... ; the benefit of their being in the hands of a friendly power in case of any future war with either the United States or France;—their importance to our West India Islands;—their situation for the East India Trade;—the ascendancy which this country will naturally exercise over the South American Continent;—the influence of her example on the other New States, were she to adopt a monarchical Government;—the circumstance of the Isthmus of Panamá belonging to Colombia;—the produce of this Country being the same in many respects as that of the United States, so as to make us more independent of that Power for the supply of cotton, Indigo, Tobacco, Rice ... ; its riches in gold mines ... ;—not to mention the imports of British Manufactures,—and, chiefly, the great and rapid advancement of which this country is capable." Campbell then went on to speak of the desire of France and Spain to gain influence in Colombia and to ask whether the foreign secretary of Britain would desire him to use his direct or indirect influence in favor of a monarchy under English patronage.[42]

In subsequent letters he declared that nearly all of the intelligent people of Colombia favored a monarchy. He was not quite certain of the attitude of Bolívar, but he did not believe that he would oppose the plan. He said that the Liberator had long been "impressed with the feeling that it was of primary necessity to eradicate . . . the great laxity of morals which existed in Colombia, owing, as well to the vices and defects of the old colonial system, as to the state of anarchy resulting from the long continuance of the revolutionary war . . . , and that only a strong and justly-wielded executive power could effect the required change in the people." He recalled Bolívar's conviction "that no democratical Government had ever united power, prosperity, and permanency"; his "surprise" that the federal system had lasted so long in the United States; his preference for the English form of Government. "I cannot therefore suppose," wrote Campbell, "that he would be an obstacle in the erection of Colombia into a constitutional monarchy—but I do not think that he would, himself, . . . accept the crown." He then concluded this particular despatch with an optimistic statement of the prospects for the plan.

[42] Campbell to Aberdeen, *Confidential*, May 14, 1829, F. O. (18), 64.

"Should the ensuing Congress [of delegates to revise the constitution] invite any Prince to Colombia, . . . he would find [in case he came] many difficulties to conquer and much to amend; but the people are docile, and the country is eminently rich, and the recompense arising from the feeling of contributing to the felicity of a whole people would be a noble reward for it." [43]

Indeed, Campbell was so anxious to obtain the definite views of Bolívar with reference to a monarchy that he wrote him (May 31, 1829) a flattering letter concerning the matter, in which he quoted excerpts from another very complimentary letter that he had received from Charles R. Vaughan. Bolívar's reply was somewhat canny. He knew better than Campbell the opposition which the project would encounter both in Great Colombia and elsewhere. He was somewhat non-committal, and yet he did not express definite disapproval. "I know not," wrote the Liberator, "what to say to you on this project, which contains within it a thousand difficulties. You must be aware that, as far as regards me, there will be none, determined as I am to resign the Government into the hands of the approaching Congress; but who shall be able to contain the ambition of our Chiefs or to assuage among the lower orders the apprehension of the destruction of equality (of rights). Do you not think that England would feel jealous at the election of a Bourbon? What an opposition would there not be made by all the New American States? And the United States who appear

[43] Campbell to Aberdeen, *Separate* and enclosed *Memoire* of June 4, 1829, F. O. (18), 64.

destined by Providence to bring on America a plague of miseries under the name of Liberty!" Still, Bolívar did not wish to be understood as disapproving the plan. "I am," said the Liberator, "very far from opposing the reorganization of Colombia, after the model of enlightened Europe. On the contrary, I should be most happy and would exert myself with increased energy in favor of a work which might be entitled one of salvation." But he hesitated to commit himself further until he learned the views of England and France. "With these potent allies," said Bolívar, "we should be adequate to everything; without them we could do nothing. For this reason, I reserve my definitive opinion until we shall learn what the Governments of England and France think of the proposed change of system, and of the election of dynasties." [44]

It is not necessary to dwell further upon the attitude of Campbell, or of other English diplomats and consuls. They made similar reports and held similar views. Alexander Cockburn, who was sent out as minister plenipotentiary to succeed Campbell but failed to reach the capital, had several interviews with Bolívar on the coast of Venezuela and rushed home to lay a plan for the establishment of a monarchy under British auspices before the foreign secretary.[45]

[44] Campbell to Aberdeen, Confidential, Sept. 13, 1829, and enclosure (Bolívar to Campbell, Aug. 5, 1829, from Guayaquil), F. O. (18), 66.

[45] Cockburn to Canning, Nos. 2 and 3, April 24 and 29, 1827, F. O. (18), 67; *idem* to Dudley, Oct. 29 and Nov. 10, 1827, F. O. (18), 67.

At Caracas Consul Robert Ker Porter conversed with the Liberator, sensed monarchical plans, sought to obtain the sentiments of the people, and wrote home the result. From Maracaibo Consul Sutherland sent reports of monarchical schemes based upon several interviews with the Bolivarian partisan, General Urdaneta.[46] Of all the prominent British agents, only Admiral Fleeming of the West India squadron and Consul-General James Henderson at Bogotá failed to be captivated by Bolívar and the plans of the monarchists. Henderson considered the project Quixotic and maintained that Campbell, in encouraging it, was injuring British interests.[47] The Admiral not only took the same view of the matter, but either intentionally or inadvertently encouraged the secession of Venezuela.[48] Minister William Turner arrived after the scheme had virtually been smashed, but he, too, fell under the spell of the Liberator.[49] If the advice of the majority of its agents had been followed by the Foreign Office, England might have attempted to estab-

[46] Porter to Canning, Jan. 15, 21, 24, and 27, 1827; April 9, July 8, and October 22, 1827, F. O. (18), 47; Sutherland to *idem*, Sept. 1, Oct. 15 and 16, Dec. 4, 1826, F. O. (18), 33.

[47] The pertinent despatches from Henderson, too numerous to cite in detail, may be consulted in F. O. (18), volumes 43, 44, 45, and 68.

[48] On Fleeming's conduct and attitude, see Fleeming to Aberdeen, Nov. 29, 1829, and Feb. 27, 1830, F. O. (18), 73, 79; Turner to *idem*, April 20, 1830, F. O (18), 75.

[49] *Cf.* Turner to Aberdeen and to Palmerston, April 19, 1830, and *passim*, F. O. (18), 75, 82.

Northern South America

lish a monarchy under its auspices in northern South America.

What were the views of Yankee diplomats and consuls during the period? As already intimated, all of them were hostile to Great Britain and the projected Colombian monarchy and most of them were unfriendly to Bolívar.

Richard Anderson reported rumors that the British commissioners would seek special commercial concessions without even acknowledging the independence of Colombia. And the terms of the treaty which he negotiated were designed mainly to reduce British sea power.[50]

Beaufort T. Watts, who as *chargé d'affaires* succeeded Anderson to the Colombian post, had frequent occasion to complain of the British. When he learned that the English treaty was more favorable than the one which had been secured by his predecessor, he interviewed Gual, the foreign minister, and heard with pleasure that the Colombian government would not refuse to admit the United States to the privileges "which had been extorted in the late treaty with England."[51] When the British *chargé* presumed to take a place ahead of him on state occasions, he protested and gave the following reasons for his action: "I based my conduct upon the principle, that the Representative of a Republic might yield from cour-

[50] Anderson to Adams, March 18 and Oct. 3 and 4, 1824, Desp. Colombia, Vol. III.

[51] Watts to Clay, May 10, 1825, *loc. cit.*

tesy, but not from compulsion. . . . English enterprize, English wealth, and intelligence have penetrated the recesses of the Andes. . . . In this capital alone there are about thirty English officers in the service of Colombia, added thereto as many merchants, miners, and adventurers. In that number I find . . . no other remarkable trait distinct from other men but the common characteristic of English effrontery. The corps diplomatique at Bogota is small. . . . Established etiquette, it seems, in point of procedure, had never been started—but Englands representative had not been unmindful of its importance. He is a Col. of Artillery in His Majestys service—with the Brevet rank of Brigr. Genl. in Spain, whilst under the command of Wellington. He had been the commissioner sent out . . . to this Country—a plenipotentiary to sign Mr. Canning's Treaty. . . . But [he] became . . . charge d'affaires several weeks after I had been presented in that character. In all assemblies with the ministry of this Government, as in the private entertainments of the country, His Majestys representative was first to assume the place of distinction." Because he thought this procedure might lead the Colombians to consider England more important than the United States, Watts protested, and the protest proved effective. Precedence was placed upon the basis of seniority and Watts took his place ahead of Campbell.[52]

Thus Watts was jealous of the British and quick to act when he saw an opportunity of diminishing British

[52] *Idem* to *idem*, Jan. 6, 1826, *loc. cit.*

prestige. But he did not always understand what was going on around him. He seems never to have learned, for instance, of Bolívar's partiality for England and his alleged monarchical leanings. It may have been due in part to this dullness of perception that he always praised the Liberator, refused to believe any charges made against him, and assumed the monarchist attitude of doubting the capacity of the people of northern South America for self-government. "If I am in error," said Watts, "in the faith I repose in Bolivar's disinterested political virtues, let it be attributed to misjudgment. I am not fearful of hazarding an opinion on the event of his retiring from public duty. I despair then of the tranquillity of the nations he emancipated." [53] Early in 1827 his admiration for Bolívar was so great that he invited him to hasten to Bogotá and assume the reins of power. A year later he outlined a very dark picture of the condition of Colombian society. He said that the politicians and military chiefs were greedy, dishonest, and turbulent, the priesthood bigoted and corrupt, the masses ignorant and indolent; and that he seriously doubted "whether the people of Colombia are [were] prepared anterior to various conflicts and changes, to regulate a representative government in the spirit and freedom with which the Institutions of the United States are [were] directed." [54]

[53] Watts to Clay, March 14, 1827, Desp. Colombia, IV.

[54] *Idem* to *idem*, March 10, 1828, *loc. cit.*

William Henry Harrison, who set sail for Colombia late in 1828 as United States minister, probably went with his mind prejudiced against both the British and Bolívar. He had hardly reached Bogotá when he scented despotism and British intrigue. On February 13, 1829, he wrote that the British government was "eagerly embracing every opportunity to increase its influence." So far as the official class and the native merchants were concerned, he thought the British had already achieved success; but he was convinced that "the great mass of the intelligent men of the country" were more friendly toward the United States than any other nation. "They hear with wonder and astonishment," said Harrison, "the progress of our country . . . and the happiness which our institutions dispense to the people, and they are extremely desirous to tread in our footsteps." [55]

Soon afterwards he heard of the monarchical project. Bolívar was to be made president for life, he wrote, and a successor found "from amongst the Princes of Europe. . . . If it were not for the obstacle which the difference of religion presents, I have no doubt that a British Prince would be selected, that nation being decidely the favorite with all the members of the Government." He then went on to reiterate his former view of the attitude of the unofficial group and the masses in general. "The institutions and people of

[55] Harrison to Clay, Feb. 13, 1829, Desp. Colombia, V.

the United States are with them constant themes of eulogy," said Harrison.[56]

By the latter part of June, 1829, he had obtained what he conceived to be reliable knowledge of the plans of Bolívar and the reactionaries of Colombia and Europe. Their "great object," he said, was "to establish Monarchical Government throughout the whole of the late Spanish possessions. The number of Kingdoms into which they may be divided, is a question of subordinate interest, which they will not suffer to interfere with their principal design." [57]

Harrison's Colombian mission proved even more unhappy than these early impressions promised. Bolívar and the Bogotá authorities were probably none too friendly toward the Adams administration. Edward Tayloe, Harrison's secretary of legation, was looked upon with suspicion because of his former service in the same capacity under Poinsett in Mexico. Harrison himself was deeply irritated by the misery and oppression which he saw around him and attributed these unfortunate conditions more to the form of government than to the character of the people and the former rule of Spain. Handicapped by inability to understand Spanish, he found his associates among the American residents and the few British who were hostile to Bolívar and the national authorities, and obtained his information largely from them. He may

[56] Harrison to Clay, March 27, 1829, Desp. Colombia, V.

[57] *Idem* to Van Buren, June 22, 1829, *loc. cit.*

have expressed his views too freely. And last, but not least in importance, was the conduct of Thomas P. Moore, a Jacksonian spoilsman who came to supersede him in September, 1829.[58] Moore appears to have gone to the already suspicious authorities and reported ominously of Harrison's connection with a plot to assassinate some of the leaders and overthrow the government.[59] Early in November Harrison was ordered out of the country.

As a parting fling he wrote the Liberator a long letter, warning him against his alleged despotic course and urging him to mend his ways. It was one of Harrison's most bombastic utterances, but it was shot through with sincerity and democratic enthusiasm. He began by remarking that projects calculated to defeat the "hopes of the friends of liberty throughout the world" had been attributed to Bolívar. He pointed out how difficult it would be to establish a monarchy over a people who had been taught by Bolívar himself to love liberty more than life. He declared that such a régime could only be set up and maintained by fre-

[58] Dorothy B. Goebel, *William Henry Harrison* (Indianapolis, 1926), 256 ff., gives a very good account of Harrison's Colombian mission.

[59] At any rate this is what *Chargé* Campbell and Consul-General General Henderson reported. (See Campbell to Aberdeen, *Secret*, Nov. 4, 1829, F. O. (18), 66; Henderson to Lord Dunglas, Feb. 7 and 14, 1830, F. O. (18), 81. Henderson had also been accused along with Harrison.) Apparently the first man to bring charges against Harrison to the Colombian government was a certain Virginian named Carr, a Lieutenant in the Colombian army.

Northern South America

quent and constant executions and that the dying groans of the victims would be rendered more poignant to the dictator by the reflection that, "like the last of the Romans," they had aimed their daggers at his bosom "not from hatred to the man, but love to the country." He maintained that a monarchy would not be best for the people, for it could not enlighten them if it would, and would not if it could. He emphatically disagreed with those who asserted that the Colombians were not prepared for democracy. He said he had observed them for almost twenty years with the greatest interest and sympathy and had found nothing to justify the assertion. "I search in vain," he declared, "for a single fact, to show that in Colombia . . . the state of society is unsuited to the adoption of a Free Government. . . . The people of Colombia possess many traits of character suitable for a republican [system]. . . . Their faults and vices are attributable to the cursed government, to which they have been so long subjected, and to the intolerant character of their religion; whilst their virtues are all their own. But admitting their present want of intelligence, no one has ever doubted their capacity to acquire knowledge; and under the strong motives which exist to obtain it, supported by the influence of Your Excellency, it would soon be obtained."

Harrison concluded his letter with a moral exhortation on the qualities of true greatness. "In bestowing the palm of merit," he wrote, "the world has become wiser than formerly. . . . In this enlightened age, the mere hero of the field and the successful leader of armies, may for the moment attract attention. But it will be such as is bestowed upon a passing meteor, whose blaze is no longer remembered, when it is no longer seen. To be esteemed eminently great, it is necessary to be eminently good. . . .

"If the fame of our Washington depended upon his military achievements, would the common consent of the world, allow him the preeminence he possesses? His victories . . . , brilliant as they were, . . . are scarcely thought of. The source of veneration and esteem which is entertained for his character . . . is to be found in his . . . devotedness to the interests of his country. . . . For his country he conquered. And the unrivalled and increasing prosperity of that country, is constantly fresh glory to his name.

". . . Are you willing that your name should descend to posterity amongst the mass of those, whose fame has been derived from shedding human blood, without a single advantage to the human race? Or shall it be united to that of Washington, as the founder and father of a great and happy nation. The choice lies before you. The friends of liberty throughout the world, and the people of the United States in particular, are waiting your decision with intense anxiety. . . ." [60]

Harrison later contended that his letter to Bolívar was partially responsible [61] for his abandonment of his

[60] Harrison to Bolívar, Sept. 27, 1829, Desp. Colombia, VI.

[61] *Remarks of General Harrison, Late Envoy Extraordinary and*

ambitious schemes, but the correspondence of the Colombians indicates that it merely enraged the Liberator and the government which he had set up at Bogotá.[62] At any rate, the document was listed as another charge against the American minister.[63]

Returning to Harrison's successor, it may be noted that Moore refused to believe that any monarchical schemes were being considered in Colombia, became an ardent admirer of Bolívar, and evinced a disposition to lament the limited vision of his countrymen in northern South America. He did not, however, fail to express jealousy of British influence or rejoice at the prospect of its diminution.

His comment upon the attitude assumed by North Americans in Colombia is worth quoting, for it was the sanest view expressed by any diplomat or consul

---

Minister Plenipotentiary . . . to Colombia, on Certain Charges Made Against Him by that Government (Washington, Gales and Seaton, 1830). Pamphlet, 69.

[62] Goebel, *William Henry Harrison*, pp. 282-285, and authorities cited.

[63] The main complaints made by the Colombian government against Harrison were as follows: He entertained hostile and insurrectionary sentiments and made them public, declaring, among other things, that the Colombian soldiers should redress their grievances by cutting the throats of their oppressors. He knew of the intended insurrection of General J. M. Córdova and refused to inform the government. He aided and abetted a plot for rebellion in the capital. He publicly boasted that the government of Colombia had sooner play with a lion than take any action against him. He wrote an insulting letter to the Liberator. (See Foreign Minister Vergara to Moore, Oct. 17, 1829, and Jan. 17, 1830, Desp. Colombia, VI.)

of the United States during the entire period now under consideration. Speaking of the improper conduct and disposition of his compatriots, he said: "Mr. Gooding . . . has mingled freely, ardently and imprudently in the affairs of Colombia; but I am well satisfied, that he is incapable of doing any wrong *intentionally* to this Govt. or to any of its citizens. His errors have originated in an enthusiastic devotion to our own institutions, and to this is to be imputed his hostility to those whom he considers as enemies of civil liberty. Like most of the citizens of the United States, who have visited Colombia, he has not reflected upon the difference between the moral and intellectual condition of the people here, and those of our own happy country. Our citizens, accustomed to a government, whose operations are all conducted upon constitutional principles, and where the exercise of discretional and arbitrary power, is unknown and inadmissible, do not seem inclined to make any allowance for measures, which though bearing the impress of harshness and injustice, and not to be tolerated under a settled government, may yet be excused, if not justified, in a country, where everything is disorder and confusion, and where vigilance and severity only, can avert the evils of anarchy. . . ."[64] In other words, their main fault consisted in the fact that, as Mier y Terán had remarked with reference to the Yankees in Texas, they carried their constitutions in their pockets!

[64] To Van Buren, No. 15, March 27, 1830, Desp. Colombia, VI.

Northern South America

The quotation also implies a lack of confidence in the political capacity of the people of Colombia, and later despatches leave no doubt of Moore's views on this matter. "I have no confidence in the intellectual fitness of this people for free institutions, and still less in the private and public virtue of the majority of the public men," he wrote in August, 1830.[65]

With such sentiments as these, he could see no reason for condemning the dictatorial tendencies of Bolívar, whom he considered one of the few noble patriots of the country. As the Liberator left Bogotá for the last time in May, 1830, the American minister wrote: "When I look back at his life; contrast his character with that of other public men in Colombia—his talents, private integrity and past services and disinterested conduct, when I recollect, that he made the first stand for liberty in Venezuela with his own slaves, liberating them to fight the battles of Freedom, when I remember that Peru offered him for his services a million of money, which he utterly refused, . . . and that he retires in poverty; although he has frequently erred, I cannot but regret his departure." [66]

These conservative tendencies did not make Campbell any less severe on the British, however. When General Rafael Urdaneta seized the government by a military *coup* in August, 1830, he accused them of having taken part in the movement. "In this effort to

---

[65] To *idem*, Aug. 28, 1830, *loc. cit.*

[66] To *idem;* No. 17, May 7, 1830, *loc. cit.*

overthrow the government the English residents have participated most boldly, and would have suffered most signally if it had failed," he said. He then expressed the fear that they would have "much to do with the conduct of Public Affairs, so long as the *now* dominant party" maintained itself in power, but he added: "It is a responsibility which I do not covet." [67]

Soon afterwards he expressed greater apprehension. "We are informed here," he wrote, "that the people of Panamá have implored the protection of the British Govt. and have solemnly offered it the sovereignty of that part of the country." "This," he continued, "on account of its present and increasing commercial importance would be a valuable acquisition; and the monopolizing spirit of that Govt.; the continued and active interference of its subjects in the affairs of this country, are strong indications in my opinion, of a disposition to acquire an influence in it, fatal to its independence and prosperity, and wholly incompatible with the interests of every other nation having commercial relations with it." Moore then went on to complain of the important rôle which William Turner, the British minister, was trying to play at Bogotá and of the activities of Admiral Fleeming on the Venezuelan coast.[68]

Late in the spring of 1831, however, General Urdaneta was driven from power and Moore exulted.

[67] See citation in note 65.

[68] To Van Buren, No. 23, Oct. 21, 1830, Desp. Colombia, VI.

"The usurpation of last August is put down at all points," he wrote Van Buren, "and all those concerned in it banished from the country.... You will recollect that I informed you ... that the English (with scarcely an exception) had embarked boldly in the revolution, and that a day of restitution would come. It has come, and from being masters of everything, they will be deprived of all, and be obliged to endure the bitterest persecution.

"The people of Colombia seem to have caught the spirit of the age, and in the recent struggle have manifested a degree [of] energy, that I was not prepared to see. Half Bogota fled to the plains, abandoning everything, and returned after months of toil and privation as common soldiers under Genls Moreno and Lopez.... In all this army there was not a *forced* recruit, it was the triumph of public opinion over a ruthless and worse than Turkish despotism. As the troops passed through the principle streets the Ladies showered roses upon their heads, and when they passed under my balcony, from which the star spangled banner was floating, they made the welkin ring with 'Viva el Ministro de Los Estados Unidos.'"

He then went on to accuse the British of using their influence to obtain in the Colombian tariffs discriminations against American flour and British goods imported by the Yankees from the United States. But now, he said, things were going to be different. The duties were going to be reduced or removed and the English were on the point of being expelled *en masse*.

He declared, however, that he himself had not been guilty of improper conduct.

"So far as we are concerned the change is not merely satisfactory but delightful. I aspired to nothing but the reputation of a fair representative of my country, neither wished nor attempted to command influence, untill [*sic*] I was fully satisfied that the govt of Urdaneta was *virtually* a British dependency, and then I waged no war upon the English, but I conceived it my duty to labor to impress all classes with just opinions of my Govt. I ceased in some measure to invite English [residents] ... to my house, and devoted my leisure hours ... to the natives, pointed out the beauty simplicity and cheapness of our govt, caused the Presdts message to be republished and circulated, etc. ... The English party are down and in my judgment forever...."[69]

The foregoing analysis of the correspondence of the Yankee diplomats renders it superfluous to dwell upon the views of the consuls. At this point, it seems necessary merely to note that all of them expressed jealousy of the British, uneasiness regarding the monarchist plots, and suspicion of the disinterested patriotism of Bolívar, although none of them was so severe as Harrison in this latter respect.[70]

---

[69] Private of May 21, 1831, Desp. Colombia, VI.

[70] On the reports of the consuls, consult the following: J. G. A. Williamson to Clay, May 9, 1827, and Dec. 12, 1829, La Guayra, Cons. Lets., I, II; A. B. Nones to *idem*, Dec. 21, 1826, Dec. 24, 1827, June 25, 1829, Jan. 27 and March 27, 1830, Maracaibo,

III. OFFICIAL ATTITUDE OF ENGLAND AND THE UNITED STATES TOWARD BOLÍVAR AND THE PLANS OF THE MONARCHISTS

Prior to 1824 British statesmen had looked with favor upon the idea of erecting monarchies in Spanish America, provided this could be done without augmenting the power of the French Bourbons. What attitude did they take toward the proposals of the Liberator and the Colombian conservatives? And what course did the United States follow, with its doctrine of two separate spheres and its ardent faith in republican forms? The story can be told briefly.

Canning seems to have made no response to Bolívar's early applications for an English alliance, a prince, and a guaranty. He wrote the Liberator on March 20, 1826, complimenting him on his moderation in dealing with the dispute with Brazil over the province of Chiquitos and tactfully urging him not to interfere in the war between Buenos Aires and Brazil, but said nothing of the monarchical proposals. The instructions drafted for Cockburn, who was sent out as minister plenipotentiary at about the same time, were likewise silent on the matter. He was told that he was

---

Cons. Lets., I; Franklin Litchfield to Clay, July 20, 1826, April 19, 1827, [October,] 1827, and to Van Buren, April 30, 1830, Puerto Cabello, Cons. Lets., I. In the letter of April 19, 1827, Litchfield gives further evidence of the views of Bolívar. He says that the "Liberator President himself told me that he was expecting advices from Mr. Canning relative to the opinion the British Cabinet formed of the constitution he had framed" for Bolivia.

being dispatched to Colombia in order that the relations of the two states might be placed upon a "higher footing." He was also informed that it was Britain's aim to promote "peace and tranquillity" between the various nations of South America, and directed to urge Bolívar to exert himself in the interest of the same cause. But nothing was said about a prince or a protectorate.[71]

Neither did the Earl of Dudley, Canning's immediate successor, make a definite response to Bolívar's proposal. He did, however, assume the attitude of a mild supporter of the Liberator. On March 8, 1828, he instructed Campbell as follows: "At the same time . . . that you carefully abstain from mixing in any intrigues for the purpose of an election, or from adopting the language of party, you will not hesitate,— temperately, and in such terms as become the Minister of a Foreign Power,—to declare that H. M. would look with satisfaction to the elevation of Bolívar to the highest station that the constitution of Colombia allows to an individual, both as an additional guarantee of amicable relations betwixt H. M. and the Republic, and as likely to contribute to its repose and happiness. . . ." The choice of the Liberator was not to be represented, however, as the price of British friendship.[72]

[71] Canning to Cockburn, No. 2, March 18, 1826, F. O. (18), 23. Canning's letter to Bolívar is published in Daniel F. O'Leary, *Correspondencia de Estranjeros notables con el Libertador* (Madrid, Editorial Amerca, 1920), II, 38-39.

[72] F. O. (18), 51.

Moreover, Dudley refused to recognize a Peruvian government which was hostile to Bolívar, but that this did not necessarily indicate a preference for the dominance of that leader in Peru, is clearly revealed by a memorandum upon which Dudley seems to have based his action. The memorandum first noted that the new government at Lima was not only military, but that it was also threatened by a revolt from within and by Colombia and Bolivia from without. It then presented a general view of the relation of recognition to the attitude which ought to be assumed toward the Liberator. If the Cabinet desired Bolívar's power to be consolidated, it should refuse to recognize the insurgent authorities at Lima. If His Majesty's government was indifferent toward Bolívar or uncertain as to its policy, the nature of the new government of Peru and the dangers confronting it would furnish sufficient excuse for delay. If it desired to oppose Bolívar by recognizing the new government, it would contribute to the consolidation of a power avowedly hostile to him. With these alternatives before it the Cabinet decided that it would be "most expedient that the British Consuls in Peru remain quiet spectators of passing events, . . . contenting themselves with using their best endeavours to protect the Interests and Property of British Subjects, and sending home full and detailed Reports. . . ."[73] Thus the failure to recognize this particular government of Peru may have represented

---

[73] Dudley to Ricketts, Jan. 12, 1828, F. O. (61), 15. The memorandum can be found in F. O. (61), 13.

merely an attitude of strict impartiality. Hitherto the state of Peru had not been recognized and it was not acknowledged at this time, nor indeed until after the period set by the bounds of the present study.

It remained, however, for Lord Aberdeen, Dudley's successor, to issue on August 8, 1829, more definite instructions on the question of monarchy in Colombia. The date[74] for the general convention in Colombia and the consummation of the monarchical projects was approaching and the foreign secretary decided to state his policy. He wrote Campbell as follows:

"In the event of your opinion being verified, that it is the intention to establish an European Prince in Colombia and of any proposition being made to you, respecting the selection of a British Prince for that purpose, you will give the Colombian Government to understand, that the King, while he duly appreciates the wish, which Colombia has always shown, to cultivate an intimate connection with England, entertains no views of aggrandizement for himself, or for his family; and you will be careful therefore, to give no encouragement to the project of placing a British Prince upon the Throne of Colombia.

"You will, however, at the same time intimate to the Colombian Govt that the elevation to that station of a Prince of any other Royal House in Europe, excepting that of Spain; and the establishment of so intimate a relation with any European Nation, other than that of the Mother Country, would form a subject of much

[74] Namely, January, 1830.

interest to His Majesty; and would demand the most mature consideration from His Government." [75]

In an interview with the Colombian minister in London (December 16, 1829) Aberdeen made his position still plainer. He stated that the British government would neither furnish a prince nor allow France to do so. He also pointed out that no prince of a prominent dynasty would accept an office of which he could not obtain possession until the death of Bolívar, and advised that if Colombia really needed a monarch, its authorities should choose one at once. When the Colombian minister rejoined that the dangerous transition from a republic to a monarchy could only be made under the direction of the Liberator, Aberdeen replied that there was accordingly no immediate need for the selection of a prince and that a Spanish monarch could be chosen later; whereupon the agent of the Colombian government answered that his nation did not desire a Spanish prince and the interview closed.[76]

By this time opposition in Colombia to a monarchy was becoming so obvious that none but the blind could fail to see it. Bolívar disavowed all connection with the project and there the matter rested.[77]

[75] Instructions No. 7, Aug. 8, 1829, F. O. (18), 53.

[76] Goebel, William Henry Harrison, p. 292, and authorities cited.

[77] Bolívar's attitude toward monarchy has been the subject of much discussion. His conversations with British and French agents may have been designed in part to sound them out. It would appear in the light of available evidence that he was not

Meanwhile, what of the attitude of the United States in face of this apparent threat to the Monroe Doctrine? The records of the State Department will be searched in vain for any clearly defined, vigorous policy with reference to the plan of establishing a member of some European royal house in Colombia. It will not be difficult, however, to find a sentiment of opposition to Bolívar's alleged ambitions and to monarchies in general.

Henry Clay first took official notice of the soaring aspirations of Bolívar in March, 1827. While drawing up instructions for Poinsett and Sergeant, who had been designated as the representatives of the United States at the Congress of Tacubaya, he took occasion to observe: "The intelligence which has reached us from many points, as to the ambitious projects and views of Bolivar, has abated very much the strong hopes which we once entertained of the favorable results of the Congress.... If that intelligence is well founded (as there is much reason to apprehend) it is probable that

---

strongly opposed to monarchy in northern South America, but that he considered its establishment in this region virtually hopeless after 1829 and preferred a quasi-republic, with a life president and vice-presidents directly under the president's control in charge of the large subdivisions (Bolivia, Peru, Venezuela, etc.). There can be little doubt of his desire for a British or possibly a Franco-British protectorate applying not only to his Great Colombia, but also to all Spanish America bound together by a sort of League of Nations. On this mooted question, see Carlos A. Villanueva, *El Imperio de los Andes* (Paris, 1914) and Vicente Lecuna's notes to the Spanish edition of Lockey's *Panamericanism* (Caracas, 1927).

he does not look upon the Congress in the same interesting light that he formerly did. . . . You will, in all your conversations and intercourse with the other ministers, endeavor to strengthen them in the faith of free institutions, and to guard them against any ambitious schemes and plans, from whatever quarter they may proceed, tending to subvert liberal systems." [78]

The urgent appeal of *Chargé* Watts to Bolívar, to return to the capital of Colombia and save the country, was disavowed and strongly disapproved. Moreover, James Cooley was commended for assuring the Peruvian government that Watts's action must have been unauthorized. "The letter of Mr. Watts . . . gave great dissatisfaction to the President," Clay wrote to Cooley. He then stated that it not only violated the rule of non-interference in the domestic politics of other nations but was also "objectionable as indicating a confidence in the views and purposes of Genl. Bolivar which the President regretted he was obliged not to feel." [79]

It is worth noting, also, that a paragraph in the instructions given to William Henry Harrison, in October, 1828, was directed at Bolívar and the schemes of the monarchists. Clay directed Harrison's attention to our general policy of non-interference and told him that the President wished no deviation from it, but he nevertheless instructed him on "proper occasions" to

[78] U. S. Insts. to Ministers, X, 274-277.

[79] Letter of Dec 18, 1827, U. S. Insts. to Mins., XII, 48.

express the "ardent hope" that Colombia's internal dissentions might "terminate in the establishment of constitutional government, so as to secure her liberty, and advance her happiness and prosperity." He also authorized him, "upon proper application," to "communicate freely and frankly the nature of our institutions, and their practical operation." [80]

Moreover, almost a year before Harrison penned his bombastic epistle to the Liberator, Clay had written that eminent leader similar sentiments in a far more effective style. Whatever else we may say of Clay, it would be difficult to prove that he was not an ardent devotee of human liberty in theory at least, if not always in practice. Early in his career he had exclaimed: "I have no commiseration for princes. My sympathies are reserved for the great mass of mankind." And his determined championship of Spanish-American independence is well known. As early as 1818 he had expressed his confidence in the capacity of these people for democratic forms. "It is the doctrine of thrones," he said, "that man is too ignorant to govern himself.... I contend that it is to arraign the dispositions of Providence ... to suppose that he has created beings incapable of governing themselves, and to be trampled on by Kings. Self-government is the natural government of man." [81] When Adams, Mon-

[80] *Loc. cit.*, XII, 152.

[81] Calvin Colton, *Works of Henry Clay* (New York, 1897), V, 146.

roe, and even Jefferson[82] himself were expressing doubts of the political ability of the former colonies of Spain, Clay appears to have remained steadfast in his early faith. And many in Spanish America had appreciated his enthusiastic championship. In November, 1827, Bolívar himself took advantage of the departure of Colonel Watts to express his admiration for Clay's "brilliant talents and ardent love of liberty." "All America, Colombia, and myself, owe your excellency our purest gratitude for the incomparable services you have rendered us,"[83] declared the Liberator. But he was preparing the way for an eloquent lecture.

"I am persuaded," replied Clay almost a year later, "that I do not misinterpret the feelings of the people of the United States, as I certainly express my own, in saying, that the interest which was inspired in this country by the arduous struggles of South America, arose principally from the hope that, along with its independence, would be established free institutions, insuring all the blessings of civil liberty. To the accomplishment of that object we still anxiously look." Clay admitted the difficulties confronted by Colombia, but he expressed the hope that "Providence would bless her ... with the genius of some great and virtu-

[82] Adams, *Memoirs*, V, 325; Monroe to Jefferson, Aug. 18, 1823, *Writings* (Hamilton, ed.), VI, 317-318; Jefferson to John Adams, May 17, 1818, *Writings* (Ford, ed.), X, 108-109, and in many other letters.

[83] Calvin Colton, *Life and Times of Henry Clay* (New York, 1846), I, 244.

ous man, to conduct her securely through all her trials." "We had even flattered ourselves," said Clay, "that we beheld that genius in your excellency. But ... ambitious designs have been attributed by your enemies to your excellency, which have created in my mind great solicitude. ... I can not allow myself to believe, that your excellency will abandon the bright and glorious path which lies plainly before you, for the bloody road passing over the liberties of the human race. ... I will not doubt, that ... , preferring the true glory of our immortal Washington to the ignoble fame of the destroyers of liberty, you have formed the patriotic resolution of ultimately placing the freedom of Colombia upon a firm and sure foundation. ..." [84]

Such, then, was the policy of Henry Clay. He endeavored to defeat the monarchical projects by moral suasion, but he went no further. Perhaps he deemed more vigorous action unnecessary. In October, 1828, he told Charles Bresson, who was on his way to Colombia as agent of the French government, that Bolívar's ambitions embraced all Hispanic America, but that they had been opportunely discovered and had already become impracticable.[85]

The leaders of the Jackson party had often criticised the Spanish-American policy of Adams and Clay, but when they ascended to power they adopted virtually the same policy. The rule of non-interference was

[84] Colton, *op. cit.*, I, 245.

[85] Carlos A. Villanueva, *El Imperio de los Andes*, 147-148.

emphatically announced, but Van Buren's initial instructions to Moore contained the following paragraphs:

"The President [Jackson] will not disguise the fact that recent events in Colombia . . . have produced in the minds of the friends of liberty in this region occasional and painful apprehensions as to the ultimate views of President Bolivar. The President, notwithstanding, is free to say that he has, at all times, been . . . sustained by an abiding hope that they would, in the sequel, be found such as the friends of freedom throughout the world could approve. . . .

"The President is unwilling to believe that he who has made such liberal sacrifices and exerted such great powers, physical and moral, to redress the wrongs and secure the liberties of his country, can ever consent to exchange the imperishable renown which posterity will doubtless award to the constant and untiring patron of public liberty for the fleeting and sordid graitfication of personal aggrandizement." [86]

Six months later, after Moore had erroneously reported that no monarchical plots existed in Colombia, Van Buren, still not entirely reassured, wrote: "The President is not disposed to disguise or conceal his desire that General Bolivar should, by the purity and disinterestedness of his course disappoint the hopes . . . cherished by the enemies of free governments, and thus secure an additional claim to the esteem and respect of the world. . . . What more gratifying exhibi-

[86] Insts. of June 9, 1829, U. S. Insts. to Am. States, XIV, 16.

tion of human glory could be presented than to see this great captain, after having successfully resisted foreign aggression, and extinguished intestine commotion, conquer also those infirmities to which noble minds have in all ages been exposed. The welfare of that country, and the interest of this in the success and stability of free institutions, combine to render such a result most desirable."

Thus far there appears to be little difference between the views of Van Buren and Clay. The instructions now under consideration contain, however, three sentences which express a spirit of compromise that Clay might not have been willing to entertain. "Public opinion," wrote Van Buren, "will not require from the Liberator . . . more than the actual condition of his country will allow. It is well known that circumstances, which are the results of centuries, cannot be overcome in an hour. The world will, therefore, give him full credit for advising . . . the establishment of institutions as liberal as existing circumstances will permit." [87] Otherwise there appears to have been no difference in the policies of the two administrations. Confronted by the unpleasant prospect of monarchies under European protection, they applied no remedy save moral suasion. Their correspondence contains no hint of more vigorous action, no evidence of remonstrance to the European courts. Perhaps they felt that

[87] Instructions of Dec. 12, 1829, U. S. Insts. Am. States, XIV, 51.

moral influence exerted in America was all that was needed, and in the end this proved to be true.[88]

The era now under consideration closed with the turbulent forces of democracy triumphant in northern South America and the influence of the United States standing at a high mark. The commerce of England was more than twice that of the United States and British capital was operating the important mines and clamoring for dividends on the government loans, but this economic lead was due largely to lack of capital and manufactures north of the Rio Grande. It is difficult to see how the political contest could have ended differently. The masses of the region had acquired a taste for freedom and accepted democratic republicanism as their creed. The Liberator himself did not contemplate the establishment of a monarchy except by the vote of a constituent assembly democratically elected. England and Bolívar would have found it

[88] On February 17, 1830, Harrison gave Adams a correct statement of British policy. Probably the same information had already reached Jackson and Van Buren. Harrison told Adams that he expected Venezuela to separate from Colombia "if Bolivar should assume the crown." "This, however, he believed he would not do: he would content himself with the title of President for life. He said that Bolivar had applied to the British Government for support to his project for establishing a monarchy, and the answer was, that Great Britain took a deep interest in the welfare of the people of Colombia, but would not interfere with their interior government. If they should, however, call a European prince to the throne, no English prince could accept it, and there would be great inconvenience should the choice fall upon any other than a prince of Spain." (*Memoirs*, VIII, 190.)

exceedingly difficult, in face of the envy of France and the opposition of the United States, to reconcile the people to a monarchy; and, besides, the attempt might have constituted a violation of Canning's open disavowal of any intention to extend the British empire at the expense of the former colonies of Spain. Northern South America, like the lands to the south, was destined to be "plagued" by governments of the Yankee type.

CHAPTER VI

FRICTION IN CENTRAL AMERICA; THE PANAMA CONGRESS

It was in 1823 that British diplomats first evinced concern with reference to the relations of the United States and Central America. At that time an agent from Salvador was in the United States seeking protection from the Mexican Emperor Iturbide. Stratford Canning learned of the negotiation and magnified it into an overture of the whole of Central America for annexation to the United States. He also connected the question with a potential canal route and enclosed a letter from George Woodbine (of Florida fame), in which this adventurer begged the encouragement of the English government in a proposed attempt to secure for the British "Crown" the "complete control of a water communication . . . through Lake Nicaragua." [1]

Canning's successor made inquiries concerning the alleged delegation from Guatemala, and John Quincy Adams gave a very agreeable reply. He said that a deputation had come from Salvador with propositions for an alliance against the threatened violence of Iturbide, but that its commission had been annulled by that Emperor's overthrow and the changed attitude of the Mexican government.[2]

[1] Stratford Canning to George Canning, Apr. 8, 1823, F. O. (5), 176.

[2] H. U. Addington to *idem*, No. 22, Nov. 30, 1823, F. O. (5) 177.

With reference to the canal, British diplomatic representatives in the United States revealed uneasiness upon only one other occasion prior to 1830. In August, 1826, Charles R. Vaughan was disturbed by a concession which the Republic of Central America had granted to an American company . He interviewed Secretary of State Clay, and was told that the United States government would "have nothing to do with" the canal project "in any shape." If the canal was to be constructed by foreigners, then Clay would be pleased if the task should fall to the lot of his own countrymen; but "he was convinced that it must be carried into effect with the consent of all Nations, studiously avoiding any privileges reserved for any one."[3] Although this conciliatory response must have been gratifying to Vaughan, he was not altogether satisfied; for he noted somewhat regretfully, when he examined the liberal terms of the concession, that the navigation of the canal would be "completely in the hands of the Company formed in the United States."[4]

I. ATTITUDE OF CONSULS O'REILLY AND SCHENLEY

The agents who revealed real jealousy of the procedure of the Yankees with reference to Central America were the consuls whom the British govern-

[3] Vaughan to Canning, No. 65, Aug. 28, 1826, F. O. (5), 212.

[4] *Idem* to *idem*, No. 72, Oct. 2, 1826, *loc. cit.*

ment sent to the region. Three of these[5] — John O'Reilly, E. W. H. Schenley, and Charles Dashwood— were dispatched between 1825 and 1830, but the last fell a victim to the climate and had to be taken out in a litter after a brief sojourn.[6] He accordingly had little opportunity for hostile criticism of the Americans, and that apparently not altogether disagreeable duty was confined to his predecessors.

The interest of the British government in Central America centered mainly around questions of commerce, investments, canal concessions, and the alleged rights of British settlers. Negotiations for a commercial treaty were considered, but the instability of the Central American government and its views on maritime matters prevented the accomplishment of anything along this line. Some British capital was invested in lands and mining operations and a small loan was made to the government. English subjects attempted to obtain a canal concession, but were defeated by their American rivals. And, finally, British nationals in Central America were irritated by the jealousy of the native population and their refusal to deliver up the fugitive slaves who escaped from the Belize settlements.

[5] George Alexander Thompson had been sent on a kind of inspection tour in 1825. He appears, however, not to have expressed any jealousy of the United States. His correspondence and reports will be found in F. O. (15), I-III. The officials of Jamaica and Belize also frequently traveled through Central America.

[6] For the Dashwood correspondence, see F. O. (15), 8, 10, 11.

The British government does not appear to have been aggressive during the period, although its agents and nationals often were. They advocated the occupation of the Island of Ruatan, in Honduras Bay, and actually took possession of it in 1830; they brought the Mosquito "kings" to Belize for coronation; and they spread their establishments for agriculture, trade, and logging southward towards the San Juan River. In these activities, however, they were not encouraged by the home government. The successive cabinets went no further than merely to safeguard what they termed the "possessory rights" of British subjects.[7]

In looking after their affairs in Central America the English agents often found reason to complain of their American rivals. Consul Schenley spent only a few months in Guatemala before he developed a "liver complaint" which sent him to England for his health, but he was there long enough to conceive a jealousy of the United States and a desire to add the island of Ruatan to the British Empire. He declared that this island could be made another Gibraltar and that it should be surreptitiously occupied. He said that the people of Central America were hostile toward the British settlements and looked forward to a day when the English should be forced to evacuate Belize, and that their attitude was largely due to the United States

[7] *Cf., inter alia*, the Thompson reports referred to in note 5; Canning to O'Reilly, Sept. 12, 1825, F. O. (15), 4; *idem* to *idem*, March 17, 1826, F. O. (15), 5; O'Reilly to Canning, Feb. 17, 1826, *passim, loc. cit.*; and an undated memorandum in F. O. (15), 11.

FRICTION IN CENTRAL AMERICA

and its "numerous emissaries." Since 1813, he said, the Washington government had shown an evident determination to prevent the further acquisition of territory by European Powers on the Continent of America, and surely the "growing influence and crafty intrigue" of the Yankees could not be unknown to His Majesty's ministers. The 'Imbecility' of Central American authorities had in fact become "dangerous in the hands of *clever* and designing agents." [8]

John O'Reilly, the first British consul, reached Guatemala City in August, 1825, and continued there in the service of his government until he was murdered by one of his household servants in January, 1828.[9] During this period he often revealed jealousy of the United States and wrote indignantly of the activities of the American *chargé*, John Williams.

O'Reilly first referred to Williams and other Yankees in May, 1826. At this time he expressed the view that the commercial treaty which the American *chargé* brought down for ratification contained an objectionable article on the subject of navigation and hence would not be ratified. On this point O'Reilly was in error, as the sequel was soon to reveal; for however disagreeable the article may have been to the British, it was finally accepted by the government of Central

[8] Schenley to Planta, Jan. 1, May 19 and 31, and June 3, 1826, F. O. (15), 5.

[9] O'Reilly to Canning, Aug. 31, 1825, F. O. (15), 4; and see the last document in volume 11, *loc. cit.*, for an account of O'Reilly's death.

America. The English agent also reported that a canal contract had been awarded to Palmer and Company of New York. This result he attributed to "the superior activity and intrigue of the American over the Agent of the English House," as well as to "the weakness and indecision of the President. . . ." [10]

To these two subjects O'Reilly returned again and again. On August 5, 1826, for instance, he reported that the treaty with the United States had been ratified because of the menacing attitude of Williams and declared that the most-favored-nation principle which was embodied in it would give the United States a privileged position. Special favors had already been granted by Central America to the sister states of Spanish origin and the United States would now be given these concessions. He had protested in vain. He had recently "met with worse than slights from the President," and, "looking to British Interests," he saw no reason to "regret any change from the present order of things." [11]

In the following December O'Reilly reported more fully and more hopefully. Williams had just left for the United States after a sharp correspondence with the Central American government and greatly displeased because of the defeat of the "high Republican party" in its recent attempt to get control of the country. O'Reilly said that he himself was now "on very friendly terms with the principal persons who

[10] To Canning, May 31, 1826, F. O. (15), 5.
[11] To Bidwell, No. 8, F. O. (15), 5.

FRICTION IN CENTRAL AMERICA   223

support and advise the President." He was convinced that the indiscretions of Williams had reacted in favor of the English.

Yet the British consul was not entirely free from anxiety. Just before his departure, Williams had gone to Salvador in order, as O'Reilly supposed, "to make representations to the leading persons" in that state "against the President and in favor of the 'Liberal' party here, through whom, in the event of their success, he expected to have a preponderating influence in their councils." Williams had told O'Reilly that he thought his efforts had not been without success, and O'Reilly feared that this might be true. While in San Salvador Williams had met an influential British merchant and apparently converted him to the American cause, federalism and all. Moreover, he had persuaded him to accept an appointment as American consul. O'Reilly objected to this plan of using the influence of an English subject in order to forward Yankee interests, and told Williams so. O'Reilly did not think that the federal government of Central America would grant an *exequatur* to this individual, but he urged that the British government should be on its guard and send out more consuls in order to "counteract political intrigues." The activities of Williams reminded him of those of Poinsett in Mexico! [12]

Before closing his despatch the consul referred once more to the canal project. In fact it was in this connection chiefly that he urged the sending of more

[12] For Poinsett's career in Mexico, see *post* Ch. VII.

agents. "Looking forward," said O'Reilly, "to the company formed in the United States for digging the Nicaragua Canal, whose engineers are soon expected . . . , and believing, as I do, that the Government of that Republic connect therewith Political views and the obtaining a footing in the Isthmus, it might perhaps be advisable to appoint two consuls, or vice consuls." [13]

In the spring of 1826 O'Reilly returned to the canal question for the last time, declaring that Williams and the agent of Palmer and Company had obtained the concession by allying themselves with the Liberal party and overawing the President. In March he was considerably alarmed, for he had heard that Secretary Clay had formally demanded the sovereignty of the canal and a certain extent of territory on each of its banks, on . . . condition that the Government of the United States would execute the work." But his anxiety was soon relieved. The canal scheme "turned out a bubble"; the contractor fled from New York carrying away "80,000 Dollars collected from credulous subscribers," and Williams's connection with the affair brought him and his country "into great disrepute." [14] All this O'Reilly reported early in April. During the following May, he declared that the "Government and people of the United States" had "become still more unpopular"; [15] and with this statement Brit-

[13] To Bidwell, No. 16, Dec. 3, 1826, F. O. (15), 5.

[14] To Canning, March 18 and Apr. 3, 1827, *loc. cit.*

[15] To Bidwell, May 7, 1827, F. O. (15), 7.

ish criticism of American policy ceased—until the close of the period now under discussion.

II. THE MILDER DISPOSITION OF AMERICAN AGENTS

Prior to 1830 the United States maintained a diplomatic representative in Central America for only a few months. One *chargé* died on the way to his post. Another reached the port of Omoa, but concluded that his presence in the disorderly country could serve no good purpose. A third was called back to Washington, after he had made less than half of the journey to Central America, in order to answer a charge of forgery. For most of the period, therefore, the interests of the United States were watched by the consuls at Guatemala City.[16]

In the correspondence of these agents jealousy of the British is not often expressed. *Chargé* John Williams said nothing of British opposition to the treaty whose ratification he was sent to secure, or of English attempts to obtain the canal concessions for themselves. In fact, he mentioned the English only once, remarking that the Central American tariff discriminated against the coarse cottons of the United States and favored British commodities. *Chargé* William B. Rochester reported that certain Central Americans were apprehensive of British prestige in Mexico[17] and

[16] Their correspondence will be found in Despatches from Central America, I (State Department MSS.).

[17] Rochester to Clay, May 12, 1827; Williams to *idem*, Aug. 4, 1826, Desp. Cen. Am., I.

some of the consuls condemned the encroachments of the English residents in British Honduras, one of them characterizing their temporary occupation of the island of Ruatan as a "gross violation of the rights" of the Central American nation.[18] Aside from these instances, little envy or hostility was evinced.

With reference to O'Reilly's accusations against Williams, it can only be stated that the correspondence in the archives at Washington neither proves nor disproves the charges. Williams had difficulty in securing the ratification of the commercial treaty, and it was probably the most favorable agreement negotiated with any Latin-American state during the period, but the methods which he used to achieve his purpose are not revealed. He deprecated the militaristic tendencies of President Manuel J. Arce, sympathized with the Liberals, gave counsel and advice on political matters, and visited San Salvador, but declared that he had taken no part in the factional contests of the country. "The failure here at representative Government has grieved me to the heart," he said. But he then added that he had kept himself "entirely aloof from their party strife," although he "would have taken great pleasure in contributing to the improvement of their institutions."[19] Consul William Phillips, who lost some three thousand dollars in the "infamous canal bubble," alleged that Williams had advised him to participate

[18] Manning, *Dip. Cor.*, II, 888.

[19] Williams to Clay, Nov. 24, 1826, and following, *loc. cit.*

in an undertaking which Williams declared to be "too important to the Government of the U. States to fall into the hands of any other power," but, aside from this reference, the correspondence throws no light upon the *chargé's* connection with the project.[20]

III. OPPOSING VIEWS OF THE UNITED STATES AND ENGLAND REGARDING THE PANAMA CONGRESS

The rivalry of the two Anglo-Saxon Powers never appeared more clearly than in connection with the Congress which assembled at Panama in the summer of 1826. The state papers drawn up by the two governments on this occasion contain a complete revelation of their motives and antagonisms, and deserve a minute examination.

The policy of Canning is set forth in the several instructions to Edward J. Dawkins, who was sent in response to the invitation of Colombia to represent British interests at the assembly. Dawkins was directed to transmit information "as to the views and policy of the American Govts—their feelings toward each other, and the degree of influence in their concerns which they may appear inclined to allow the United States. . . ." He was told that England would not object to a "league among the States lately Colonies of Spain," but that "any project for putting the U. S. ... at the head of an American Confederacy as against Europe, would be highly displeasing. . . . It would be felt as an ill return for the service which has been ren-

[20] Phillips to *idem*, Aug. 8, 1827, *loc. cit.*

dered to those States, and the dangers which have been averted from them by . . . Great Britain; and it would too probably at no very distant period endanger the peace both of America, and of Europe."

Here, then, was one phase of the antagonism. Canning feared that a league of American liberalism and democratic republicanism would be formed in opposition to European conservatism, monarchy, and aristocracy; moreover, that such a combination might have other implications equally dangerous to the system of which Canning was the exponent. It might constitute a threat to the familiar maritime rules which England had established by long domination of the high seas. On this matter Canning was quite vigorous. "You will . . . avow . . . the wish of Your Govt," he wrote Dawkins, "that the principles of Maritime Law, to be adopted by the new States, may be those which Great Britain has always contended to be the true principles of the law of Nations; principles growing out of long established usage, and of prescriptive authority in the Old World: upon which Great Britain has uniformly acted, and of which she has uniformly respected the exercise of others, and by none more than the new States of America themselves.[21] And you will take care to have it duly understood that our determination to act upon these principles . . . has not been shaken by European Confederacies, [and] . . . will not be

[21] This clause has reference to the naval operations of Chile, Brazil, and Buenos Aires.

altered by any Resolution or combination of the States of the New World."

These instructions were filled with significance for the United States. They meant the right of search; they meant the refusal to recognize as national any vessel not built in the country whose flag floated above its deck, not owned by citizens of that country, and not manned by a crew three-fourths of whom, at least, were citizens of the same; they meant the restriction of the carrying trade between the Spanish-American states and England to British and Spanish-American bottoms; they meant contraband lists pages long; they meant that a neutral flag could not cover the goods of an enemy; they meant an extensive exercise of the power of blockade; they meant opposition to almost every political and maritime principle for which the United States had contended for half a century!

The remainder of the instructions merely specified certain means of increasing the prestige of England at the expense of the United States. If the dispute between Buenos Aires and Brazil over Banda Oriental came up, Dawkins was authorized to offer British mediation. If plans for driving Spain out of Cuba were discussed, he was to contrast the position of England with the meddlesome disposition of the United States to restrict belligerent operations, and tactfully to warn the Spanish Americans that a general war might therefore result from an attempt to change the status of Cuba. Dawkins was also directed to urge the Spanish-American diplomats to seek a reconciliation with the mother country even at the cost of a pecuniary contribution as the price of recognition.[22]

Hence, it was not without good reason that Adams and Clay desired to send representatives to Panama. They had not seen these instructions to Dawkins, but a perusal of them was not necessary to a knowledge of England's views. This had been obtained in the course of long political careers characterized by almost continuous protests against English "pretensions"; and both men must have felt keenly the hostility of George Canning. For "was it not he who disavowed Erskine's arrangement [1809], which, had it been sanctioned in England, might have prevented a war? Was it not he who in 1823 infused the unfriendly tone into that long negotiation at London, almost refusing to listen to nine out of ten of our claims, obviously just as most of them were? And was it not he who in 1826 most abruptly closed the West India trade against us, upon pretexts the most unexpected and flimsy? . . . He esteems civil and political liberty no more than Lord Londonderry [Castlereagh] did, though circumstances have made him appear to be somewhat more their champion. . . . Mr. Canning never liked the United States nor their institutions, and never will. . . . He will watch all our steps with sharper and more active jealousy than perhaps any other English statesman living. Of all their public

[22] Canning to Dawkins, Nos. 1, 2, 3, 4, and 5, March 18, 1826, F. O. (97), 115.

men, we have the least to expect from him." [23] So wrote Richard Rush to Clay in 1827, and doubtless this is the way Clay felt in 1826. At any rate, there can be no doubt about the feelings of Adams, for as early as 1816 he had confided to his *Memoirs* that Canning had been "invariably noted for ... bitterness ... toward the United States"; and news of the English statesman's death called forth the following prayer in October, 1827: "May this event, in the order of Providence, avert the evils which he would, if permitted, have drawn down upon us... !" [24]

The policies of the two Powers were certainly antagonistic, and this in spite of the fact that the majority of Americans were too completely converted to the notion of no entangling alliances to think of organizing a Pan-American political league. This antagonism can have no more striking exposition than one which may be obtained by a comparison of Canning's instructions to Dawkins with Adams's messages referring to the Panama Congress and the directions given by Clay to the delegates chosen to represent the interests of the United States at that assembly.

Indeed, Adams's message to the House of Representatives set forth the policy of the United States with such thoroughness and eloquence that it left little for Clay to add when the time came to draft instructions to the American commissioners. Adams had England

[23] *The Private Correspondence of Henry Clay* (Calvin Colton, ed., New York, 1856), 165-166.

[24] *Memoirs*, III, 437, VII, 328.

and the Neo-Holy Alliance in mind, as well as the opposition to the mission which had developed in Congress. His state paper deserves to be quoted at length.

"The great revolution in human affairs which has brought into existence, nearly at the same time, eight sovereign and independent nations in our own quarter of the globe has placed the United States in a situation not less novel and scarcely less interesting than that in which they had found themselves by their own transition from a cluster of colonies to a nation of sovereign States. The deliverance of the Southern American Republics from the oppression under which they had been so long afflicted was hailed with great unanimity by the people of this Union as among the most auspicious events of the age. . . ." These republics have now invited the United States to send agents to Panama for "consultation upon *American interests*," and the invitation has been accepted. "To meet the temper with which this proposal was made with a cold repulse was not thought congenial to that warm interest in their welfare with which the people and Government of the Union had hitherto gone hand in hand through the whole progress of their revolution. . . . I would have sent ministers to the meeting had it been merely to give them such advice as they might have desired, even with reference to *their own* interests, not involving ours. I would have sent them had it been merely to explain . . . to them our reasons for *declining* any proposal of specific measures to which they might

Friction in Central America

desire our concurrence, but which we might deem incompatible with our interests or our duties. . . .

"But objects of the highest importance, not only to the future welfare of the whole human race, but bearing directly upon the special interests of this Union, will engage the deliberations of the Congress of Panama whether we are represented there or not. Others, if we are represented, may be offered by our plenipotentiaries for consideration having in view both these great results—our own interests and the improvement of the condition of man upon earth. It may be that in the lapse of many centuries no other opportunity so favorable will be presented to the Government of the United States to subserve the benevolent purposes of Divine Providence. . . ."

And what were these objects that so accorded with the purposes of Divine Providence? They related to commerce, maritime rules, and democratic institutions. In opposing the views of the United States on these matters, Canning and England were in league with the Devil himself!

"It will be within the recollection of the House," Adams continued, "that immediately after the close of the war of our independence a measure closely analogous to this congress of Panama was adopted by the Congress of our Confederation, and for purposes of precisely the same character. Three commissions with plenipotentiary powers were appointed to negotiate treaties of amity, navigation, and commerce with all the principle powers of Europe. They met and resided for that purpose about one year at Paris, and the only result of their negotiations at that time was the first treaty between the United States and Prussia—memorable in the diplomatic annals of the world. ... The treaty ... consecrated three fundamental principles. ... : First, equal reciprocity and the mutual stipulation of the privileges of the most favored nation in the commercial exchanges of peace; secondly, the abolition of private warfare upon the ocean, and thirdly, restrictions favorable to neutral commerce upon belligerent practices with regard to contraband of war and blockades. A painful, it may be said a calamitous, experience of more than forty years has demonstrated the deep importance of these same principles to the peace and prosperity of this nation and to the welfare of all maritime states. ...

"At that time ... they [the commissioners] were able but to obtain the sanction of one great and philosophical, though absolute sovereign in Europe to their liberal and enlightened principles. They could obtain no more. Since then a political hurricane has gone over three-fourths of the civilized portions of the earth, the desolation of which it may with confidence be expected is passing away, leaving at least the American atmosphere purified and refreshed. And now at this propitious moment the new-born nations of this hemisphere, assembling by their representatives at the isthmus ... to settle the principles of their future international intercourse ..., ask in this great exigency for our advice upon those very fundamental maxims which we from our cradle at first proclaimed. . . .

"If it be true that the noblest treaty of peace ever mentioned in history is that by which the Carthagenians were bound to abolish the practice of sacrificing their own children . . . , I can not exaggerate to myself the unfading glory with which these United States will go forth in the memory of future ages if by their friendly counsel, by their moral influence, by the power of argument and persuasion alone they can prevail upon the American nations at Panama to stipulate by general agreement among themselves, and so far as any of them may be concerned, the perpetual abolition of private war upon the ocean. And if we can not yet flatter ourselves that this may be accomplished, . . . the establishment of the principle that the friendly flag shall cover the cargo, the curtailment of contraband of war, and the proscription of fictitious paper blockades —engagements which we may reasonably hope will not prove impracticable—will, if successfully inculcated, redound proportionately to our honor and drain the fountain of many a future sanguinary war."

Adams then assumed his characteristic attitude of hostility toward the "exclusive and excluding" colonial system, alluding to the non-colonization clause of the Monroe Doctrine and setting forth the motives underlying it. This clause, said Adams, "rested upon a course of reasoning equally simple and conclusive. With the exception of the existing European colonies, which it was in nowise intended to disturb, the two continents consisted of several sovereign and independent nations, whose territories covered their whole surface. By . . . their independent condition the United States enjoyed the right of commercial intercourse with every part of their possessions. To attempt the establishment of a colony in those possessions would be to usurp to the exclusion of others a commercial intercourse which was the common possession of all." The plenipotentiaries soon to assemble at Panama were to discuss means of making this principle of freedom of trade effective, and the United States could not afford to be without representation.

Nor did Adams neglect the political phase of the subject. The Hispanic colonies, he declared, had been "transformed into eight independent nations, . . . seven of them Republics like ourselves, with whom we have an immensely growing commercial, and *must* have and have already important political, connections; with reference to whom our situation is neither distant nor detached; whose political principles and systems of government, congenial with our own, must and will have an action and counteraction upon us and ours to which we can not be indifferent if we would . . . *America* has a set of primary interests which have none or a remote relation to Europe; . . . and if she [Europe] should interfere, as she may, . . . we might be called in defense of our own altars and firesides to take an attitude which would cause our neutrality to be respected, and choose peace or war, as our interest, guided by justice, should counsel."

FRICTION IN CENTRAL AMERICA

In conclusion, Adams declared that the design of the congress was great, benevolent, and humane. "It looks to the melioration of the condition of man. It is congenial with that spirit which prompted the declaration of our independence, which inspired the preamble of our first treaty with France,[25] which dictated our first treaty with Prussia . . . , which filled the hearts and fired the souls of the immortal founders of our Revolution."

Such were Adams's larger intentions with reference to the assembly at Panama. He would not form entangling alliances, he would not bind the nation with formal pledges; but he would employ counsel, argument, moral pressure in support of those great commercial, maritime, and political principles which were the distinguishing ideals of his country. These were not the only reasons for urging the dispatch of a commission to the isthmus, but they were the main reasons. And in promoting these views Adams was placing himself in opposition to the British government as it was then organized and operating.[26]

The instructions which Clay transmitted to the Panama delegates in May, 1826, were designed to carry out the purposes set forth in Adams's message to the House. They contained little that was new and almost nothing new that related to England. The dele-

[25] This preamble (1778) had much to say about "perfect equality and reciprocity . . . and the just rules of free intercourse" in matters of trade.

[26] J. D. Richardson, *Messages and Papers of the Presidents*, II, 329 ff.

gates were directed to insist upon the most-favored-nation principle in commercial intercourse, a broad definition of the rights of neutrals in time of war, and a restriction of the power of blockade. They were also instructed to urge that "whatever may be imported from any foreign country into any one American nation or exported from it in its own vessels may, in like manner, be imported into or exported from the same" in vessels of other American nations. Lastly, they were authorized to encourage these new states to resist European interference or encroachments and to strengthen their faith in republican institutions.[27]

The commercial features of these instructions were obviously aimed at Great Britain, and the British did not fail to grasp their significance. When they were made public in 1829, Vaughan, who had kept a careful watch over the entire proceedings, sent home a copy with full comment.[28] The London *Times* remarked: "There is an obvious anxiety throughout these long documents to assume . . . that all 'American' states are to constitute a system and a community of their own, recognizing interests and establishing maxims for their common regulation as affects each other, and for their separate, exclusive, nay, repulsive use, as regards the other nations of the world. The first obvious consequence of such a scheme, if adopted by Mexico and the states of South America, would be to

[27] *International American Conference, 1889-1890*, IV, 113 ff.

[28] To Aberdeen, No. 18, March 25, 1829, F. O. (5), 248.

Friction in Central America 239

place the United States at the *head* of the new federation, in virtue of superior strength, maturity, safety, commercial and political resources." [29]

An anonymous pamphlet published in London at about the same time presented a more extensive view. Its authors declared that the United States had urged "infant states without maritime force, without the possibility of becoming maritime states for many generations, if at all," to adopt in their relations with Europe "the highest pretensions, which, in the maturity of her naval strength, the United States herself ever ventured to urge—and even then, without the remotest hope of success." Instead of advising these budding nations to cultivate a friendly intercourse with Europe and avoid meddling where their interests were not concerned, the United States had said: "Take the highest ground in your negotiations with Europe, that an old-established, powerful state wolud propose. Insist that free ships shall make free goods. Demand also a definition of blockade."

Moreover, this was not the only objection which the writer raised to the content of the instructions. "Having recommended to the new states," he continued, "that they should call upon us, to renounce in their favor, a belligerent right which we have never yet conceded to any other power, the elder branch of the American family further suggests to them the experiment of prevailing upon us to make a slight inroad into our navigation act. One of the principles of this code is,

[29] Issue of May 18, 1829.

that we admit from other nations their own produce, in their own shipping, or in our own; but in no other, unless such produce be again exported from this country. Thus, a ship of the United States brings us cotton or tobacco from New York; but she cannot do so from Colombia; it must come from the latter country either in a Colombian or British ship. Now, the government of the United States says to these young republics, 'America is one continent—insist in your treaties with Europe that it is one nation—and that it shall be so considered for all commercial purposes—that we, your elder brethren, may come to your ports, and be the carriers of your produce.' " [30]

IV. DAWKINS AT PANAMA

What was accomplished by the two rivals at Panama? Nothing, so far as the United States was concerned. The delegates appointed by Adams never arrived. One of them, Richard C. Anderson, died on the way from Bogotá to the isthmus; the other, John Sergeant, had not yet set out when news came of the adjournment of the congress to meet later at Tacubaya. Perhaps it was just as well that they did not attend. Disparaging remarks made during the debate over their appointment had offended certain Spanish Americans; the Mexicans and Colombians were not pleased at the position taken by the United States with

[30] *Spanish America. Observations on the Instructions given by the President of the United States of America to the Representatives of that Republic at Panama in 1826* . . .

reference to Cuba; the policies of the two peoples differed on the slavery issue; and the attitude of aloofness forced upon the United States government by a strong isolation sentiment probably would have failed to satisfy some of the delegates of Spanish America.[31]

The British agent, on the contrary, was present at the Congress from its beginning to its end. Although he did not actually attend the formal deliberations of the assembly, he held frequent informal conferences with the Spanish-American delegates. What he said and did may be ascertained from his own accounts and the correspondence of the other representatives.

Dawkins first endeavored to ascertain the views of the deputies on the question of reconciliation with the mother country. This matter, if properly adjusted by British effort, would increase English prestige in Latin America where it was meeting the competition of the United States, and in Spain where it was being threatened by France. The basis proposed by Dawkins, a pecuniary consideration as a reward for recognition, involved insuperable obstacles. Colombia and Peru were bound by an agreement not to submit to a

[31] See the instructions of May 8, 1826, *loc. cit.* in note 27, above.

Chargé Beaufort T. Watts wrote from Bogotá with reference to the debate in Congress: "The intemperate and ungenerous expressions of Senator Berrien, and Mr. Randolph towards these Republics, have been seized by the English Editors at Caracas, and in Bogota, to prejudice the government and people against our character." He thought the effort had failed, but he gives no good reason for so thinking. (To Clay, Nov. 7, 1826, Manning, *Dip. Cor.*, II, 1302-1303.)

demand for tribute; Chile and Buenos Aires were not represented at Panama; and such an exaction as the price of acknowledgment was prohibited by the instructions of most of the deputies who were present. The idea met with little favor. Señor Michelena, one of the Mexican delegates, talked magniloquently and impractically, but ended by opposing a settlement on the basis proposed.

On the closely related question of the meditated attempt to drive Spain out of Cuba, Dawkins found Pedro Gual of Colombia in a fairly satisfactory mood. Gual was "no stranger to the declaration of the United States upon the subject." Moreover, he appeared to be "sensible of the heavy Responsibility Colombia would incur towards all the Maritime Powers, and the alarming contingencies to which She might expose Herself by embarking in such an undertaking."

Dawkins next turned to the subject of commerce and maritime regulations in the supposition that the Congress might formulate a treaty on this subject. Gual said that he did not advocate the "privileges of the neutral flag" as a general principle, but that, in the present crisis, he was willing to accept that principle in order to obtain the good will of the United States. The Mexican delegates professed themselves to be "decidedly hostile to the principles of Maritime Law put forth by the United States for the adoption of America." In fact it was apparently for this reason mainly that Michelena was urging the disbanding of the congress before the arrival of the American delegates. He desired to avoid open opposition to the United

States on these matters. Manuel Vidaurre of Peru said that he would never sign a document binding his country to the commercial principles of the United States, and Pérez Tudela, the other Peruvian delegate, told Dawkins that he and his colleague had been instructed to "follow the opinions of Great Britain." The Guatemalan delegation appeared to be divided, but Dawkins thought that Guatemala would adopt the contentions of the United States.

The relations between Dawkins and the Spanish-American deputies, with the exception of one minor incident, were entirely harmonious. On June 26, when Dawkins made one of his almost daily visits to the residence of Gual, he found the Colombian delegate somewhat cold and skeptical regarding the good wishes of the British government toward the new states. This mood was quite in contrast with Gual's previous attitude, and Dawkins soon discovered the cause. Gual had been reading the despatches of Alexander Everett, United States minister to Spain. Everett had written that the efforts of the British diplomats in behalf of Spanish recognition for the insurgent governments had been very feeble. He asserted, among other things, that in a period of five months the British ambassador, Frederick Lambe, had had only two conversations with the Spanish government on the question. Everett then went on to remark: "No offer of formal mediation has been made by England since her recognition of Mexico, Colombia, and Buenos Aires. Indeed her interest as a commercial and manufacturing country, is now on the other side. The longer the war continues, the longer she enjoys a monopoly of the Spanish American market for her fabrics, and the more difficult will Spain find it to recover her natural advantages upon the return of peace. England will, therefore, probably be very easy in regard to this matter, and will leave Spain to pursue, unmolested, the course she may think expedient. I suggested this point both to Mr. Zea [head of the Spanish foreign office] and to the Russian Minister. . . . They both admitted the justice of my remarks. . . ."[32]

Here was a delicate situation and Dawkins was much concerned. He asked Gual if he could for a moment suppose that England, "the strenuous opposer of the [maritime] principles which the United States are [were] urging this Congress to adopt," could possibly profit by a continuation of the war between Spain and the colonies. And a few days later he succeeded in convincing the Colombian deputy that "the errors and indiscretions" of Everett had done injury to the cause of Spanish recognition. Indeed, Gual even went so far as to promise that he would bring before the Congress a proposal for mediation through Great Britain, a promise which he fulfilled on July 13! All friction had been removed, and Dawkins was invited to go along with the delegates to Tacubaya.

This invitation the English "observer" could not accept, because he had no authority to do so. Instead of going to Tacubaya, he returned to London and made his final report to Canning in October. The

[32] Everett to Clay, Oct. 20, 1825, *Sen. Doc.* No. 68, 19 Cong., 1 Sess. (Ser. 127), 84-85.

mission cost the British government more than $16,000, but it was probably worth it. In his final report Dawkins stated his conclusions on the main topics which he had discussed with the Spanish-American delegates. All of the delegates favored an accommodation with Spain, but it involved a responsibility beyond the powers which they had been granted. The Colombians favored the adoption of the "Maritime Rights" advocated by the United States, but Mexico and Peru would successfully oppose the introduction of these "false principles" into a Pan-American treaty. "The general Influence of the United States" was not "to be feared." It would be resisted by Mexico and Peru. It existed in Colombia; "but it has [had] been very much weakened even there by . . . protests against an attack on Cuba, and by the indiscretions . . . committed at Madrid." Moreover, Dawkins even found the "principles of the Republicans" much less radical than he had expected.[33]

Thus Dawkins's despatches show that he had been very busy in his attempts to counteract the influence of the United States. Reports of his work by delegates of the Spanish-American states do not differ materially from those of the British agent himself. Briceño Méndez of Colombia characterized the conduct of Dawkins as "noble, frank, and loyal." "We have had no cause for complaint against Mr. Dawkins," said Méndez, "and no reason to distrust him; on the contrary all the delegations manifested toward him

[33] The correspondence relative to the Dawkins mission is in F. O. (97), 115.

very flattering marks of respect and consideration. We Colombians, particularly, were the object of his special attentions and I am not ashamed to confess that my famous friend and colleague, Señor Gual, received greater consideration than any of the rest. ... He [Dawkins] limited himself to counseling that we show respect for the institutions of other countries, whatever they might be; that we not only avoid everything that might serve to increase the fears and misgivings which Europe already had relative to revolutionary principles, but that we make an effort to demonstrate that republicanism in America is not what France professed under a republican régime; that we do not confirm the suspicion that we are aiming to form a separate political system in opposition to Europe, but that we confine ourselves to looking after our own interests and to providing for our national security; that above all it was important that we give proof of a love of peace and of a disposition to embrace it, even though it were at the cost of some pecuniary sacrifice. ..." Vidaurre said that Dawkins urged the Spanish Americans to "proceed in such a way as to avoid coming into conflict with the system of Europe, as well as to avoid arousing the prejudices of America," meaning by the term "America," the United States.[34] Britain had apparently achieved another triumph, although, due to the meager results of the congress, it was of no great significance.

[34] The quotations from Méndez and Vidaurre are taken from Joseph B. Lockey, *Pan-Americanism: Its Beginnings* (New York, 1920), 372, 375.

CHAPTER VII

SPIRITED CONTESTS IN MEXICO

If much of England's early Hispanic-American policy was inspired by a desire to checkmate the United States, Mexico was considered the key to that policy. And this is true whether one refers to George Canning or to his successors at the Foreign Office.

Late in 1824, in a memorandum urging recognition of certain of the new states of Spanish America, Canning wrote: "I believe we now have the opportunity (but it may not last long) of opposing a powerful barrier to the influence of the U. S. by an amicable connection with Mexico, which from its position must be either subservient to or jealous of the U. S. In point of population and resources it is at least equal to all the rest of the Spanish colonies; and may naturally expect to take the lead in its connection with the powers of Europe. . . ."[1] Early the following year, after his recognition policy had been accepted by the Cabinet, he remarked to his friend John Hookham Frere: "The thing is done. . . . The Yankees will shout in triumph; but it is they who lose most of our decision. The great danger of the time . . . was a division of the world into European and American, Republican and

[1] Temperley, *The Foreign Policy of Canning*, 553.

Monarchial; a league of worn-out Gov[ernmen]ts, on the one hand, and of youthful and stirring Nations, with the United States at their head, on the other. *We slip in between; and plant ourselves in Mexico. The United States have gotten the start of us in vain; and we link once more America and Europe....*" [2]

The instructions written by the Earl of Dudley for Richard Pakenham three years later revealed the same sentiments. Dudley feared that Poinsett's intrigues had about succeeded in establishing the ascendancy of the United States, and Pakenham was told that England, the "natural Ally" of Mexico, could not "allow so formidable an accession to American power." [3]

I. THE BEGINNINGS OF DIPLOMATIC RELATIONS

More than two years before Canning had drawn up his recognition memorandum suspicion of the designs of the United States in Mexico had become a part of the atmosphere of the Foreign Office. Patrick Mackie, who had long resided in Mexico and established connections with the Iturbide government, had warned Canning of alleged commercial ambitions of the United States. "I am most anxious and eager," said Mackie, "to avail myself of the credit and influence I enjoy with the Emperor, the principal Officers of State, and the Congress, to counteract designs so injurious to the Interests of Great Britain."

[2] Temperley, "The Later American Policy of George Canning," *Am. Historical Rev.*, XI (1906), 782.

[3] Dudley to Pakenham, No. 9, April 21, 1828, F. O. (50), 41.

Spirited Contests in Mexico

During the course of his conferences (July and August, 1823) with Guadalupe Victoria, an agent of the provisional government which had followed the overthrow of Iturbide, Mackie had tried in vain to pledge the Mexican authorities not to sign a commercial treaty with any other Power until one had been arranged with England. Mackie doubtless had the United States mainly in mind. He also reported that Victoria held a "contemptible opinion" of the Americans and "represented them as an ambitious people always ready to encroach upon their Neighbors."[4]

The commissioners—Hervey, O'Gorman, and Ward —sent to Mexico near the close of 1823, had likewise sensed the Yankee danger. "The Mexicans," they wrote, "are looking anxiously around them in quest of an Alliance with one of the great Maritime Powers of Europe and if they should be disappointed in their hopes, they will ultimately be forced to throw themselves into the arms of the United States, already opened wide to receive them."[5]

The commissioners had been instructed (1) to report on the advisability of recognition; (2) to assure the Mexican government that Great Britain did not desire dominion over any portion of Spain's former colonies in America and would not allow them to fall "under the dominion of any other power"; and (3) tactfully to encourage the establishment of a monarchy in case

[4] The Mackie correspondence is found in F. O. (50), 1.

[5] The Mexican Commission to Canning, *loc. cit.*, III

they found Mexican leaders favorably disposed.[6] The commission was so blinded by enthusiasm for the authorities in power in Mexico and so convinced of the friendly disposition of these authorities toward England that they reported in favor of recognition after only three weeks' observation and in spite of the fact that an important revolution was then in progress. A few days later one of them (Hervey) actually guaranteed a loan in the name of the English government in order to support the Mexican officials in the crisis. For this act he was recalled and J. P. Morier was sent out to replace him.[7]

Finally, on January 3, 1825, Canning announced his intention of recognizing some of the new states of Spanish America, Mexico among them. On the same day he prepared instructions to guide his agents in the negotiation of a commercial treaty with Mexico. By April 6 they had signed an agreement which aroused great enthusiasm among the Mexican leaders. Indeed, it was so favorable to Mexico and so at variance with British policy that Canning refused to accept it.

But this did not immediately become known in Mexico City. Throughout the year 1824 and a good portion of the year 1825 Mexican officials repeatedly revealed sentiments of gratitude and cordiality toward England. In April, 1824, a public celebration of the birthday of His Majesty was seriously considered.

[6] Canning to Lionel Hervey, No. 1, Oct. 10, 1823, F. O. (50), 3.

[7] The Canning-Hervey Correspondence is found in F. O. (50), 3, 4, 5.

Early in the following January, Lucas Alamán, minister of foreign relations, evinced in his report to Congress great partiality for the British government, giving it chief credit for checking the designs of Continental Europe and mentioning the United States only incidentally.[8] Then came news of British intention to consider Mexico a member of the family of nations. Mexican officials were profoundly touched and celebrations lasted more than a week. From London the Mexican agent wrote: "The Supreme Head of all things, who directs the fate of Nations, has seen the merits and sacrifices of ours, ... and has decided the great cause in our favor. Everything is complete: England recognizes our independence...."[9] Deeply impressed, President Victoria sent for Morier, and "every word he uttered was expressive of his great satisfaction at the occurrence of an event which has [had] been the constant object of his ardent wishes." Attended by all the national authorities, Victoria proceeded in state to the cathedral in order to render thanks to the Almighty.[10] On the last day of May Ward was enthusiastically received as *chargé d'affaires.* Victoria publicly referred to England as the great nation which was accustomed to sustain the liberties

[8] Manning, *Early Diplomatic Relations between the United States and Mexico*, 52 ff.

[9] Morier to Canning, No. 22, March 12, 1825, contains this letter as an enclosure. See F. O. (50), 11.

[10] *Idem* to *idem*, Nos. 21 and 23, March 10 and 17, 1825, *loc. cit.*

of the world.[11] British popularity in Mexico had risen to a flood.

The influence of the United States, on the other hand, was on the wane. The Mexican insurgent movement had received aid and inspiration from certain citizens of the United States, although the government had maintained a strict neutrality. The extension of recognition and the proclamation of the Monroe Doctrine had been worth something. This assistance and encouragement had not been entirely unappreciated. Iturbide had expressed admiration for Henry Clay and gratitude for his services in Congress on Mexico's behalf. He had also predicted intimate relations between the two neighboring nations for the future. The provisional government which followed Iturbide's brief reign had shown an equally friendly attitude, and Mexico's first republican constitution had been closely modeled after that of the United States. But Don Luis de Onis, while agent of the Spanish government in Washington (1809-1820), had filled the Mexican archives with alarming accounts of the ambitions of the Americans of the North and had published a memorial (1820) representing them as desiring to expand southward immediately to Panama and ultimately to all the regions of the New World. These reports must have been sufficient to arouse distrust among the Mexican leaders. The menacing attitude of North American frontiersmen and utterances of dis-

[11] Ward to Canning, No. 5, June 1, 1825, and enclosure, F. O. (50), 13.

SPIRITED CONTESTS IN MEXICO

satisfaction with the western boundary of Louisiana deepened this distrust into anxiety;[12] and before the first minister of the United States arrived in Mexico the Mexican envoy at Washington had been directed to sound the Adams administration on the question of limits.[13]

Joel R. Poinsett, who reached Mexico early in May, 1825, in the capacity of envoy extraordinary and minister plenipotentiary of the United States, was not slow to grasp the situation. From Vera Cruz, on May 5, he wrote: "The British government has anticipated us. . . . Their treaty is made, and . . . has been ratified by the lower house. . . . It is now before the Senate [and] . . . no doubt appears to be entertained of the result." [14]

In some respects Poinsett was not a happy choice for the position. He was a man of culture, with a command of the Spanish language and a knowledge of the world obtained from extensive travel, but he was also a flaming evangel of republicanism and his previous career in Spanish America had given him a reputation for aggressiveness and intrigue. Information of his activities in Buenos Aires and Chile had long since reached Mexico. During his former visit

[12] It is possible that these suspicions were stimulated by Mackie, Hervey, O'Gorman, and Ward.

[13] Manning, *Early Diplomatic Relations* . . . , pp. 1-88; Onis, *Memoir*, p. 23; *La Diplomacia Mexicana. Pequeña Revista Historica* (Mexico City, 1925), 9-12.

[14] To Clay, No. 1, Mex. Desp., I (U. S. State Dept., Bureau of Indexes and Archives).

(1822) military and civil officials of the Iturbide government had shadowed his movements[15] and a secret agent who conferred with him had received the impression that Poinsett coveted for his country not only important commercial and mining concessions, but also large territorial acquisitions.[16]

II. WARD VERSUS POINSETT

President Victoria's response to Ward's presentation speech filled Poinsett with envious apprehension. It convinced the American envoy that the time had come to place the attitude of the United States toward Spanish America "in its true light." Accordingly, he took advantage of his public reception, which occurred on June 1, to congratulate the Mexican leaders upon the adoption of a republican form of government, to remind the audience of the sympathetic interest with which the people of the United States had viewed the struggle of their neighbors for independence, and to point out that England, in its official procedure toward Mexico, had merely followed the example set by the United States.[17] Three days later he wrote in a letter to Clay that the British had evidently "made good use of their time and opportunities." He then went on to

[15] On August 26, 1826, *El Sol* published what was alleged to be an order, issued by the Iturbide government in October, 1822, directing the military commanders along the coast to "keep a strict watch over Mr. Poinsett."

[16] Manning, *Early Diplomatic Relations* . . ., 289-290.

[17] Poinsett to Clay, June 4, 1825, Mex. Desp., I.

explain that the Mexican president and three members of his Cabinet were pro-British, but he also noted, hopefully, that "we have a respectable party in both houses of Congress" and that a "vast majority of the people" were friendly toward the United States and suspicious of Great Britain.[18] Longer residence in Mexico served only to deepen these convictions. "I am made sensible every day," said Poinsett on August 5, 1825, "of this disposition to court the favor of Great Britain by taking as little notice of the United States as possible."[19]

That the American envoy's summary of the situation was essentially correct is borne out by the testimony of the British *chargé* himself. On September 30, 1825, he wrote: "Mr. Pointsett [*sic*], upon his arrival here, found His Majesty's Government in possession of that influence to which it has so just a claim. He found the President and Ministers satisfied with the conduct of England, and her character standing high with the generality of the people. . . . Although the idea of an intimate union between the former colonies of Spain had long been entertained, nothing was further from the wishes of the Mexicans than to see the United States included in this fraternal bond." In brief, the two diplomats agreed respecting the sentiments of the executive and his Cabinet and disagreed only with reference to the uncertain attitude of the people.[20]

[18] *Loc. cit.*
[19] *Loc. cit.*
[20] Ward to Canning, Most private and confidential, F. O. (50), 14.

Poinsett's instructions directed him, among other things, to negotiate treaties of commerce and limits and to encourage republicanism in Mexico.[21] He soon concluded that nothing could be accomplished until a transformation had been effected in the sentiments of the Mexican executive department. He accordingly appears to have associated himself with the opposition in order to influence the Mexican president and Cabinet through the Mexican Congress. He encouraged the formation of lodges of York Rite Masons which soon became the political machine of the opposition party. The president and the conservative members of the Cabinet were alarmed. They hastened to Poinsett and assured him of their friendly disposition toward the United States. Alamán, the member most hostile to Poinsett, resigned.[22] Soon afterwards news came that Canning would not accept the treaty of April 6. It was now Ward's turn to become frightened.

The British *chargé* immediately commenced sending to his chief accounts of American designs and ambitions which corresponded exactly with the apprehensions which Canning had expressed at the time he was

[21] Clay to Poinsett, March 26, 1825, U. S. Inst. to Ministers, X.

[22] Manning, *Early Diplomatic Relations*, p. 190 ff., and authorities cited. Manning makes too much of the Cabinet reorganization. There had been friction between Victoria and Alamán for some time, and Ward was as much responsible as Poinsett for Alamán's resignation. The alleged change in the sentiments of the president and Esteva (secretary of the treasury) was mostly pretense and Poinsett knew it.

pressing his recognition policy through the British Cabinet. "It is the great object of the United States," Ward had written a few days before the Mexican Cabinet crisis, "to convince the natives of Spanish America, that there exists between them and their brethren of the North, a community of interests, in which no European power can share." "I think it highly probable," he added, "that they will take the earliest possible opportunity, of cultivating any disposition ... which might be turned to account, in event of a rupture, at any future period, with Great Britain." [23] After Ward had obtained a more complete revelation of Poinsett's views and influence, he reported: "The formation of a general American federation, from which all European Powers, but more particularly Great Britain, shall be excluded, is the great object of Mr. Poinsett's exertions." And he admitted that "many members of both chambers" had been induced to favor the project and were desirous of sanctioning it by a treaty.[24] Ward observed with no little anxiety the plans for the proposed Panama Congress, for he looked upon this gathering as the possible occasion for perfecting these Pan-American ambitions. He was particularly alarmed at the prospect that Poinsett would use his influence to secure as one of the Mexican delegates to Panama, or possibly as head of the Mexican foreign office itself, Señor Michelena, who had been

[23] To Canning, No. 32, Sept. 6-22, 1825, F. O. (50), 14.

[24] To *idem*, Most private and confidential, Sept. 30, 1825, *loc. cit.*

recalled from London at Canning's suggestion and was therefore decidedly anti-British.[25]

Under any circumstances it would have been Ward's duty to counteract the influence of the United States in Mexico. With reference to Mexico, as indeed to all Spanish America, as has already been noted, the interests and ambitions of the two branches of the Anglo-Saxon family appeared to be widely divergent. Now that Ward was convinced of the hostile purposes and power of Poinsett, he was spurred to even greater exertions. Believing that the United States had three objects in view—namely, to stultify European projects and influence in America, to procure Mexican territory, and to negotiate a commercial treaty which would embody the maritime principles of the United States and grant important privileges to its merchants—and that all of them were opposed to British interests, the British *chargé* set himself all the more firmly to checkmate every move of the American envoy.

The next two years, therefore, witnessed a spirited contest between Ward and Poinsett, in which neither employed methods entirely above reproach. Each professed an unwillingness to enter the fray, but Ward appears to have been more aggressive and uncompromising. "I cannot but regret that the Agent of the British government should imagine that whatever influence I may acquire here must of necessity be averse to the interests of the nation he represents."[26] "I never

[25] To *idem*, No. 51, Oct. 31, 1825, F. O. (50), 15.
[26] Poinsett to Rufus King, Oct. 24, 1825, Mex. Desp., I.

SPIRITED CONTESTS IN MEXICO

have and never will oppose the establishment of friendly relations between the new American States and Great Britain on such principles as are not hostile to the United States." [27] This was the spirit of Poinsett. At the same time Ward declared: "Nothing could have been further from my wish, on Mr. Poinsett's first arrival, than to enter into any contest of this description." [28] Once the struggle had begun, the British diplomat pursued his supposed foe far more relentlessly. If Poinsett sought to put through his negotiations by a sort of alliance with the *Yorkinos,* or Liberals, Ward, with greater caution and more finesse, associated himself with the opposing groups. Ward accused Poinsett of resorting to slander in order to mar the domestic felicity and destroy the influence of a fair favorite (Countess Regla) of President Victoria, but he admitted that he himself had made use of this favorite in order to carry out his purposes. He accused the American envoy of encouraging the publication of propaganda calculated to foment suspicion against Great Britain and advance the commercial and political aspirations of the United States, but Poinsett alleged that Ward had published literature designed to prevent the negotiation of a satisfactory commercial treaty by the United States, and Ward's own correspondence shows that, with the view of fomenting suspicion of the Yankees, he had expended funds in pre-

[27] *Idem* to Clay, July 12, 1826, *loc. cit.*

[28] Ward to Canning, *Most private and confidential*, Sept. 30, 1825, F. O. (50), 14.

paring a map of Texas and in reprinting the abusive Onis memorial. Each diplomat gave banquets and omitted to invite his rival in order that the occasion might be used to disparage and destroy the prestige of the nation whose minister was conspicuous by his absence. Ward eagerly seized upon every opportunity to discredit Poinsett, carrying to the Mexican president numerous reports of the American's utterances and making frequent appeals to the personal prejudices of the chief executive. Recalled early in 1827, the British *chargé* reported, with evident exultation, that Poinsett had not been invited to the farewell reception given in Ward's honor.[29]

As a matter of fact, Ward was largely responsible for the beginning of the diplomatic conflict in Mexico and the line which it followed. In the summer of 1825 he was still under thirty, but he had back of him nearly ten years' *attaché* experience at the minor courts of Europe. He had come to Mexico with a young wife and a growing family, ardent patriotism, great enthusiasm for his chief, and an eagerness to make a career in the service. Although his later activities in the House of Commons were to win for him the reputation of an "advanced liberal," in Mexico he did not find his associates among men of that temper. In order to

[29] The statements in this paragraph are based upon letters of Poinsett and Ward, too numerous to cite in detail. They may be consulted in the archives of the State Department and the Foreign Office. Ward was in very close touch with the conservative leader Nicolás Bravo, as well as with Victoria, Pedraza, and Esteva.

secure the signature and ratification of the treaty of April 6, 1825, defective as it later appeared to Canning, he had distributed small gifts with a free hand and entertained at elaborate banquets. His expenses for the quarter beginning April 5 had amounted to over $7,000, and the following was his apology: "From the peculiar circumstances in which I was placed, with regard to the ratification of the Treaty, and the difficulty of carrying it through the Senate, it was necessary to make the house of the mission a rendezvous for all those, who had declared themselves in favour of the cause of Great Britain." [30] Most of the newspapers and reactionary politicians had been lined up on his side and he had virtually become the head of a party. Even the president's private secretary (Tornel) and the Colombian minister (Santa María) had appeared in print as the champions of Great Britain.[31] "I found the British united with the Aristocratic and Monarchical party who governed the country . . . ," [32] Poinsett afterwards declared when summing up the situation as it appeared to him in the summer of 1825; and he was probably not far wrong.

At the very beginning of his negotiations (August, 1825) and before he had made any attempt to organize his friends, Poinsett found himself handicapped by Ward's interference. Separation of the boundary and

[30] Ward to Canning, Aug. 17, 1825, F. O. (97), 272.

[31] *Idem* to *idem*, May 17-20, 1825, F. O. (50), 12.

[32] To Van Buren, March 10, 1829, Manning, *Diplomatic Correspondence*, III, 1679.

commercial issues was soon agreed upon, but when Poinsett pressed the latter in the hope of a speedy settlement, he encountered insuperable difficulties. Following his instructions, he urged the principle of reciprocity, but met with firm opposition on this point. The part played by Ward in this initial disagreement is revealed by his own letter: "From M. Esteva, I learnt, at an early period of the negotiations, that perfect reciprocity was at first insisted upon.... Against this, I of course told him that I should protest, as Mexico had refused to assent to it in the treaty with Great Britain, and assigned the non-existence of this reciprocity as a plea for her refusal. It certainly did not exist in a greater degree between Mexico and the United States, and consequently the principles, which had been applied to us, must be applied to them. To this Mr. Esteva gave his full assent...."[33]

The question of reciprocity was therefore dropped for a time and Poinsett and the Mexican negotiators took up the closely related topic of the "most-favored-nation." Once more he found the way blocked, and in part by the attitude of Ward. The Mexican government was not opposed to this principle in general, but it desired to make an exception in favor of the Spanish-American states, as had been done in the British treaty of April 6. Ambitious to play an important rôle among these states, Victoria looked upon this preference in their favor as a means of increasing Mexico's prestige among them. Accordingly, the

[33] To Canning, No. 32, Sept. 6, 1825, F. O. (50), 14.

SPIRITED CONTESTS IN MEXICO

Mexican diplomats insisted upon this exception. Poinsett, foreseeing trouble, had already gone to Ward and urged him to protest against the clause in the British treaty which related to the matter; and, strangely enough, Ward had complied by sending in such a protest on August 9.[34] The note had remained unanswered, however, and Poinsett, determined not to admit the discrimination in favor of the Spanish-Americans and convinced that he could accomplish nothing until the sentiments of the executive authorities had undergone a modification, had played some part in the Cabinet change which occurred between September 23 and 26.[35] At about the same period, Poinsett appealed again to Ward, urging him to demand an answer to his protest against the special concession in favor of the Spanish-American states. But by this time, if not indeed before,[36] Ward had become suspicious and hostile. He had learned both from Poinsett and Esteva that the American minister was so violently opposed to the discrimination that he would never consent to the negotiation of a treaty embracing it. He had also been given the impression that Poinsett's opposition arose from the feeling that the provision would interfere with the Pan-American

---

[34] Ward to *idem*, No. 42, Sept. 27-28, 1825, *loc. cit.*; Poinsett to Rufus King, Oct. 10, 1825, Manning, *Dilpomatic Correspondence*, III, 1634.

[35] *Antea*, 256.

[36] Ward's change in attitude appears to have occurred between September 22 and 27.

schemes of the United States. Thus there were two reasons why Ward became unwilling to insist upon the removal of the exception in the interest of the Spanish Americans. An impediment which tended to delay the negotiation of a Mexican-American commercial treaty and at the same time appeared to interfere with Poinsett's project of unity among the states of the Western Hemisphere must not be removed by the hand of a Briton. Ward therefore decided to withdraw the note altogether![37] On September 28 the United States and Mexican plenipotentiaries dropped the entire negotiation and it was not resumed for almost seven months.[38]

Thus Ward had won the first contest. But he was still uneasy. From the last days of September to the end of October he beheld the growing influence of Poinsett with terrified amazement. The treaty between Britain and Mexico was still pending and

[37] "I had protested against the clause in question; and reserved to His Majesty's Government the right of taking, with regard to it, such measures as might be deemed expedient:—Circumstances occurred afterwards, connected with Mr. Poinsett's views here, which induced me to withdraw this note, in order to prevent the conclusion of a treaty between Mexico and the United States, on terms which I could not but regard as detrimental to the interests of Great Britain; and I have even gone so far . . . as to express to General Victoria my opinion, that His Majesty's Government would admit the exception in favor of the former Spanish colonies, provided the United States were obliged to submit to it likewise:—My object in taking this step has been attained, and the treaty with the United States is still pending in consequence. . . ." Ward to Canning, No. 68, Dec. 15, 1825, F. O. (50), 14.

[38] Manning, *Early Diplomatic Relations*, 220.

there was a chance that Canning would demand very substantial modifications. Ward had little hope that a treaty so modified would be accepted by the Mexican government. As he surveyed the Cabinet he saw only one member, Señor Esteva, whose coöperation could be counted upon, and even this member might be "kept in awe by Mr. Poinsett's party in the chambers, which he is [was] anxious to conciliate." President Victoria's disposition toward England was still very favorable, but unless he felt sure of success he would never risk his popularity. Everything depended, therefore, upon the Mexican Congress, and its temper was certainly not encouraging. The influence of the American "Junta" was "so great, that on any question, in which the interests of England came into competition with those of the United States, Mr. Poinsett, in despite of the efforts of the Government, ... would obtain a majority in both chambers against us." [39]

On October 10 Ward became so excited that he sent a special messenger to England in order to lay the situation before Canning and counsel moderation and delay. Meanwhile, he continued, as before, to make his mission "a rendezvous" for the friends of England, in order, as he said, "to prepare the way for the Treaty." From the first of October to the end of the year 1825 the expenses of his establishment amounted to more than $15,000! [40]

[39] To Canning, No. 44, Oct. 8-17, 1825, F. O. (50), 15.

[40] Separates to Canning and to Planta, F. O. (97), 272.

Ward's excitement even caused Poinsett some uneasiness. Poinsett's hostility toward England appeared to be far less than that of Ward toward the United States. In fact, Poinsett felt, or pretended to feel, that the two countries had many common interests and few irreconcilable differences in the matter of their relations with the new states of America. When he heard that Ward was preparing to dispatch a special courier to London he requested a conference with his antagonist. He also sent an explanatory letter to Rufus King in which he suggested that the subject might be discussed with Canning.

Ward's account of the interview with Poinsett is important. "In the conversation," said Ward, Poinsett "most solemnly denied many things which had been attributed to him, and which had tended to inspire me with a belief, that his Hostility towards England, and European Interests in General, had evinced itself in a Manner which might almost be called *personal*. — He protested that with regard to commerce, he neither demanded more than a fair competition, nor had ever lent himself to any Project, by which the commercial interests of Great Britain could be affected. As to the Junta, of which so much had been said, he had not created it, but had been almost forced into it:—He had never yet made use of it for political purposes, although he could not deny that he regarded it as a means of acquiring political Influence; but that I might rest assured that he had neither there, nor any where else, expressed sentiments calculated to discourage the Mexicans from entering into the most intimate connexion with the Nations of Europe, *if they preferred it;* although, as a good American, he had naturally endeavoured to inspire them with Feelings of a still more amicable nature towards his own Country.

"I told Mr. Poinsett in reply, that it was with the utmost Satisfaction that I heard him disavow Expressions of a very unpleasant nature, which certainly had been very generally attributed to him, and which were calculated to disturb that good understanding which I hoped would always prevail between us:—that after what he had said, with regard to himself, I should forget that entirely; but that as to the Junta at which he presided he must excuse me if I did not consider it as any thing *but* a Political Machine, and one which might become highly dangerous to the Interests of Great Britain;—Without rendering him in any way responsible for the imprudent Language held by the Members of the Junta, he must be aware that from the circumstance of Eighty Persons having been present at some of the Meetings, it was impossible that what passed there could have remained long a Secret: and that I consequently, was perfectly aware that Sentiments had been expressed, which, as an Englishman, could not but alarm and irritate me: I added, that so long as this system was persevered in, and opinions circulated which I could not but consider as detrimental to the Interests of my Country, he could not expect my Feelings towards those who took the leading part in this Assembly to be of the most friendly nature.

"Mr. Poinsett asked to what Opinions I had alluded?—I told him more particularly to the Continental System of the New World, (as it is pompously entitled)—the Grand American Federation,—of which the United States were to be the Head, and every Member of which was to enjoy Privileges, in which no European Power could share:—Mr. Poinsett replied that these Privileges were merely *political;* that with regard to commercial Advantages, none could exist—and that we should always find his Government ready to *respect* the commercial Interests of every other Nation, and more particularly those of Great Britain: As to a more intimate Political connexion with the New States of South America, the United States certainly thought themselves entitled to it from the circumstance of their being in possession of no inconsiderable Portion of the same Continent; but upon this Subject their Sentiments had been communicated to you, and had received your unqualified Approbation:— The only Bar which existed at present to the execution of the Plan, which, he must again assure me, had received the Sanction of the British Government, was the Art. in our treaty with Mexico, by which we consented to allow certain special privileges to be conceded to each other by the Spanish American States, and thus separated them from the rest of the Continent.—This Art. he will never consent to; and yet, from the Fact of its having been admitted in our

Spirited Contests in Mexico

Treaty, he found the Mexican Government very unwilling to dispense with it in that with the United States. He was therefore, most anxious that I should insist upon an Answer to my note of the 9th of August, in which, as I had myself informed him, I had protested against this very clause; a Step by which he was perfectly sure that I had only consulted your wishes.

"I informed Mr. Poinsett in Reply that such, of course, was the Impression under which I had thought it my Duty to write this note; but that circumstances had since occurred, which had induced me to change my opinion entirely: I had no instructions at all with respect to the Plan of an American Federation . . . , — and I was therefore bound to be guided by those general Principles which His Majesty's Ministers had invariably laid down, and which certainly did not provide either for political, or commercial Privileges. . . . I myself looked upon political Influence as the only guarantee for commercial Security; I should . . . certainly not take upon myself to determine whether the Influence of Great Britain would be increased or not, by rendering the American Federation, if it must exist, partial, instead of general: This was a point which His Majesty's Government must decide; and in order to leave them at perfect Liberty, I had withdrawn my note and referred the question Home.

"Mr. Poinsett did not . . . conceal his Disappointment at this Intelligence, and expressed very strongly his conviction that my reasons for doing what I had done, would not meet with your Approbation: Indeed, so convinced was he of this, he said, that he had sent a Letter through me to Mr. King, . . . requesting him to see you upon this subject, and to represent to you that upon this Point, as indeed upon all, at present, the two Countries had but one Interest.

". . . I may undoubtedly be mistaken, and Mr. Poinsett may be right, in asserting that His Majesty's Government conceives the interests of the United States and England in the New World to be intimately connected; but as there is nothing in the present state of affairs, in which I can trace this perfect community of Interests, I do not feel myself justified in acting as if I had received Instructions upon the Subject from yourself: I shall therefore, do my utmost to encourage a Feeling in favour of Europe, and of England in particular, and shall even endeavour to promote that Predisposition, which already exists, in favour of a Federation amongst the Spanish American States, provided I can convince the Mexicans, that none *but* these States ought to be admitted into it.

"Mr. Poinsett told me candidly that this was impossible: that the question was not to be decided here, or in any other single State: but that at Panama it *would* be decided, in spite of all the Endeavours of England to oppose it. I admitted the possibility of this, but added that the Decision would be very much facilitated, if His Majesty's Diplomatic Agents, in each single State, allowed those of the United States to disseminate their Opinions without Contradiction, and thus to prepare the way for the Attainment of their Views." [41]

In his letter to King, Poinsett presented an account of the contest then being waged as well as his own version of the interview with Ward. "I . . . stated," wrote Poinsett, "that if G. Britain ratified the treaty with an exception so injurious to her commerce, her only motive could be to create distinctions, which might divide the Republics of America, whereas it was our interest and that of both the Americas, that they should be closely united. This opinion became public, for there are no secrets in Mexico, and opened Mr. Ward's eyes to what he imagines to be the true interests of Great Britain. In consequence, he withdrew his note, and set about forming an European party in opposition to that he thinks organized by me. Both these measures are, in my opinion, impolitic and calculated to prejudice the interests of Great Britain. The withdrawal of his note has confirmed the opinion I expressed, and the attempt to form a party strictly European in this country will only produce the effect of confounding Great Britain with the other European powers, whereas it appears to have been her policy, as it is manifestly her interest, to separate herself as much as possible from them in relation to American affairs. I never have confounded Great Britain with the powers of Europe that are hostile to the independence and liberties of these countries. I have considered her interests identified with ours in the cause of Amer-

[41] Ward to Canning, No. 45, Oct. 17, 1825, F. O. (50), 15.

ican emancipation and in the defence of free government, and came here disposed to make common cause with her envoy for the extension of liberal principles of trade for the mutual protection of our industry and capital and for the diffusion of more tolerant religious sentiments. In this sense I have hitherto acted; but if Great Britain seeks to divide the Americas, or strives to destroy the principles of Republican Government which are taking root in these countries, or to create a party strictly European and therefore adverse to our interests, her Ministers must not complain if we exert all our influence to counteract their views. If I were inimical to the interests of Great Britain in these countries, I would invite such a contest; I am not, and therefore deprecate it. It does not appear to me to be consistent with the policy of Great Britain to provoke it; I can venture to predict, that it will not prove her interest to do so.

"Learning that Mr. Ward was about to dispatch a courier to London . . . , I sought an interview with him and frankly explained my opinion of the course he seems disposed to pursue—of its impolicy and inefficacy. I am afraid he thinks I have made a tool of him, and is vexed and mortified because he was induced to send in the note protesting against the exception made in the 4th article of the Treaty; there certainly was no intention on my part to injure him or the interests of the nation he represents by advising him to take that step. In my opinion, the interests of Great Britain have been much more seriously affected by the withdrawal of that note." [42]

Thus the two diplomats were in opposition to each other and the conference had failed to bring about a reconciliation. Poinsett was encouraging a system of liberal, federal republics politically isolated from Europe; Ward was opposing the "division of the World into European and American, Republican and Monarchical," with the United States at the head of the American republican group. Moreover, each feared that the influence of his rival would be employed for economic ends and—in the case of Ward, but not so surely in that of Poinsett—in support of hostile maritime principles. Poinsett doubted whether Ward represented the real views of his government; Ward never doubted that Poinsett was acting upon orders received from headquarters. Their relations never again became cordial. For the chasm which separated them some of the Mexican politicians had been, and continued to be, partially responsible.[43]

That the fears and jealousies of the two diplomats were shared by their respective governments hardly needs to be repeated. Poinsett's early reports of British ascendancy in Mexico had brought instructions on this point. Poinsett was told that, although the prevailing influence of England in Mexico was regretted, it could hardly be made the subject of formal complaint unless

[42] Manning, *Diplomatic Correspondence*, III, 1634-1635.

[43] *Cf.* Poinsett to King, Oct. 14, 1825, Mex. Desp., I; Ward to Canning No. 42, Sept. 27-28, 1825, F. O. (50), 14.

it should be employed so as to secure special privileges for the British to the detriment of American interests. Against any such use of English power and prestige he was directed to remonstrate.[44] From London Ward received a letter approving his opposition to Poinsett. "In all that relates to the watching and counteracting of the Intrigues of the American Minister Mr. Poinsett, you appear to have exercised a judgment as sound, as your zeal has been meritorious." [45] These were the words of Canning after he had read the despatches written by Ward during the period of his greatest anxiety. Rufus King's interview, which occurred a little later, may have effected a slight modification in Canning's views of what Poinsett was doing. At the beginning of the interview King had placed all of Poinsett's letters — all that Poinsett had written to King—before the British foreign secretary. "Mr. Canning expressed his satisfaction with the conduct of Mr. Poinsett in all respects, with the single exception of his establishing a Lodge of Free Masons, this he had no inclination to condemn, but as it was a measure liable to the interpretation of political views, it was discouraged by them [the English], as respects their own agents—that the course of Mr. Ward had been incorrect, he ought to have left the whole matter in which he interfered, to his own government. . . ." [46]

[44] Manning, *Early Diplomatic Relations*, 75.

[45] Canning to Ward, No. 1, Jan. 7, 1826, F. O. (50), 19.

[46] King to Clay, Feb. 21, 1826, Manning, *Diplomatic Correspondence*, III, 1581.

But this somewhat non-committal statement should not be taken too seriously. Canning's conviction that the policies of the two nations were antagonistic could not lightly be removed, and their policies were fundamentally different. This is clearly revealed by Canning's decision, already reached in the summer of 1825, to reject the treaty of April 6. With the exception of the provision reserving the power to grant special favors to the Spanish-American states, there was probably nothing in this document that the United States would not have been willing to put into its own commercial treaty with Mexico. Yet—and it was for this very reason—Canning and the men who advised him strenuously objected to many of its stipulations. William Huskisson, upon whose advice Canning mainly relied, summed up his own opposition by the statement that the treaty contained "everything which the United States could wish for in such an Instrument." [47]

Englishmen perused the document with the spectre of American privateers and merchantmen constantly before them. Did it define a national vessel so as to encourage the growth of a Mexican merchant marine? In time of peace the Yankees might profit by placing their vessels under the Mexican flag, and in case of a war between England and the United States, in which Mexico should be a neutral, they would certainly transfer the whole of their commerce to the Mexican flag and thus nullify the effect of the British blockade.

[47] Huskisson to Canning, Aug. 20, 1825, Huskisson Papers, XIV (MS., British Museum, London).

Did the treaty reserve to Mexico the right, as the price of recognition, to grant to Spain certain privileges which would not be extended to any other European Power? The clause was worded so loosely that it might allow the United States to obtain special concessions in the matter of tonnage dues and customs duties; moreover, it would leave Mexico "at liberty to grant to Spain greater privileges than to England," while restraining her "from giving to Spain the like advantage over the U. States of America." Did the agreement contain a stipulation in favor of the provinces of America which had formerly been Spanish possessions? Louisiana and the Floridas might be embraced under this clause! In brief, the treaty contained too many provisions in favor of neutrals without navies, and Britain was seeking to guard the interests of a great belligerent maritime power. Perhaps Mexico should not aspire to sea power anyway. She had no shipbuilders or seamen, "no convenient Ports or safe Harbours." She should concentrate her efforts on military power as the means of territorial security and defence and seek intimate relations with Great Britain. "The natural connexion of such a State is with the great Maritime Power of Europe, from which she can be under no apprehension of encroachment on her Territory, or of interference with her Station and Rights on the continent of America." [48]

[48] William Huskisson (head of the Board of Trade) to Canning, July 25, Aug. 3, and Sept. 8, 1825, F. O. (50), 18; Canning to Ward, No. 9, Sept. 9, 1825, F. O. (50), 9.

Nothing ever occurred afterwards which essentially changed Canning's views with reference to the pact of April 6 and its relation to the maritime ambitions of the United States. In fact, news of the publication of the document before its ratification and the appearance of hostile attacks on England in the Mexican press led him to assume an even more uncompromising attitude. On October 14, 1825, he wrote Ward that the new treaty must be "signed precisely according to the Project which you are instructed to bring forward, or not at all." [49]

The several instructions relating to the negotiations did not reach Mexico City until near the middle of December, and Morier, who was again associated with Ward in the task, did not arrive until almost a month later.[50] By this time Ward was in a calmer mood with reference to the machinations of Poinsett. In fact he had for some time felt that the "American Junta" was beginning to disintegrate. Yet he was still far from confident. His instructions were rigid and the Mexican Congress would again have to be confronted.

Negotiations on the new project began on January 20, 1826, and continued without interruption for four days, at the end of which it became clear that the Mexican government was very loath to agree to the provisions which tended to limit the development of its shipping. The project defined a Mexican vessel as

[49] F. O. (50), 9.

[50] Ward to Canning, No. 51, Oct. 31, 1825; *idem* to *idem*, No. 68, Dec. 15, 1825; and *passim*, all in F. O. (50), 15 and 16.

one built in Mexico and owned by a citizen or citizens thereof, provided its master and three-fourths of its crew were Mexicans; but the Mexican government was eager to employ sailors of all countries and ships of every construction, and therefore objected to the definition. On January 26 it was decided that Sebastián Camacho, the Mexican foreign secretary, should accompany Morier to England in order to discuss this point with Canning. Apparently it had not occurred to President Victoria at this time that the Senate's approval of Camacho for the mission would be necessary. The foreign secretary became ill, however, and another agent had to be chosen. Victoria appointed Gómez Pedraza, who was at that time secretary for war, and then asked the Senate to give its consent. The Senate refused and the British agents at once concluded that Poinsett was largely responsible. Another contest was on.[51]

Morier interviewed Poinsett in regard to the matter. Poinsett said that his interference had been limited to advising, when his counsel was asked, that the Senate had the right to confirm or reject diplomatic appointments; but he expressed the conviction that the Senate would never allow one of the ministers to proceed to England. The situation was not promising, and Morier set out for London on March 18, without waiting for the appointment of the Mexican agent.[52]

[51] The correspondence relating to the new treaty will be found in F. O. (97), 271.

[52] Morier and Ward to Canning, March 17, 1826, F. O. (97), 272.

Spirited Contests in Mexico 279

After Pedraza's rejection the president seems to have decided definitely upon Camacho for the London mission. To this Poinsett objected, as he reported to Clay,[53] because the absence of the foreign secretary would delay his own negotiations regarding pecuniary claims. He prepared to rally his friends and exert his influence.[54]

At the same time, Ward began to call together the pro-English leaders, playing upon the prejudices of Victoria, urging those who were absent—particularly General Bravo—to hasten back to the City, throwing the doors of the legation wide open, spending lavish sums on food and wine, and threatening a rupture in the relations of England and Mexico and a complete exposure of this "tissue of intrigues," in the British Parliament, if Camacho was not sent to London. He even went so far as to circulate a letter threatening a break unless the Senate ratified the appointment.[55]

While in the heat of the fight both antagonists found time (March 29) to attend an Irish banquet. It was a perilous thing to do. Not only the Irish in Mexico, but also "all the principal persons of the country" were present. An Irishman gave a toast to "The President of the United States, and the uninterrupted prosperity of that great Republic." In response, Poin-

[53] Feb. 1, 1826, Manning, *Diplomatic Correspondence*, III, 1651.

[54] For Ward's account of this interference, *see* Ward to Canning, No. 22, Secret and confidential, March 25, 1826, F. O. (50), 20.

[55] *Ibid.* and Separate of March 18, 1826, *loc. cit.*

sett referred to the Irish struggle for civil and religious liberty. He expressed the hope that they would soon enjoy these liberties in their own country as fully as they might now enjoy them in the United States. It was a clever move. "To the Irish," as Ward remarked, "he was sustaining the cause of liberality; to the Mexicans, that of the Catholic Religion:—To the English, he could maintain that he only used the language of many, whose names were most deservedly dear to them;—and yet, the result of the whole was, to produce an impression as unfair as it was unfavourable to the Government and Country."[56] The sensitive Ward was furious. He waited for his chance, and arose, alluding in no uncertain terms to Poinsett's alleged interference in the politics of Mexico. He said that there was one noble restraint which the Irish had always exercised: "during the whole course of their struggle for those Rights to which they conceived themselves so justly entitled, they had never either sought the interference, or solicited the sympathy of a Foreign Power!" The atmosphere suddenly became chilly and tense. Some of the principal personages decided it was time to leave, and Ward himself soon withdrew.[57]

The event furnished the occasion for the second attempt of Poinsett to conciliate his rival. He went to O'Gorman, now the British consul-general, with an explanation. He had meant no offense by his speech

[56] Ward to Canning, No. 24, March 30-April 1, 1826, *loc. cit.*
[57] *Ibid.*

Spirited Contests in Mexico 281

at the St. Patrick's Day Banquet. Moreover, "during the whole period of his stay" in Mexico, he had "never ... uttered ... the slightest expression either inimical or unfavourable to Great Britain." He had "always ... had (excepting during the late war ...) a strong personal partiality towards the English, and ... as a public man he [knew] too well the cordiality and intimate Relations subsisting between the two countries and their perfect agreement as to the Line to be adopted with these New States, to have thought of crossing us in any way." He was "persuaded" that Ward had suffered himself to be misled by tale-bearers. Plenty of tales had been brought to him regarding Ward, but he had refused to listen to them, and he defied "any man to bring home to *him* any one Action or Expression" which could rightly cause the British *chargé* the slightest displeasure or give him "any uneasiness as the Representative of Great Britain." [58]

O'Gorman carried the explanation to Ward and the British *chargé* made the consul-general the medium of a reply. Ward said he would forget the unfortunate speech at the Irish banquet, but frankly declared that he considered the general line of Poinsett's conduct in Mexico to be hostile toward England and hence one which it was the duty of England's agent to oppose. "This Impression may originate in Prejudice, or in a want of proper Information," said Ward. He then continued: "Mr. Poinsett will, however, do me the Justice to acknowledge that if, upon his Arrival, there

[58] O'Gorman to Ward, March 30, 1826, *loc. cit.*

existed any Prejudice or Predisposition on my Part, it was all in his Favour: I went with him Heart and Hand, until I thought I could not conscientiously do so any longer: nor did I affect any sort of mystery when I changed my Opinion, and my Conduct: I did it with Reluctance,—nay more,—with Regret, and I told Mr. Poinsett so in the month of October last. . . . Since then, I will not affect to deny that my Sentiments have continued the same;—and Mr. Poinsett must himself allow that either he has more reason to complain of Public Opinion than any man breathing, or that he is a decided political Enemy of Great Britain.

"I wish the greatest stress to be laid on the Term *Political*, because, in every other respect, I not only admit, but acknowledge with real Gratitude, that personal partiality towards England which Mr. Poinsett has evinced by his uniform Kindness to every Englishman whom chance has thrown in his way:—*Personally* he must be looked up to, and liked by us all, and you can bear witness that I have invariably been the first to do justice to his Abilities, and to say, what I really feel, that were I fortunate enough to meet Mr. Poinsett in any part of the World, where I could be convinced that the Interests of our Countries were, indeed, the same, there is no man whose Intimacy I should more court. . . ." [59]

So the second attempt at reconciliation failed and the fight for the Senate's acceptance of the Camacho mission continued. On April 7 that body finally gave

[59] Ward to O'Gorman, April 1, 1826, *loc. cit.*

its sanction, and on the next day Ward wrote in high exultation that the "Americans" had been "fairly forced to quit the Field." The vote was 23 to 4. Victoria had been "indefatigable"; Bravo had hurried to the Capital to aid the cause; "all those who regard[ed] a connexion with England as essential to the interests" of Mexico "sided with the Government; and ... many, even of Mr. Poinsett's adherents, finding that there would be a majority against them, endeavoured to make a merit with the President by offering him their votes."

The fight had been won, and Ward congratulated himself and England. "Had I not had recourse to most decided measures ... the People here would have been hurried blindly on, and wd. not have been aware till too late of the Scheme which had been laid for their Destruction. That this Scheme was to involve Mexico in a Dispute with England, ... to create a Feeling of Hostility between the two Countries, and thus to induce the President to throw himself into the arms of the United States, I have not the least doubt. Thank Heaven, it has failed; and we stand on higher Ground at present, than we have done for long." [60]

Poinsett's terse note to Clay showed that he had not failed to observe something of what was going on around him. "Yesterday," wrote Poinsett on April 8, "the appointment of Dn. Sebastian Camacho ... was approved by Senate. It appears, that the President, before he had communicated his intentions to Senate, had solemnly engaged himself to send one of the Secre-

[60] To Planta, Private, April 8, 1826, F. O. (50), 20.

taries composing the Cabinet to continue the negotiations and conclude the Treaty in London." "The British *Chargé*," Poinsett continued, "went so far as to say, that none other but a Minister of State would be received, and, that by refusing to ratify the nomination of Camacho, the Senate would occasion a rupture between the two powers—conduct, which could only be imputed to the secret influence of those who sought to divide the old world from the new, in order that they might govern the latter—meaning, of course, the United States." Poinsett also expressed the conviction that the "hints thrown out from time to time by the English, of the ambitious views entertained by our government, would be disregarded, if they were not corroborated by statements" coming from other sources.[61]

Ward naturally felt much easier in regard to the influence of Poinsett during the ensuing year. After much delay Camacho got off to London. The English government made some slight concessions in the course of the further negotiations, and, late in February, 1827, the treaty was brought back to Mexico for ratification. It was accepted without difficulty. The British had their way.[62]

Meanwhile, Poinsett encountered no end of difficulty. Owing in part to Ward's hostility, negotiations

[61] To Clay, Manning, *Diplomatic Correspondence*, III, 1656.

[62] Ward to Canning, No. 39, March 2, 1827, F. O. (50), 31; and for a copy of the final treaty, *see British and Foreign State Papers*, XIV, 614 ff.

on the commercial treaty were not resumed until May, 1826. By July 10, Poinsett had agreed to a pact far less favorable to the United States than Ward's had been to England but embodying some of the maritime principles of the United States and a few safeguards for its merchants. Yet the Mexican government was so suspicious that it refused at first to submit the document to the chambers, and when it finally did so the agreement was repeatedly rejected.[63]

The main objection to the pact was due to the absence of a stipulation accepting the boundary fixed by the Spanish treaty of 1819 as the dividing line between the United States and Mexico. And here, too, the hand of Ward can probably be seen; for he had constantly sought to alarm Mexico with reference to the security of Texas, and on March 31, 1827, he wrote the following admission to Canning: "I have no hesitation . . . in expressing my conviction, both publicly and privately, that the great end of Mr. Poinsett's Mission . . . is to embroil Mexico in a Civil War, and to facilitate . . . the Acquisition of the Provinces to the North of the Rio Bravo. . . ." [64]

Still, Ward's path was not all lined with roses, despite his successful encounters with his rival. In the course of less than two years he had spent more than $50,000 in making his mission the "rendezvous of the friends of England" as Poinsett had made his establishment a meeting place for those of the United States:

[63] Manning, *Early Diplomatic Relations*, Ch. VII.

[64] F. O. (50), 31.

—and the British government was bent on economy. Ward was accordingly recalled for his extravagance, but commended for his zeal, and he left Mexico in April, 1827, with income diminished by disallowed accounts, a liver injured by malaria, and a gloomy pessimism regarding his future career. The British merchants had been more appreciative, but this was small consolation. They had given him a farewell reception, with many tokens of esteem, and he had concealed a broken heart while he declared it to be "one of the proudest moments of" his life. President Victoria, too, had tendered a farewell dinner; but Ward departed from the scene of his contests with only three consoling thoughts: he had done his duty, the designs of the United States had been checked, and neither the American minister nor a single Yorkino Mason had been invited to share Victoria's hospitality at the valedictory feast![65]

III. POINSETT AND PAKENHAM

After the exciting contests of the previous months, the relations between Poinsett and Richard Pakenham, who came to Mexico in the spring of 1827 as the *chargé d'affaires* of the English government, appear smooth and calm. Yet the two diplomats were far from cordial. Their sympathies were with opposing

[65] The correspondence regarding Ward's accounts and his recall is in F. O. (97), 272. *See* also Ward to Canning, Separate and Private, April 18, 1827, F. O. (50), 32; and his No. 58, of the same date, to Canning, *loc. cit.*

parties in Mexico and they were ever suspicious of each other. Given the same incentives, their clashes might have been just as exciting.

Poinsett always considered the new British agent as a rival ready to oppose the interests of the United States and eager to inculcate in Mexico both a leaning toward monarchy and a disposition to face toward Europe. In his correspondence and publications Pakenham was seldom referred to by name, but he was frequently alluded to in a manner which leaves little doubt as to his identity. In 1828, for instance, Poinsett wrote that "the agents of certain European powers" had represented the United States as the "natural" enemy of Mexico, and so had interfered with the conclusion of a treaty of limits.[66] At about the same time he reported that the diplomatic corps in Mexico City had openly advocated the cause of the insurgents led by Nicolás Bravo.[67] Near the close of the following years he wrote: "If we were disposed to judge of the views of the British Government from the conduct of their representatives in Mexico, we should see in them much that was . . . very unfriendly to the United States. We refer to the singular coalition which they formed, as far as their influence extended, to exclude the Minister of the United States from all their social parties, as if there was contagion in his republicanism; to their not only permitting, but encouraging, toasts to be given at their convivial meet-

[66] Manning, *Early Diplomatic Relations*, 319.

[67] *Ibid.*, 354.

ings, hostile to the government he represents; to their intimate union with the aristocratic faction, even when in open rebellion against the government to which they are accredited." [68] It seems evident that in some of these statements Poinsett had Pakenham in mind.

Against these policies, real or imaginary, Poinsett continued to proceed with firm resolution. They furnished the mainspring of his activities from 1827 to 1829 as they had during the previous two years. His sympathies were with the plain people and the disinherited masses. To Martin Van Buren, a lieutenant of the new democracy in the United States, he expressed his anxieties in a somewhat alarming fashion: "The great Powers of Europe have established their separate influences over the inferior Nations of that continent after a long struggle with each other; and it must be manifest, that the contest for power will be renewed in America. Are we to take no part in this contest? ... If we do not exercise a direct and salutary influence over the councils of the American States we ought not to permit any European Nation to do so. Is it not obvious that if Great Britain should establish such a dominion over this Country as she exercises over Portugal, that this state of things might prove highly detrimental to our Interests? That this ambitious Nation has attempted and will continue to exert her vast means to effect this object cannot be doubted. In my opinion the United States ought not to permit it,

[68] Quoted from a long article which appeared in the Philadelphia *National Gazette* of Dec. 14 and 15, 1829.

SPIRITED CONTESTS IN MEXICO

and with this view of the Subject I have acted...."[69] Here, then, is a viewpoint and an admission, and in his efforts to counteract European influence in Mexico, Poinsett became more and more involved in Mexican politics, until finally the very men he tried to assist turned upon him and demanded his recall.

Pakenham, for his part, was scarcely less apprehensive with reference to his rival, but he held himself more aloof from the domestic affairs of Mexico. He observed and reported—sometimes calmly, sometimes with considerable agitation, but he seldom violated diplomatic decorum. He appears to have made up his mind in regard to his antagonist from the outset. Before he had been in Mexico a month he declared that Poinsett's "recall, particularly at the present moment, would be a very fortunate occurrence."[70]

From this early conclusion he never varied. After a conference with John Sergeant, American envoy to the Congress of Tacubaya, he reported his belief that Sergeant would inform the United States government "of the opinion entertained of Mr. Poinsett, by all persons interested in the welfare" of Mexico. He then added: "It cannot be denied, that he [Poinsett] has identified himself with a set of people whose object appears to be nothing short of bringing about a revolution...."[71] The British *chargé* was convinced that

[69] Despatch of March 10, 1829, Manning, *Diplomatic Correspondence*, III, 1678-1679.

[70] To Canning, No. 8, May 7, 1827, F. O. (50), 34.

[71] To *idem*, No. 22, June 17, 1827, *loc. cit.*

the "American party," as he called it, embraced most of the rascals and ignoramuses of Mexico and he felt that the sympathies of "respectable" people must be on the other side.[72] Moreover, he declared in this connection that Poinsett was "endeavouring by any means, or at any expense of character and principle, to prevent the tranquillity and prosperity of Mexico, either from jealousy . . . , or with the view" of "establishing the influence of the United States, to the exclusion of any other Country."[73] It seems never to have occurred to Pakenham that the party in power was employing unfair methods to retain their hold upon the government of the states and nation, or that the insurgent Indians and mestizos, who had borne the brunt of the struggle for independence but had been deprived of its fruits, had any rights that were sacred.[74] To respectable men of his type there was only one way of dealing with the aspiring masses—suppression.

There was no predicting the outcome of this mass uprising, and by the opening of the year 1828 Pakenham was beginning to be thoroughly alarmed. The Yorkinos had been winning national and state elections, calling for the expulsion of the pure-blooded

[72] Ward expressed similar views. See his two letters of Oct. 25, 1826, and his letter of March 31, 1827, to Canning, F. O. (50), 25, 31.

[73] Pakenham to Canning, No. 72, Oct. 13, 1827, F. O. (50), 35.

[74] For an excellent summary of the political situation in Mexico at this time, *see* Herbert I. Priestley, *The Mexican Nation, A History* (New York, 1923), Chs. XIV-XV.

SPIRITED CONTESTS IN MEXICO

Spaniards, and threatening to undermine and control the army. "Their leaders are men of no character," he said. "In forwarding their plans of ambition and personal aggrandizement they have shown that the means, by which they attain their objects, are to them a matter of indifference." Worse still, they might prove subservient to the schemes of their American coadjutor. "With reference to British Interests it must be borne in mind, by whose exertions and intrigues this party has been called into existence, and forced up to the degree of power and influence which it has attained. Mr. Poinsett has shown, whenever an opportunity has presented itself, that he is no friend of England. . . . If at the election which according to the constitution, is to take place at the end of the year, the choice of a President were to fall upon a member of his party, it is not improbable that the mission would have to contend against an influence which might frequently cause to it considerable embarrassment." [75]

Such reports caused the Foreign Office great uneasiness. Canning had passed away, but Viscount Dudley took up his pen and composed instructions which leave no doubt that the Canning Policy was still to be maintained. No more significant instructions on Mexico and Spanish America were written by the English government prior to 1830.

"You are already aware," said Dudley, "that it is

[75] Pakenham to Dudley, No. 1, Jan. 5, 1828, F. O. (50), 42; and *see* also, for an elaboration of this disparaging view of the Yorkinos, Pakenham to Vaughan, Jan. 13, 1829, F. O. (50), 53.

not the intention of H[is] M[ajesty's] Govt. to interfere in the internal affairs of the South American States. Such an interference would be sometimes ungracious, oftener unavailing:—And at this distance it would be difficult to frame Instructions adapted to a rapid succession of unexpected events. The duty therefore of any person intrusted with the conduct of H. M.'s affairs in these countries, is in general confined to the protection of the property, rights, and trade of English Subjects, and to furnishing his Govt. with such information as may be necessary in order to form a correct judgment of the temper and political situation of the State to which he is accredited. He must be careful not to compromise the dignity of his Sovereign by taking part in those intrigues and quarrels, which occur occasionally in all Countries, but to which new and unsettled Govts. are peculiarly liable."

Dudley then stated that the *de facto* principle was the one generally followed by the English government. "This is a broad, clear, and intelligible rule," he continued, "and would serve for your guidance in all cases, if other nations would conduct themselves with equal moderation and forbearance:—but some qualifications of it may be rendered necessary by an opposite conduct on their part.

"It appears . . . that from the first establishment of Mexican Independence up to the present moment, the wishes of his Govt.—powerfully seconded by his own ambitions and intriguing temper—have engaged the American Minister, Mr. Poinsett, in a constant and active interference with the internal affairs of the new State:—He has made himself a partisan, and almost a chief, in the domestic factions of Mexico. . . . Even this might be of less importance, were not the active interference with Mexican politics connected with designs injurious to this Country. The American is also an anti-Anglican party, and it is evidently the object of the United States to establish an exclusive ascendency in all the [states near the?] Isthmus of Panama, which they may afterwards exercise in a manner prejudicial to the interests of England. . . .

"Without a dereliction of the interests of his own country, the English Minister could not remain wholly passive, whilst his American colleague was employing against him an unceasing and pernicious activity. A Mexican faction, guided by the councils and animated by the spirit of an artful and enterprising Minister from the United States, might . . . become as available for any purpose of political ambition, as if it were actually part of the Union:—nor could this country allow so formidable an accession to American power to be effected by no other efforts than those of dexterity and intrigue.

"You will, therefore, continue to watch the conduct of this gentleman, and you will furnish to H. M.'s Govt. the best information you can procure as to the nature and extent of his designs. The proper mode of counteracting his views as a partisan, will not be by making yourself equally a partisan on the other side. . . . But no exclusive advantage, commercial or political, must be allowed to the U. States, nor will you pass over without remonstrance any mark of confidence or respect shown to its Govt. which is not equally shared by that of H. M. Should any disposition appear in the ruling party to place themselves decidedly under American influence, you will endeavour by advice and expostulation, to recall them to a more correct notion of the real situation of their country.—It is true that the interest of Mexico requires that she should be on a friendly footing with a State bordering on her own territory along an extensive line of frontier, with which she maintains advantageous commercial relations, and [which is] dis-inclined from various causes, to favour the pretensions of Spain. . . . But the Mexican Gvt. will be guilty of a great and palpable error by allowing the ascendency, or even encouraging the interference, in its internal concerns, of so powerful a Neighbour.

"From the position of the two Countries, it is hardly possible that from time to time points should not arise, on which their interests are incompatible:—and a party governing Mexico through the patronage of the U. States would be under continual temptation to submit to undue sacrifices for the sake of preserving this foreign connection, and their own power founded upon it.

"It should be represented to them, on the other hand, that England is their natural Ally:—the commercial intercourse between the two Countries is mutually beneficial:—we have no political objects that are likely to set us at variance:—we neither possess, nor covet, any advantages which we have not purely reciprocal:—nor can the English Govt. be so much as suspected of a desire to establish any influence in Mexico, injurious to her interests or her independence.

"The relation in which Mexico stands to the United States is, in many important particulars, not dissimilar to our own. We are willing, and indeed anxious, to cultivate their friendship, but we watch them with care, as a Power from whom encroachments may be apprehended, and with whom differences may arise. While therefore you entirely abstain from professing or circulating a hostile feeling toward America, you will lose no opportunity of reminding the Mexican Govt., that she ought not to be the object [victim?] of a blind and indiscriminate confidence.

"It would be unwise as well as ungrateful to estrange themselves without necessity from a Country which countenanced their first efforts for independence, but they should constantly bear in mind that the complete ascendency of an United States party would render their independence little better than a name." [76]

Such were Dudley's views in the spring of 1828. They reiterate the Canning tradition and authorize, while disavowing it, a sort of moral interference in Mexico's politics. They not only hold out the suggestion of an alliance against the ambitions and encroachments of the United States, which are referred to in no uncertain terms, but they also authorize Pakenham to advise, remonstrate, and utter warnings against a pos-

[76] Dudley to Pakenham, No. 9, Apr. 21, 1828, F. O. (50), 41.

sible subserviency of Mexico to its neighbor on the north. In certain contingencies this might have called for an even more decided interference in the domestic affairs of Mexico, and the instructions, indeed, contain a hint of a possible departure from the *de facto* principle: "some qualifications" of the rule might be "rendered necessary by an opposite conduct" on the part of the United States.[77]

What Pakenham did in order to carry out the directions of his government does not clearly appear either in his own correspondence or that of his rival. It seems probable that little action against Poinsett and the United States proved necessary. Poinsett's influence over the Yorkinos was never so great as Pakenham and Dudley supposed, and when these instructions reached Mexico his power was already revealing evidences of decline. He was, in fact, becoming the object of denunciation on every hand, suspicion of the United States was developing into hostility, and the Yorkinos themselves were beginning to abandon him. Indeed, the Yorkino party was splitting into factions which were soon to prove fatal to its success.[78]

Pakenham understood the situation. In June, 1828, he noted, as proof that Poinsett was not yet all-powerful, "that the Chamber of Deputies, ... composed, by a

[77] In September, 1828, the Mexican secretary of state came to Poinsett and "revealed his fears that England or some other foreign power would interfere" (Manning, *Early Diplomatic Relations*, 357). Had Pakenham given him that impression?

[78] Manning, *Early Diplomatic Relations*, 349 ff.

SPIRITED CONTESTS IN MEXICO

great majority, of persons belonging to the 'Yorkino' party, steadily refused to ratify the Treaty" of amity and commerce between the United States and Mexico.[79] In September he was able to report, after some uneasiness, that Gómez Pedraza had been elected president of the Mexican nation. Pedraza, erstwhile monarchist and Scottish Rite Mason, elected in part by Yorkino votes and by administrative pressure exerted through the army, of which Pedraza, as secretary of war, was chief! It was an evil omen, but it also indicated a certain weakness on the part of the group known as Poinsett's friends, and Pakenham was delighted. "I think I may safely congratulate Your Lordship," he hastened to write Dudley, "not so much from my own opinion, that under General Gómez Pedraza such a Government may be expected, as will afford the greatest probability of the connexion of this country being honorable and advantageous to England, but because his election has been conformable to the wishes of the great majority of Persons, Foreigners as well as Mexicans, having property at stake in this Country, whose interest in the preservation of order is, I conceive, the best guarantee of the soundness of their opinion upon such a question." Here one has a characteristic utterance. Pakenham preferred Pedraza because Pedraza was a friend of order—the established order—, England, and "respectable" people with property. Pakenham had no use for the plebeian Vicente Guerrero,

[79] Pakenham to Dudley, No. 74, June 28, 1828, F. O. (50), 44.

Pedraza's opponent. Moreover, he feared that Guerrero was under the domination of Poinsett.[80]

There was only one factor in the situation in the fall of 1828 that gave Pakenham any uneasiness. Under the constitution of Mexico, Pedraza could not take possession of his office until the following April, and there was danger in the meantime that the rising partisan spirit would lead to revolution. The danger was real. The election of Pedraza had violated men's sense of justice and they took up arms. President Victoria could not, or would not, protect the president-elect. Pedraza fled. Guerrero first became secretary of war and then, soon afterwards, president. Mexico had had its first national election revolution and the party in power had been largely responsible.[81]

Yet Pakenham and many Mexicans blamed Poinsett. "Mr. Poinsett has carried his point," he wrote Dudley, "but the triumph is a melancholy one, and it is difficult to conceive what advantage the United States, as a Commercial nation, can possibly derive from the confusion in which his intrigues have involved the Country." [82] Pakenham was outraged and somewhat anxious. He expected Poinsett secretly to rejoice at the success of Guerrero, but he had supposed that "decency would have prevented him from making any publick demonstration of his satisfaction." Yet this

[80] Despatch No. 121, Sept. 26, 1828, F. O. (50), 45.

[81] Priestly, *The Mexican Nation*, pp. 266-266; Manning, *Early Diplomatic Relations*, 357-361.

[82] No. 6, Jan. 14, 1829, F. O. (50), 53.

SPIRITED CONTESTS IN MEXICO

proved not to be the case, for "on the day after the entrance of the insurgents into the Capital, which was marked by excesses that filled the whole of the well-disposed inhabitants with terror and dismay, he [Poinsett] gave a dinner to celebrate the event, at which Mr. Zavala and the principal leaders of the insurgents were present. . . ."[83] It did seem criminal, but Zavala said that the British had supported Pedraza and, although Pakenham declared that Zavala was drunk when he made the charge, it is not difficult to believe that some of the English residents, if not Pakenham, carried their sympathy for the conservatives to the point of actual assistance.[84]

Yet, with all of his irritation at the success of the plebeians, Pakenham still felt that Poinsett was far from establishing "a permanent American influence in Mexico," and his impression was soon confirmed. Shortly after Guerrero entered the president's palace, Pakenham approached him with some degree of anxiety, but the new president received him cordially and assured him that he desired to cultivate intimate relations with England. A few days later he told Pakenham that he felt "the discredit brought upon his Government" by the prevailing idea that he was "acting under the influence of the Agent of a Foreign Power" and expressed the intention of demanding Poinsett's recall.[85]

[83] Pakenham to Dudley, No. 152, Dec. 19, 1828, F. O. (50), 45.
[84] *Idem* to *idem*, Nos. 153-154, Dec. 19, 1828, F. O. (50), 45.
[85] Pakenham to Dudley, No. 52, May 3, 1829, F. O. (50), 54.

Pakenham, suspicious of the mestizo general, did not place "entire credit" in what he asserted, but he might well have done so. The current of hostility was now actually running so strong against Poinsett that Guerrero was compelled to disown him in order to save his own face. Not only the state legislatures, but at least half a dozen newspapers were demanding his expulsion, and there were even hints of assassination.[86] On July 1, 1829, Guerrero wrote President Jackson a tactful letter requesting that Poinsett be called home. "The public clamor against Mr. Poinsett has become general," said Guerrero, "not only among the authorities, and men of education, but also among the vulgar classes; not only among the individuals who suspected him, but also among many of those who have been his friends." [87] On Christmas Day, 1829, Poinsett took formal leave of the president whose party he had helped to organize.

During the more than five years which he had spent in Mexico, Poinsett had accomplished little and done some harm. The zealous friend of democracy and the republican system had become known as the "scourge of the continent" that he had tried to serve. He was a somewhat imprudent man of good intentions, whose failure was due in part to his propensity for intrigue, but even more to the opposition of the British and the suspicious atmosphere in which he moved. Of course,

[86] Manning, *Early Diplomatic Relations*, Ch. 10.

[87] *Ibid.*, 369.

SPIRITED CONTESTS IN MEXICO

Pakenham was delighted at his departure from Mexico. English influence now stood high in the country, and Van Buren, the suave secretary of state, even felt that he must approach the British minister in Washington on the subject. He informed Vaughan that Poinsett's conduct was not approved and expressed the hope that British "ascendancy" might be used to dissolve Mexican hostility toward the United States![88]

A few months after Poinsett's departure, the scheming Alamán sounded Pakenham on the subject of a European protectorate. He was once more in charge of foreign affairs and he said that he and his colleagues in the government, perceiving that monarchical sentiment had lost no ground, would like to help establish a prince from Europe in Mexico, provided the prince were not a Spanish Bourbon. "Humanity had induced Great Britain, France, and Russia, to undertake the adjustment of the political state of Greece, and why should not a like feeling induce them to take the state of this Country into consideration, and provide a remedy for the evils which afflict it?" Alamán, like Bolívar, had little faith in democratic republics, and he was longing for a monarch and a protectorate.

But the project aroused no such enthusiasm in Pakenham as the Colombian scheme had in Ricketts, Cockburn, and Campbell. "There is a numerous class of persons in the Country who would gladly see brought about the change advocated by Alaman, pro-

[88] Vaughan to Aberdeen, No. 44, July 31, 1829, No. 15, March 20, 1830, F. O. (5), 249, 259.

vided it were effected by no risk or trouble to themselves," said Pakenham; "but I cannot but apprehend," he added, "that the task of improving the condition of this Country by that means, or any other act of interference with it's concerns, would in the end prove a very thankless office, and might, if the success . . . were to depend upon the cordial and manly cooperation of any set of men in this Country, end, not improbably, in total failure." [89] Moreover, the refusal to consider a Bourbon prince from Spain meant the rejection at the outset of the only feature of the plan which would have recommended it to England. Mexico was to have no monarch until Maximilian came—and experienced the tragic fulfillment of Pakenham's prediction regarding the nature of the task.

[89] Pakenham to *idem*, No. 30, March 25, 1830, F. O. (50), 60.

CHAPTER VIII

CONCLUSION — A CENTURY OF SUBSEQUENT CONTESTS

The contests of the United States and Great Britain in the major regions of Hispanic America between 1808 and 1830 have now been narrated in detail and the main motives and issues of the struggle set forth. It seems appropriate, in bringing the study to a conclusion, to attempt a general estimate of the achievements of the rivals, to trace the later history of some of the controverted questions, and to place the story in its proper setting by presenting a brief summary of the subsequent competition of the two Powers in the areas concerned.

I. ACHIEVEMENTS OF THE RIVALS

In the matter of commerce, England started somewhat behind the United States and came out in 1830 far in the lead. Her trade with the Spanish colonies was less than twenty-five million dollars in value in 1808; but it rose to thirty million in 1822, nearly sixty million in 1825, and then dropped to about thirty-two million in 1830. The commerce of the United States with the region amounted to almost thirty million in 1808, decreased to less than fourteen in 1822, rose to twenty-four in 1825, and dropped again to twenty in 1830. With respect to Brazil, where for most of the period British merchants had the advantage of discriminatory duties, the position of the United States was even worse. The Brazilian trade of England amounted to nearly twenty million dollars in 1825 and almost thirty million in 1830, while that of the United States was valued at about four million two hundred thousand dollars for each of these years, respectively. With Cuba alone, of all Hispanic America, did the United States maintain its commercial predominance. British trade with this island probably never reached a value of four million dollars at any time between 1808 and 1830, while that of the United States averaged about nine million dollars annually.[1]

So far as investments were concerned, the United States, as has been frequently noted, was hardly in the race at all. Without capital to invest abroad and even borrowing money for the development of their own country, American citizens placed small amounts in

[1] Trade statistics for the period have been difficult to obtain. It is believed, however, that those given are sufficiently accurate for comparative purposes. They are based upon the following sources: G. B., *Parliamentary Papers* (1828), XIX, 479, (1831-1832), XXXIV, 207; Timothy Pitkin, *A Statistical View of the Commerce of the United States of America* (Hartford, 1816), 36 ff.; *American State Papers, Commerce and Navigation*, II *passim*; Robertson, *Hispanic-American Relations of the United State* 188, *passim*. It should be noted that the Hispanic-Anerican trade of the two rivals was an unimportant item in their total foreign commerce. The total trade of the United States was approximately $152,000,000 in 1810, $141,000,000 in 1822, $181,000,000 in 1825, and $134,000,000 in 1830; that of Great Britain was $435,000,000 in 1810, $420,000,000 in 1822, $500,000,000 in 1825, and $580,000,000 in 1830.

Mexico, Cuba, and Central America, but little or nothing elsewhere. The British, on the other hand, probably invested not less than £40,000,000 in Hispanic America by 1830. Yet, it may be doubted whether, on the whole, these investments had become profitable. The numerous mining enterprises paid little or no dividends prior to 1828 and probably had not yet begun to prove valuable even by 1830.[2] Of the government loans amounting to more than one hundred and ten million dollars made to seven of the new states, those granted to Brazil alone continued to pay interest in 1830. Owing to the low price at which they had been bought, they had yielded excellent profits up to 1826, but this must have been small comfort to those who held the bonds in 1830.[3]

With reference both to investment opportunities and commerce, the British were succeeding to the Spanish heritage, but financial corruption and domestic disorders were greatly diminishing its importance. Seventy years later it was to prove very valuable, but by that time lusty competitors had entered the field.

In the territorial phase of the contest England had little or no success. The British government did not prevent the United States from acquiring Louisiana and the Floridas. It may have delayed our acquisition of Texas and Cuba, but this is doubtful. The failure

[2] These statements are based upon numerous reports of British consuls from all parts of Hispanic America.

[3] G. B., House of Commons, *Reports of Committees* (1831-1832), VI, 587.

of the United States to secure these areas prior to 1830 was probably due mainly to other causes. It must be noted, however, that the British government did not desire to add any of these four areas to the British Empire. It was interested not so much in the territories themselves as in the defense of an ally and in the bearing of these areas upon the control of the Gulf of Mexico, that is, upon sea power.

The outcome of the maritime rivalry of the competitors is more difficult to ascertain. The development of the merchant marine of the United States was running that of England a fairly close race. The tonnage of the American merchant marine was 1,383,739 in 1800, 2,137,174 in 1810, 1,920,251 in 1820, and 1,787,663 in 1830; that of Great Britain was 4,586,069 and 5,458,599 and 5,959,334 and 5,696,592 for these respective dates. But it has not been possible to ascertain what influence Hispanic America had upon this comparative growth. It is certain, however, that the development of American shipping between 1793 and 1820 bore an intimate relation to the carrying trade between France and Spain and their American colonies; and, what is more significant, both the United States and England considered the commerce of Hispanic America an important factor in the maritime rivalry of the two Powers.[4]

With respect to maritime law, regulations, and

[4] U. S. Shipping Board, *Third Annual Report* (1919), 59; J. R. Soley, "The Maritime Industries of America" (in N. S. Shaler, *The United States*, I, Ch. X).

agreements, we can only compare the provisions of the treaties obtained by the rivals. Great Britain secured four with the Hispanic-American states prior to 1830 while the United States obtained only three, and those of England were with more important countries than were those of the United States. England ratified treaties with Buenos Aires (1825), Great Colombia (1825), Mexico (1826), and Brazil (1827). The United States did not secure any pacts with Buenos Aires and Mexico prior to 1830, but ratified treaties with Great Colombia (1824), Central America (1825), and Brazil (1828). American diplomats succeeded, however, in writing into all of these agreements their favorite provisions regarding the most-favored-nation principle, the shortening of contraband lists, the restriction of the power blockade, and the inviolability of property on board neutral vessels. English statesmen, on the other hand, although able to maintain their views on these questions, were forced to permit a slight encroachment upon their navigation laws by a liberal definition of "national vessels."[5] Moreover, when Brazil attempted to apply the old system in the blockade of the River Plate, the United States successfully resisted and its commerce and shipping suffered less than did England's. Nevertheless, it does not appear probable that these negotiotions of the rival Powers exerted any very significant influence upon the maritime rules and procedure of the period.

[5] Malloy, *Treaties*, I, 133, *passim*; G. B. *State Papers*, XII, 29 ff., 661 ff., XIV, 609 ff., 614 ff.

In regard to political forms, it may be noted that the democratic republic prevailed in all Spanish America, and that this was due in no small measure to the moral influence of the United States. And yet, it must be admitted that the policy of British statesmen, despite their preference for constitutional monarchy, tended to stultify the monarchical plans of the period. They would neither furnish princes of the English dynasty for thrones in Spanish America nor permit French Bourbons to occupy them; and since the monarchists of the New World would have none of the Spanish Bourbons, all their projects failed.[6]

Whether the attempt of the United States and England to advance their rival ambitions by means of Hispanic America resulted in the promotion of the best interests of the people of this region, is a question difficult to determine. In so far as the United States and England encouraged—directly or indirectly, intentionally or unintentionally—the Wars of Independence in Spanish America, they may be censured for promoting a movement for which the natives were probably not ready. To the degree in which the United States and its citizens stimulated the erection of federal republics in these countries, they were guilty of sponsoring the establishment of institutions for which the people were unprepared. When Americans and British championed rival political systems and groups, they

[6] In this connection the reader should also bear in mind the influence which French radicalism exercised over the political sentiments of the people to the south of the Rio Grande.

helped in some degree to lay the volcanic fires which have caused a century of eruption. But to endeavor to determine whether it were better had the Spanish Americans continued for a time under the mother country and then separated under limited monarchies would be to leave the realm of history for that of speculation.

In all that related to the matter of prestige England appears to have had some advantage from start to finish, and it was perhaps natural that she should. Britain was the wealthiest country in the world, the mistress of the seas, the object of the admiration or of the envy and apprehension of every nation, with an experienced group of diplomats and consuls. The United States was young, small in population, comparatively poor, and somewhat careless in the training of its agents. Moreover, the Yankees were greedily in pursuit of Spanish-American territory, while Englishmen, with few minor exceptions, not only sought none, but made a futile effort to prevent the United States from acquiring any.

II. THE AFTERMATH

In less than a century, however, the comparative position of the two rivals was virtually to be reversed. By that time the United States had taken the lead in the commerce of Hispanic America, though probably not in the affections of the Hispanic-American peoples. Its political influence in the Western Hemisphere had become more powerful than that of its rival; its wealth, its significance in world politics, its investments in the lands to the south, had equaled, and were threatening to surpass those of England. In the meantime, moreover, England had reconciled herself to the Monroe Doctrine, surrendered many of her ancient maritime contentions, and superimposed her democratic system upon her House of Lords and her monarchy; and Brazil had exchanged her emperor for a president. But England and the United States continued to be rivals not only in economic matters but in sea power, not only in Hispanic America but all over the world, although their relations during the last forty years have been more harmonious than ever before.

England's navigation laws were the first portion of the old structure to give way. These had long provided, among other things, (1) that no produce of America could be imported into the United Kingdom except in British ships or in those of the country of which the goods were the produce, (2) that no British coastwise trade could be carried on save in British bottoms, (3) that no goods could be exported from the United Kingdom to any of the British possessions in America except in British ships, (4) that no goods could be carried from one British possession in America to another in any but British vessels, and (5) that no goods could be imported into any British possession in America in any but British bottoms or those of the country of which the goods were the produce. By 1830 slight modifications had been made in favor of the United States, but no important concessions were granted until more than a decade later, when by a series of enactments extending from 1849 to 1856 the whole system was abandoned.

The influence exerted by the Yankees upon this change is not easy to measure. In the 1820's the United States passed several retaliatory laws directed at British trade with the United States; and our later treaties with the other Latin-American states, like the earlier ones with Brazil, Colombia, and Central America, as well as others negotiated with the Powers of Continental Europe, provided for the liberal system of reciprocity in navigation. These measures probably had considerable weight, but it may be that the British navigation edifice tumbled from pressure exerted from within rather than from without.[7]

At any rate, it collapsed and the merchant marines of both countries continued their rival growth until after 1860, when that of the United States, due largely to official indifference and the change from wood to iron, began to decline. The tonnage of the United States was three million in 1840, five million in 1850, eight million in 1860, and considerably less than seven million in 1890, while that of England increased steadily during the period from something over seven million to almost twenty-two million. Then came the

[7] W. S. Lindsay, *History of Merchant Shipping* (London, 1876), Chs. III-X; F. C. Dietz, *A Political and Social History of England* (N. Y., 1927), Ch. XXII; John Bassett Moore, *The Principles of American Diplomacy* (New York, 1918), Ch. III; J. H. Latané, *A History of American Foreign Policy* (New York, 1927), Ch. III, *passim*.

World War and, with it, the most remarkable growth that America's merchant marine ever experienced. In 1900 its tonnage was less than eight million and in 1920 it was more than twenty-four, as compared to a British tonnage of twenty-four and thirty-three million, respectively.[8] The effect of this new development upon the relations of the two countries remains to be seen.

Soon after the navigation laws were repealed, English statesmen joined in the Declaration of Paris (1856), which meant the acceptance of the principles for which the United States had contended in reference to other maritime matters. The important provisions of this declaration are as follows: "1. Privateering is and remains abolished; 2. The neutral flag covers enemy's goods, with the exception of contraband of war; 3. Neutral goods, with the exception of contraband of war, are not liable to capture under the enemy's flag;[9] 4. Blockades, in order to be binding, must be effective," that is, they must be maintained by an effective naval force in adjacent waters. But it was one of the ironies of history that the United States declined to accept these provisions because of the stipulation abolishing privateering, just as it has always refused to admit foreign shipping to its coastwise trade. Nor was it any less ironical, perhaps, that during the Civil War the North should have expanded

[8] U. S. Shipping Board, *Third Annual Report* (1919), 59.

[9] This provision went beyond the earlier contentions of the United States.

belligerent operations by a large extension of contraband lists, the exercise of the right of search, and the promulgation of the doctrine of continuous voyage so as to break up the neutral trade with Nassau and Matamoros. This procedure proved very embarrassing fifty years later, when in the midst of the World War the United States once more attempted to champion neutral rights.[10]

In the meantime, the commerce of the United States with Latin America, after lagging behind for another sixty years, eventually passed that of the United Kingdom during the last decade of the nineteenth century and far exceeded it after the outbreak of the World War. Moreover, by the turn of the century, the commerce of Hispanic America had become a valuable consideration. The trade of the United Kingdom with the region amounted to approximately $258,000,000 in 1900 and $993,000,000 in 1925, as compared to $282,000,000 and $2,110,000,000 for the United States.[11]

The investment of British subjects continued, however, to exceed those of the citizens of the United States. In 1913 the latter were valued at $1,330,000,000 and the former £999,236,000; in 1925 they

[10] On this recent controversy, see *Diplomatic Correspondence between the United States and Belligerent Governments Relating to Neutral Rights and Commerce*, American Journal of International Law, Special Supplement, IX-XI.

[11] U. S. Dept. of Commerce and Labor, Bureau of Statistics, *Statistical Abstract of Foreign Countries, passim*; The Pan-American Union, *Latin-American Foreign Trade for 1925*.

were estimated at $4,000,000,000, or more, and £1,139,659,000, respectively.[12]

Lastly, the British government, after 1856, began slowly to relax its opposition to the expanding influence of the United States in America and to reconcile itself to the Monroe Doctrine and Yankee predominance in the New World. After a half-century, British statesmen began to realize that the attempt to prevent the United States from enlarging its boundaries was futile and unwise. They not only ceased to oppose the advance but welcomed it, and recognized in 1898 the paramount position of the United States in the Caribbean by removing their squadron from the region. Moreover, they made other concessions. After asserting their claim for more than fifty years to the joint control of the isthmian trade routes, they consented to the control and fortification of the Panama Canal by the United States and made no remonstrance when American diplomats secured exclusive canal privileges in Nicaragua. After criticising the Monroe Doctrine for nearly seventy-five years, they finally commenced to disavow hostility toward the manifesto and ended by accepting it.

For the United States and the harmonious relations of the two nations it was a notable victory. But it will be well to examine the motives and extent of the concessions. British diplomats abandoned the attempt to prevent the southward expansion of the United States because they saw that their efforts stimulated rather

[12] *South American Journal* (London), Nov. 20, 1926; Robert W. Dunn, *American Foreign Investments* (1926), 3, 183.

than checked American aggressiveness, endangered the peace of the two countries, and threatened to interrupt a trade with their kinsmen which was far more important than their commerce with all Latin America combined. Moreover, they felt confident that the control of the United States over the regions to the south would result in stability and increased purchasing power and hoped that the United States would take no official step to exclude British trade with the area. Accommodations with reference to the Isthmus were the expressions of a growing cordiality which may possibly be explained by the democratization of England, the menace of Britain's European rivals, and the decline of our merchant marine. The acceptance of the paramount position of the United States in the Western hemisphere was based upon the assumption that the United States would not take advantage of that position to discriminate against British economic interests in Hispanic America. Provided prudent restraint is exercised on this point, there seems to be no reason to fear any interruption of the harmony of their relations in this region.[13] The recent development of the merchant marine and navy of the United States are more serious matters, but they lie beyond the field of the present investigation.

[13] For a fuller discussion of the rivalry of the United States and England over Hispanic America after 1830, see J. Fred Rippy, *Latin America in World Affairs* (New York, 1928), Chs. VI and VII. Recently, considerable rivalry has occurred over the oil reserves of Mexico, Venezuela, and Colombia, the government of each country apparently backing its nationals with a realization of the importance of this commodity for industry and war operations in the air and on the sea.

INDEX

Aberdeen, 4th Earl of, and proposed monarchy in South America, 206-207.

Acquisition, of Louisiana, 30; and British attitude, 26-31; of the Floridas, 34-38, 69-70; British attitude toward, 32-70.

Adams, E. D., view on Anglo-United States harmony, vii.

Adams, J. Q., peace commissioner at Ghent, 49n.; and the Florida question, 57-70; and Texas, 76, 91n.; and disagreements with George Canning over Latin America, 112-124, 231ff.; and Cuba, 77, 80-82, 83, 85-86; and Salvador, 217; and the Panama Congress, 231-237.

Addington, British prime minister, 26-27.

Aftermath, of early United States and British rivalry in Latin America, 309-315.

Alamán, Lucas, Mexican minister of foreign affairs, 103-104n., 105, 251; his pro-British attitude, 251, 255; his resignation, 256; desires European protectorate, 301.

Allen, Heman, U. S. minister to Chile, 126; his instructions, 123n.; his jealousy of the British, 126-127.

Alliance, the Anglo-Spanish, 2, 4-5; and the Floridas, 32-43; and the peace negotiations of 1813-'14, 44-45, 50-54.

Ambrister and Arbuthnot, in Florida, 55; execution of, 68-69.

Anderson, Richard C., U. S. minister to Great Colombia, 121; his instructions, 121-122; apprehensions regarding British aims, 189; negotiates a treaty, 189; dies while *en route* to Panama, 240.

Antagonism, of Canning and Adams, 112-124, 231; of Raguet and Gordon, 133-134; of Forbes and Parish, 138-142; of Forbes and Ponsonby, 145-148; of O'Reilly and Williams, 221ff.; of Poinsett and Ward, 254-286; of Poinsett and Pakenham, 286-301.

Apodaca, Spanish ambassador in London, 34, 73.

Argentina, see United Provinces of Rio de la Plata.

Aston, Arthur, British minister to Brazil, 131.

Bagot, Sir Charles, British minister to the United States, 63; his instructions regarding Florida mediation, 63-66; offers to mediate in the Florida dispute, 66-68.

Baker, Anthony St. John, British *chargé* in Washington, 57; disavows procedure of British subjects in Florida, 57-58, 67.

Banda Oriental, British mediation regarding, 143-149.

Baton Rouge, procedure of U. S. citizens in, 34.

Belize, procedure of British subjects of, 219-220.

Bland, Theodorick, member of the South American commission, 13; envious of British influence, 14-15.

Blockade, U. S. disagreements with G. B. over definition of, v, vii, 2, 6, 7-8, 109, 111, 118-119, 148, 180, 228, 234, 235, 238, 275, 307, 312.

Blount Conspiracy, the, 24-25.

Bolívar, Simón, favors British alliance, 152-160, 181-188; hostility of American diplomats toward, 171-174; Watts a partisan of,

317

191; Harrison remonstrates with, 194-196; Moore admires, 197-199, attitude toward monarchy, 152ff., 207n.; Clay's attitude toward, 208-212; Van Buren and, 213-215.

Bowles, Captain William, criticizes U. S. agents in South America, 11-13.

Bravo, General Nicolás, Ward in touch with, 260n.; pro-British, 279, 283, 287.

Burr, Aaron, 31.

Calhoun, John C., and Cuba, 80-81, 83.

California, U. S. alleged to desire a part of, 60, 68.

Camacho, Sebastián, Mexican secretary of foreign relations, 278, 279, 284.

Campbell, Patrick, British commissioner to Great Colombia, 177; *chargé* in Bogotá, 178; apprehensions regarding the United States, 178-181; intimate with Bolívar, 181-187; and the establishment of a Prince in Colombia, 184-185.

Campuzano, Francisco, Spanish ambassador in London, 60.

Canada, British desire to protect, 23, 24, 25, 48, 51, 56-57.

Canal, Nicaragua, the, 217, 222, 223-224.

Canning, George, British foreign secretary, 32, 79; suspects U. S. designs upon Cuba, 79-80, 85, 87; policy regarding Cuba, 86-87; thinks of attacking Havana, 88; proposes joint declaration against European interference in America, 84, 107; attitude toward monarchy in the New World, 112-114; antagonistic toward Adams and the policy of the U. S. in America, 112-116, 123-124, 227-230; policy in southern South America, 128ff.; attitude toward Bolívar, 203-204; and Panama Congress, 227-229; death, 231; and Mexico, 247-248; approves Ward's activities, 274.

Canning, Stratford, British minister to the U. S., 79; uneasiness regarding Cuba, 80-84; interview with J. Q. Adams, 116.

Castlereagh, Viscount (later Marquis of Londonderry), British foreign secretary, 58; and Florida, 58-70; and Texas, 75-76.

Central America, U. S. and British friction in, 217-227; British interests in, 218-219.

Chamberlain, British consul-general at Rio de Janeiro, 130-131.

Chile, rivalry of the agents of the U. S. and Britain in, 9-11, 124-128.

Clay, Henry, 5, 49n., 119, 120, 123; uneasiness regarding Britain's commercial policy, 132, 169; and Bolívar, 208-212.

Cockburn, Alexander, 187.

Cockburn, Sir George, 55.

Cockrane, Admiral Alexander, 45.

Colombia, see Great Colombia.

Colonial system, Adams opposed to the old, 116-119.

Commerce, share of G. B. and U. S. with Latin-American states compared, 129-130, 136, 143, 150-151, 176; comparative share of Latin-American as a whole, 303-304, 313-314.

Congress of Panama, 227ff.

Congress of Tacubaya, 208, 244, 289.

Cook, Daniel P., U. S. agent to Cuba, 90.

Cooley, James, U. S. minister to Peru, 150; attitude toward Bolívar, 170-171.

Cuba, Jefferson's desire for, 72-73, 80-81; uneasiness of the U. S. and Great Britain over, 72-90; Mexico and Colombia think of liberating, 85ff., 229ff.

INDEX

Dashwood, Charles, British consul in Central America, 229.
Dawkins, Edward J., British agent at the Panama Congress, 227ff.
Declaration of Paris, the, viii, 312.
Dudley, Earl of, British foreign secretary, 204; and the blockade of the Río de la Plata, 149; friendly toward Bolívar, 204-205; attitude toward monarchy in Colombia, 206ff.; jealous of influence of the U. S. in Mexico, 248, 291ff.

Emancipation of Spanish America, Britain opposes early movement, 4-5; U. S. favors, 5-6, 19-20; clashing policies regarding, 1-8.
Essex, U. S. S., in Chilean waters, 10-11.
Everett, Alexander H., U. S. *chargé* at Brussels, 77; U. S. minister to Spain, 90, 243.

Federation of American states, 115, 180, 181, 227-228, 257, 268-270.
Fleeming, British admiral, 188, 200.
Florida, East and West, 23ff.; British opposition to U. S. acquisition of, 32-43, 70; activities of U. S. citizens in, 34ff.; acquisition of, 69.
Forbes, John M., U. S. *chargé* in Buenos Aires, 137; jealousy of the British, 138ff.
Forsyth, John, U. S. minister to Spain, 82.
Foster, Augustus J., British diplomat in Washington, 38-43, 67.
Frere, J. H., 247.
France, the British fear and oppose the designs of in America, 4, 6, 8, 12, 14, 22, 23ff.; cession of Louisiana to the U. S., 30, 49, 51, 53; procedure regarding Cuba, 84, 86; Canning fears combined maritime power of U. S. and, 114; U. S. jealousy of, 131; and proposed intervention in Hispanic America, 163-165, 187.

Freedonian rebellion, 97, 103.
French Bourbons for thrones in America, 186; Britain opposes their establishment in, 203, 206-207, 308.
French designs in America, 78.

Gallatin, Albert, peace commissioner, 49n.; U.S. minister to London, 88.
Ghent, the Treaty of, 48-56.
Gordon, Robert, British diplomat in Brazil, 133-134, 144.
Great Britain, policies of, clash with those of the United States, 1-4; disagrees with the U. S. regarding the insurgents of Spanish America, 4-8; potentialities of harmony with the U. S., 4, 7-8; attitude toward U. S. expansion, viii, 22, 28-30, 32-70, 71, 73, 74, 76, 78-106; fears political influence of the U. S., 114-115, 164, 227-228, 247-248, 292-295; maritime rivalry and disagreements with the U. S., vi, 108-111, 114, 115, 118-119, 148-149, 162-163, 179, 218, 228, 229, 233, 234, 237, 238, 239-240, 242-243, 245, 306-307, 311-312, 315; commercial rivalry with the United States in Latin America, 7, 15, 20-21, 79, 108, 116-118, 127, 132, 135, 141, 148-149, 150-151, 162-163, 166, 169-170, 176, 238-240, 275, 303-304, 313; attitude toward monarchy in Latin America, 203-207, 308; prestige in Latin America, 229, 309.
Great Colombia, U. S.-British rivalry in, 176ff.
Gual, Pedro, Colombian minister of foreign affairs, 177, 180, 189; at Panama Congress, 242ff.
Guerrero, Vicente, 297-298, 300.
Gulf Coast, British fears U. S. acquisition of, 71, 96.

Handy, Charles O., 18.

Harrison, William Henry, minister in Colombia, 192ff.; writes Bolívar, 194-196.
Hawkesbury, British foreign secretary, 23ff.
Henderson, James, 19-21; British consul-general in Colombia, 188, 194n.
Hervey, Lionel, British commissioner to Mexico, 249, 250.
Heywood, Captain Peter, 9-11.
Hillyar, Captain of the British Navy, 11.
Hunter, J. D., British settler in Texas, 96, 97n.
Huskisson, William, advises Canning, 275.

Indians, of Florida, 45, 46, 57.
Investments, in Latin America, British, 108, 304-305; U. S., 305.
Iturbide, Augustine, Emperor of Mexico, 248, 255.

Jackson, Andrew, 48, 56, 68.
Jefferson, Thomas, attitude toward England, 5; desire for Louisiana and the Floridas, 27-29; for Texas, 72-73; for Cuba, 72, 80-81; doubts political capacity of Latin Americans, 211.

Kelly, Patrick, 151, 166.
Kilbee, Henry Theo, British agent in Cuba, 79, 82n.
King, Rufus, minister to England, 23, 26-27, 29.

Lansdowne, British foreign secretary, 25.
Larned, Samuel, U. S. *chargé* in Chile, 127; in Peru, 167; unfriendly toward Bolívar, 167, 172-173; attitude toward British, 169-170.
Liston, Robert, British minister in the U. S., 24.
Liverpool, Lord, British prime minister, and U. S. expansion into Florida, 52; and U. S. sea power, 109-110.

Loans, to Latin-American states, British, 108, 125, 129, 158, 168, 169, 219, 250, 305; U. S. projected, 107-108.

Mackie, Patrick, British agent in Mexico, 92-93; jealous of the U. S., 248-249.
Madison, James, 5; sympathy for Latin America, 6; and the Floridas, 35ff.
Maling, Captain Thomas, interview with Bolívar, 152-153.
Maritime riva'ry, see Great Britain, United States, etc.
Mathews, George, U. S. agent in East Florida, 41, 43.
Méndez, Briceño, 245-246.
Merchant marine, British versus U. S., 109-110, 306, 311-312, 315.
Merry, Anthony, British minister at Washington, 31, 72.
Mexico, the key to Canning's American policy, 247-248; British-U. S. rivalry over, 91ff., 248ff.
Mier y Terán, Manuel, Mexican agent in Texas, 94-95; suspicious of Yankees in Texas, 100-103, 198.
Mining in Latin America, British investments in, 108, 125, 130, 168, 190, 219, 305.
Mississippi River, British desire for navigation of, 31, 54.
Monarchies, for Latin America, San Martín desires, 12; desire for in Colombia, 152ff.; in Mexico, 301-302; and British attitude, 113, 203-207, 302, 308.
Monroe, James, 5, 119, 120; and the Floridas, 39ff.
Monroe Doctrine, and British policy, 107, 111, 314; aimed in part at Great Britain, 117-118.
Moore, Thomas P., U. S. minister to Great Colombia, 194; comment on attitude of North Americans

in, 197-198; treachery to Harrison, 194; praises Bolívar, 199; hostility toward the British, 199-202.

Morier, J. P., minister to the U. S., 34, 61; and U. S. expansion into the Floridas, 34-38; commissioner to Mexico, 250, 277ff.

Napoleon I, and Spanish America, 6, 20, 72.

Navigation system, British, 2, 109, 111, 118, 136, 228-229, 238, 240-241, 310-311.

Neo-Holy Alliance, and Spanish America, 8, 84, 107, 117.

Neutrals' rights, U. S. champions, 1, 2, 109, 111, 119, 234, 235, 238, 239, 307, 312.

Nicolls, Major, activities in Florida, 46, 55, 56, 57, 58.

Núñez, Count Fernán, Spanish Ambassador in London, 44.

Núñez, Don Ignacio, Argentine diplomat, hostile to British, 145.

O'Gorman, John, British commissioner and consul-general in Mexico, 249, 280-281.

Onis, Juan Luís de, Spanish agent in the U. S., 44n., 69, 73, 252.

O'Reilly, John, British consul at Guatemala City, 221; hostile toward the U. S., 221-224.

Pakenham, Sir Edward, 47-48.

Pakenham, Richard, British *chargé* in Mexico, 89, 105, 286ff.

Palmer and Company, and canal concession in Nicaragua, 218, 222, 224.

Panama, Congress at, 227ff.

Parish, Woodbine, British diplomat at Buenos Aires, 138, 140, 141; friction with North Americans, 142.

Pedraza, Gómez, 278, 297, 298.

Pedro I, of Brazil, 131, 144.

Perry, Captain Oliver H., 17-18.

Peru, U. S. and British rivalry in, 150ff.; Bolivar and British agents in, 152-160, 166; political disorders in, 160-161, 167, 168; hostility of American agents in toward Bolívar, 170-176.

Poinsett, Joel R., in southern South America, 9-11; opposed to recognition of Buenos Aires government, 15-16; in Cuba and Mexico (1822), 82-83; opposes Ward and Pakenham in Mexico (1825-1829), 254ff.; mentioned, 193, 223.

Polignac interviews, 112.

Ponsonby, Viscount John, at Rio and Buenos Aires, 144; indignant at Forbes, 148.

Porter, Captain David, of the U. S. Navy, 10-11.

Porter, Robert Ker, British consul at Caracas, 188.

Prevost, John B., U. S. commissioner in South America, 12-13.

Raguet, Condy, U. S. consul and diplomat in Brazil, 130; jealous of the British, 130-134.

Regla, Countess de, 94n., 259.

Republics, favored by the U. S. in Latin America, 2, 8, 115, 119, 120-123, 147, 210-211, 213, 214, 308.

Rivalry, see Great Britain, United States, Peru, Mexico, etc.

Rodney, Caesar A., U. S. minister in Buenos Aires, 137-138.

Ross, British major-general, instructions to, 47.

Rowcroft, Thomas, British consul-general in Peru, 151-152.

Rush, Richard, U. S. minister in London, 77, 84, 91, 231.

Russia, 4, 6, 8, 14, 49, 86, 117, 118, 120, 164, 301.

San Martín, José F. de, friendly toward English, 12; favors monarchies for South America, 12-13.

Santander, F. de Paula de, vice-president of Colombia, 177, 180.
Schenley, E. W. H., British consul in Guatemala, 220-221.
Sea Power, see Great Britain, United States.
Sergeant, John, U. S. agent to Panama and Tacubaya, 208, 289.
Slavery and the slave trade, 47, 48, 71, 77, 78ff., 241.
Smith, John S., U. S. secretary of state, 33.
Spain, and Great Britain, 2ff., 22, 33ff., 85, 87, 88, 229, 242, 244; and the U. S., 6, 26, 27, 35, 38ff., 72, 74, 86.
Spanish America, see the various states.
Stuart, Charles, British diplomat in Brazil, 128-129.

Tayloe, Edward, secretary of U. S. legation in Mexico and Colombia, 193.
Texas, U. S. interest in, 70-77, 91ff.; British agents and, 91-100.
Thornton, Edward, British minister to the U. S., 27, 28-29.
Todd, Charles S., U. S. confidential agent at Bogotá, 19.
Treaties of amity and commerce with the Latin-American states: British, 130, 133, 141, 250ff., 307; U. S., 134, 142-143, 178-179, 221, 262ff., 307.
Tudor, William, U. S. *chargé* in Brazil, 134-135; in Peru, 168; hostile to Bolívar, 173-174.
Turner, William, British minister to Colombia, 188, 200.

United Provinces of Rio de la Plata (later the Argentine Confederation), 15-16; U. S. and British rivalry in, 137ff.; war with Brazil, 143ff.

United States, main objectives of early diplomacy of, 1; attitude toward Latin-American insurgents, 5-7; desire for Louisiana and the Floridas, 22ff.; interest in Texas and Cuba, 71ff.; see also Great Britain, Henry Clay, J. Q. Adams, etc.
Uraguay, see Banda Oriental.
Urdaneta, General Rafael, Colombian dictator, 188, 199.

Van Buren, Martin, U. S. secretary of state, 106, 213-214.
Vaughan, Charles R., British minister to U. S., 89, 99, 105-106, 186.
Venezuela, see Great Colombia.
Victoria, Guadalupe, Pres. of Mexico, 92, 94, 99, 256, 259, 279; ambitions of, 262-263.
Vidaurre, Manuel, Peruvian diplomat, 161, 243, 246.

War of 1812, Louisiana and the Floridas in, 45-54.
Ward, Henry George, British *chargé* in Mexico, 93; and Texas, 93-100; contests with Poinsett in Mexico, 254-286.
Washington, George, held up as an example to Bolívar 196, 212.
Watts, Beaufort T., U. S. *chargé* in Colombia, 189; jealous of British, 189-190; admires Bolívar, 191.
Wavell, General A. G., in Texas, 96, 97n.
West Indies, British, relation of the Floridas to the security of, 23, 28, 41, 64.
Wilkinson, General James, 32, 74.
Willimott, Thomas S., British proconsul in Peru, 166, 168; attitude toward Bolívar, 166; hostility toward Yankees, 166-167.